TRANS

FORMATIONS

Growth
and Change in
Adult Life

ROGER L. GOULD, M.D.

A TOUCHSTONE BOOK

Published by Simon and Schuster
New York

First Touchstone Edition, 1979
Published by Simon and Schuster
A Division of Gulf & Western Corporation
Simon & Schuster Building
Rockefeller Center
1230 Avenue of the Americas
New York, New York 10020
TOUCHSTONE and colophon are trademarks
of Simon & Schuster

Manufactured in the United States of America

1 2 3 4 5 6 7 8 9 10
3 4 5 6 7 8 9 10 Pbk.

Library of Congress Cataloging in Publication Data

Gould, Roger L
Transformations : change and growth in adult life.

(A Touchstone book)
Includes index.
1. Adulthood.   2. Marriage.   I. Title.
BF724.5.G68   1979   155.6   79-13388

ISBN 0-671-22521-9
ISBN 0-671-25066-3 Pbk.

Permission to excerpt from the following is gratefully acknowledged:

"Elm" in *Ariel* by Sylvia Plath. Copyright © 1963 by Ted Hughes. Used by permission of Harper & Row, Publishers, Inc.

Child Studies Through Fantasy by Rosalind Gould. Copyright © 1972 by Rosalind Gould. Reprinted by permission of Quadrangle/The New York Times Book Co.

"Love and Hate: How Working Couples Work It Out" by Mary Murphy, from *New West*, February 14, 1977. Copyright © 1977 by Mary Murphy. Reprinted by permission of the author.

Of Other Worlds: Essays and Stories by C. S. Lewis. Reprinted by permission of Harcourt Brace Jovanovich, Inc.

"I Travel Alone" by Noel Coward. Copyright © 1934 Chappell & Co., Ltd. Copyright renewed. International copyright secured. All Rights Reserved. Used by permission.

Freud: Living and Dying by Max Schur, M.D. Copyright © 1972 by the Estate of Max Schur. Reprinted by permission of International Universities Press, Inc.

Memories, Dreams, Reflections by C. G. Jung, recorded and edited by Aniela Jaffe, translated by Richard and Clara Winston. Copyright © 1962, 1963 by Random House, Inc. Reprinted by permission of Pantheon Books, a Division of Random House, Inc.

Autobiography of Bertrand Russell, Vol. I, 1871–1914, published by Little Brown & Company. Copyright by The Bertrand Russell Peace Foundation Ltd. Used by permission of the copyright owners.

ACKNOWLEDGMENTS

Three people helped deliver this book. My thanks to Richard Kletter, whose timely editing moved the last draft a crucial step forward. The bulk of my gratitude goes to Pat Meehan, my editor at Simon and Schuster, and to my wife, Renee. Pat made this book happen: by dint of talent, insight, doggedness, devotion and unflagging friendship, she forced this unwieldy subject into a workable structure and then worked to ensure the clarity of expression. Renee generously poured her creative juices into my thinking throughout the history of this book and really co-authored many of the crucial ideas.

It is to Renee, with love, that I dedicate "our" book.

Contents

Introduction   9

Section I: • Childhood Consciousness vs. Adult
Consciousness   17
1. Origins of Childhood Demons   22
2. Protective Devices: A Childhood Armor and Adult
   Barrier   26
   Omnipotent Thoughts/Fantasies   26
   Omnipotence of Parents   28
3. Mastery: An Adult Opportunity and Childhood
   Impossibility   30
   The Concept of Fairness   30
   The Rule of Necessary Limitations   30
   The Seven-Step Inner Dialogue for Mastering Childhood
   Demons   31
   The Evolution of Adult Consciousness: 16–50   37
4. The Four Major False Assumptions   39
   Illusory Safety to Adult Self   39

3

Section II: 16–22: Leaving Our Parents' World   43

Major False Assumption: "I'll always belong to my parents and believe in their world."   43

Five Component Assumptions   47

1. Component Assumption 1: "If I get any more independent, it will be a disaster."   49

2. Component Assumption 2: "I can see the world only through my parents' assumptions."   57

3. Component Assumption 3: "Only my parents can guarantee my safety."   61

4. Component Assumption 4: "My parents must be my only family."   62

5. Component Assumption 5: "I don't own my own body."   64

Romance and Expectations   66

Identity Formation   67

Section III: 22–28: I'm Nobody's Baby Now   71

Major False Assumption: "Doing things my parents' way, with willpower and perseverance, will bring results. But if I become too frustrated, confused or tired or am simply unable to cope, they will step in and show me the right way."   71

Denial of Our New Adulthood   74

Four Component Assumptions   76

1. Component Assumption 1: "Rewards will come automatically if we do what we're supposed to do."   77

Life Dreams   78

Forming a Life Out of Our Talents   81

2. Component Assumption 2: "There is only one right way to do things."   88

New Rules with New Roles   90

Masculine/Feminine   93

Career Outside the Home   97

Domestic Career   98

Having a Child: Effects on Images of Maleness and Femaleness   99

3. Component Assumption 3: "My loved ones can do for me
   what I haven't been able to do for myself."   108
   Coupling   108
   Forming the Conspiracy   109
   Conspiracy and Forms of Coupling   119
   Single Life   120
   Living Together/Marriage   120
   The Two-Career Marriage Without Children   121
   The Two-Career Marriage with Children   127
   The Traditional Marriage   130
4. Component Assumption 4: "Rationality, commitment and
   effort will always prevail over all other forces."   137
   Social Class   148

Section IV: 28–34: Opening Up to What's Inside   153
Major False Assumption: "Life is simple and controllable.
There are no significant coexisting contradictory forces within
me."   153
   Breaking the Outdated Contract of the Twenties   159
   Making a New Contract   160
   Four Component Assumptions   164
1. Component Assumption 1: "What I know intellectually, I
   know emotionally."   165
   The Inner Dialectic   165
   Discovering the Truth of Clichés   170
   Work in the Thirties   172
2. Component Assumption 2: "I am not like my parents in ways
   I don't want to be."   184
3. Component Assumption 3: "I can see the reality of those
   close to me quite clearly."   193
   Marriage and Demonic Images   193
   Shifting Conspiratorial Compacts   199
4. Component Assumption 4: "Threats to my security aren't
   real."   205
   Divorce: Breaking Up a Family   207
   Who's the Enemy? The Critical Question for Divorce   210
   Aftermath of Divorce   213

Section V: 35–45: Mid-Life Decade   217

Major False Assumption: "There is no evil or death in the world. The sinister has been destroyed."   217

Five Component Assumptions   219

1. Component Assumption 1: "The illusion of safety can last forever."   220

The Loss of the Intact Family   220
Parents: Power Play in Three Generations   222
Children   223

2. Component Assumption 2: "Death can't happen to me or my loved ones."   226

The Illness or Death of a Parent   226
Other Messages About Death   229
The Male Response to Death   229
Work as a Protective Device   236
Transformation of the Meaning of Work for Men   241

3. Component Assumption 3: "It is impossible to live without a protector." (Women)   246

Taking Back the Power   247
Career Development for Women Executives   263

4. Component Assumption 4: "There is no life beyond this family."   267

Renegotiation of Sex in Marriage   267
Monogamy Is a Solution to the Oedipal Conflict   271
Questioning the Rules About Infidelity   275
Engaging the Change Process   277
Conspiracies Must Be Broken   279
Divorce as a Casualty of the Process   291
Living with the Conspiracies Unchanged   292

5. Component Assumption 5: "I am an innocent."   294

Our Darker, Mysterious Center   294

Section VI: The End of an Era: Beyond Mid-Life
"The life of inner-directedness finally prevails: I own myself."   309

CONTENTS

Section VII: Individual Growth and Its Effect on Social Issues: Marriage, Careers and Women's Liberation   321

Marriage   323

Careers   325

Our Response to Change   327

Women's Liberation   331

Epilogue   335

Index   337

Introduction

This book was born ten years ago, when a dream I had cherished collided with reality.

Having grown up in Milwaukee, Wisconsin, I went to college in Madison, where, during the second week of school, I fell in love with my extraordinary-in-every-way wife, Renee. Our first daughter, Lauren, was born in Chicago during my second year of medical school (she hated to go to bed and I needed to study). Our second daughter, Cheryl (who, thank God, loved to play by herself), was born in Los Angeles a few years later during my medical internship. Then there were two miserable years in Fort Polk, Louisiana, renowned as the worst possible assignment in the Army (108 degrees Fahrenheit during the summer, with 99 percent humidity). We returned to Los Angeles after the Army so that I could complete my residency. By the time I'd finished my psychiatric training, we'd lived in seven different rented houses and apartments.

The dream was that Renee and I would own our own house. We had been in Los Angeles long enough to like it, and it was time to buy a house and settle into a neighborhood. I now had a good salary guaranteed by the state of California: I was to be assistant director of the UCLA Psychiatric Outpatient Department. So Renee and I rushed out and bought the house we had fallen in love with. We had no financial hedge against hard times: there was only one salary and no savings. We were a bit jittery, but it all worked out on paper, and, besides, we each had parents we could lean on temporarily if some financial disaster did occur.

So the dream came true on moving day. Each of us claimed a room, filled it with our personal belongings, lined the cupboards, set up the lamps, kept the cats out of the way, and made ourselves visible to the neighbors in case they wanted to welcome us. In the moments between moving men, I proudly surveyed the house and yard from every angle. When the last moving man closed the door, we were alone in this strange place.

We slept fitfully that night even though we were exhausted. The next night, we each tried to manufacture our share of cheerfulness, but despite our friends' ceremonial bottle of champagne in the afternoon, we both felt profoundly depressed. "What's wrong?" we asked. "Why are we so depressed just at the crest of fulfilling our dream?" Although we didn't know it, we were caught by the forces of a powerful, predictable contradiction.

The dream of owning a house is constructed in childhood and becomes a myth about our adulthood. We prefigure the experience and then expect pure joy when it actually happens. However, the experience of owning a house carries with it realities never imagined in our dream. It has a meaning our young minds had no way of knowing. We felt sadness the second night in our dream house because something had died. What died was a protective illusion connecting us to childhood and our parents. We could no longer believe that we were children on loan to California, destined to return to our "real" home. Only after the illusion died did we recognize its silent presence. In the back of our minds, we were protecting ourselves against the full realization that this was really *our* life, to be lived into an unknown future. A tether to our parents was torn, and we mourned it. We were a bit less fettered by the codes of life our parents had woven into the tether, but we were left temporarily unanchored in time and space.

This forgotten childhood assumption, that I would live my adult life in my hometown near my family and friends, is not the same kind of assumption one thinks of in a debate or an exploratory conversation. It is more like a wish and therefore leads to unrealistic expectation—and disappointment, which in this instance was expressed by feelings of sadness. As I later discovered, my disappointment at having to give up this rather minor false assumption of my childhood is part of a process of shedding a whole network of assumptions, rules, fantasies, irrationalities and rigidities that tie us to our childhood consciousness. This network of assumptions allows us to believe, on a nonrational, emotional level, that we've never really left the safe world provided by omnipotent parents. The act of taking a step into an adult life—our moving into our new house—exposed this second, unsuspected emotional reality: a *childhood consciousness* coexisted alongside our rational, adult view of reality.

This event in my life, which I might have passed over as another peculiar reaction, unworthy of explanation, has become an impetus for the book that follows. For this book is about that second, unsuspected reality: how it supports and stabilizes us, how it interferes with our life, and how we can and must master it if we're to have an unfolding creative life.

Over the next few days, these sad, unanchored feelings gradually subsided. We resumed our lives but with a new sense of immediacy and fullness. Renee and I felt fortunate that we had experienced this unexpected discontent simultaneously, for we both realized that if one of us had been completely satisfied with being in the new house, the happy one wouldn't have understood the other's "morbid" reaction to this long-awaited event. An argument of some kind would have undoubtedly followed because either she or I would have "ruined" the pleasure of the other. As a psychiatrist, I would have looked for the neurotic origins in myself or in her and tried to search out the memory of a traumatic move in childhood.

However, it began to dawn on us that our response had nothing to do with a forgotten childhood event. Instead, it was a response to our *current* position in life and to the transition that had brought us there. In fact, it was a reaction set in motion *because* we had moved a step further into our own created life. The unexpected sadness we felt upon realizing our dream was probably inevitable. If only we had known. Wouldn't it be nice, we thought, if someone had written a Dr. Spock for adults so that we could have expected this? Someone should have predicted and labeled the mourning and discomfort that accompany every growth step. Perhaps then adults could be spared some of the pain and misunderstanding of significant life events. How many other major, hazardous growth steps awaited in the future? How many had we already muddled through without knowing? Yes, someone, we thought, ought to write a Dr. Spock for adults. And then we forgot about it.

Several years later, while supervising psychiatric residents, I became acquainted indirectly with the life stories of approximately a hundred and twenty-five people over a five-year period. The supervisory position turned out to be crucial to the development of my theories about normal adult changes, for I began to see patterns that I couldn't have seen if I had known the people more directly. The resident psychiatrists filtered for me the compelling but obscuring uniqueness of each individual.

When I asked the simple orienting questions—"What is the patient's major area of concern? Why did this person seek treatment at this time?"—I began to hear answers that sounded age-related. All teenagers were preoccupied with their parents. Un-

12

deniably, people in their twenties were preoccupied with vocational choice, with their new roles as spouses and parents, or with their inability to get into those roles. People in their early thirties talked about being stuck and mired down; the same important topics of life suddenly seemed vague, more diffuse and more difficult for them to understand. People in their late thirties and early forties all were experiencing an intense discontent and were feeling an urgency about determining what their lives had been and what they still could be.

As I brought these observations home, Renee and I began to ask ourselves if this was not preliminary evidence of a predictable sequence of changing patterns and preoccupations during the adult years. We began to see that certain key events—buying a house, a first car, experiencing a first job, a first baby, the first loss of a parent, first physical injury or first clear sign of aging—force us to see ourselves more as the creators of our lives and less as living out the lives we thought were our destiny. Only gradually do we let go of the values and programs of our parents' way of life. Progressively, we become freer to determine our own lives.

I started a research project at UCLA to track this hunch a little further. For six months, my colleagues and I had cotherapist investigators sit in on all therapy in the outpatient department. The groups were organized by age. At the end of six months, we rotated each investigator to a different age group. During the first year, we compared the preoccupations of each age group. By discarding problems common to all age groups—for instance, anxiety and depression—and by eliminating individual patterns of hostility or self-defeating behavior—fundamental differences between one age group and another became obvious.

This first study led to a second project. We constructed a questionnaire to be given to people aged 16 to 50 who were *not* patients, using the particularly salient or emotional or repetitive statements from the previous year's treatment groups. The questionnaire forced people to rank these statements according to their personal applicability. There were no right answers, so the ranking was a measure of each person's intuitive reading of himself.

When the questionnaire was given to 524 people, mostly between 16 and 50, who were not patients, the results matched the patient-group observations. Patients and nonpatients of the same age shared the same general concerns about living. As a result of this study, we had a rough catalog of the march of concerns and the changing patterns of self-awareness that occur in men and women between ages 16 and 50.

After reporting the findings of this study in the *American Journal of Psychiatry* in 1972 and to various lay and professional audiences, I received hundreds of letters and personal anecdotes saying, essentially, "Right on!" Not all those who said "right on" were relating anecdotes that conformed to my descriptions. Yet these people felt they were covered by my general explanation even though it didn't apply exactly to their experience.

I concluded that my report on the "posturing of the self" over the adult years was useful to all because it brought home the obvious fact that *adulthood is not a plateau;* rather, it is a dynamic and changing time for all of us. As we grow and change, we take steps *away* from childhood and *toward* adulthood— steps such as marriage, work, consciously developing a talent or buying a home. With each step, the unfinished business of childhood intrudes, disturbing our emotions and requiring psychological work. With this in mind, adults may now view their disturbed feelings at particular periods as a possible sign of progress, as part of their attempted movement toward a fuller adult life.

In 1973, Gail Sheehy, a journalist who had decided to write on the subject of adult development, came to interview me. After a second interview, she asked me to join her in writing a book on the subject. I told her I wasn't quite ready—it wasn't quite clear to me how these vague notions and descriptions connected with the deep unconscious workings revealed by psychoanalysis, and without that connection, any book on the subject would have to be superficial. I thought I would write a book in about three or four more years, after I had thought about the problem more.

This book is the product of the three years of maturing that I correctly guessed I would need. It is about the evolution of adult consciousness as we release ourselves from the constraints and ties of childhood consciousness.

Section I
Childhood Consciousness
vs. Adult Consciousness

*The greatest derangement of the mind is to be-
lieve in something because we wish it to be so.*
—Louis Pasteur, 1876

We're adults, you and I, with a healthy sense of self-confidence
and well-being. We're in control now. The pubescent horrors,
the daily private chaos of our youth have given way to a rational, ordered life—less volatile, of course, but finally dependable. Our parents' shadow has been cast off. We're our own
people now—Roger's Roger, Janey's Janey—and we chose this
life we lead.

Sure. A few minor irrationalities linger on, but they're just
little personality quirks. Right?

Well, not exactly. To brew up an adult, it seems that some
leftover childhood must be mixed in; a little unfinished business
from the past periodically intrudes on our adult life, confusing
our relationships and disturbing our sense of self. I call this unfinished business *childhood consciousness*. Every time we feel
anxious, depressed, afraid, inadequate or inferior and say to
ourselves, "There's no good reason to feel this way," childhood
consciousness has invaded our adult consciousness. We won't
outgrow it, and we can't will it away. To achieve adult consciousness we must overcome childhood consciousness.

Wistful adults see childhood as carefree and exuberant, but to
children it is also painfully difficult and filled with frightening

17

experiences. This negative and largely forgotten part of childhood consciousness that haunts our adult life is produced by the powerful, larger-than-life anger and hurt all children experience as they cope with the world. The pain of childhood grows out of the basic fact of biological helplessness and immaturity. The physical hazards of life and our intense needs overwhelm our fledgling controls. We want to walk before we're able; we demand more attention than we can possibly get; we fight for greater rights and power than we can manage; and our sensual desires and passions are insatiable. In short, as young children we want what we want, when we want it. We feel our every need as an inalienable right. Our smallest wish is an extension of ourselves. Deny us, even slightly, and we experience overwhelming frustration and unnecessary, humiliating disappointment.

Initially we blame our interminable pain and disappointment on our parents, for we feel that they are "required" to use their omnipotent power to help us and that they are not doing enough. It is this childhood sense that our inalienable rights have been violated that makes our early experience of anger larger and more fearsome than simple everyday adult anger as we know it. This childhood anger is covered over but not destroyed as we grow up. The larger-than-life anger of childhood does not reappear directly in our adult life. It reappears in a subtle but very real new form, in which we overestimate our own hostile powers and the hostile powers of others to control us. It is this fear of monstrous, potentially uncontrollable destructiveness that I will call *demonic anger* in this book. It is the key ingredient of childhood consciousness that *must* be mastered.

Because of a lingering belief in demonic anger, we misinterpret the actions and attitudes of others as well as misjudge our own motives. When we confuse the forgotten demonic reality of childhood with the current manageable adult reality, our life is disturbed in two costly ways:

1. We limit our love relationships because we feel someone is "controlling" or "smothering" us. We are crediting them, erroneously, with demonic powers and intentions that we feel will limit our freedom.

2. We don't fully realize our talents because we stop our-selves short of fulfillment, fearing a demonic motive might be at work in our ambition.

When we stop ourselves from realizing our full potential in love and work because of a misinterpretation, a lingering belief in demonic motives, we are experiencing an *internal prohibition*—a key concept of this book.

Demonic reality can cripple our work and our love, as the following two examples demonstrate.

WE LIMIT OUR LOVE RELATIONSHIPS: RAYMOND (THE SAME EXAMPLE WOULD ALSO BE TRUE FOR A FEMALE)

Raymond, 27, was happily married until last year, when his wife, Pat, began to point out a pattern he had deliberately ig-nored. Whether at work, where he is a draftsman, or socializing with friends, with his 3-year-old son, or with Pat, Raymond typi-cally has a hang-loose style and is very friendly. Yet periodi-cally, without apparent reason, he will begin to pick and snipe at Pat for the littlest things she does. "That dress doesn't quite fit," or "You left your eyelash liner on the sink again," or "Why do you read trash like that?"

Raymond always apologizes later. "I had a bad day at work," or "I'm just in a funny mood, that's all," or "I just talked to my mother on the phone, OK?" But Pat is not so easily put off. She points out that there is a strong pattern underlying these epi-sodes. Raymond's jumble of explanations will no longer hide what is really happening.

Whenever Pat gets too close to him, Raymond attacks her, yet they both want a close, trusting emotional relationship. His irra-tional act—destroying the closeness he wants—protects Ray-mond from an old childhood fear. "When we get close, I feel like she owns me. It's like I have to please her no matter how I feel. I can't even argue or disagree with her about anything."

Whenever Pat gets too close, Raymond thinks only of her wants. He orders his time to fit her schedule; he ignores his own needs. He allows Pat to become too important to him and thereby forfeits his own importance and the right to conduct his own life. Raymond flashes back to the past: he feels that Pat is deliberately controlling him the way his mother did. He is reduced to a helpless child needing to please his mother. He can't do what he wants because she'll stop loving him. She'll continue to love him only if he gives up his life for her. Pat, Raymond feels, is smothering him, keeping him from living his life as fully as he wants. He feels that she has all the power in the relationship (demonic projection) and that he has no options.

WE DON'T FULLY REALIZE OUR TALENTS: VIRGINIA (THE SAME EXAMPLE WOULD ALSO BE TRUE FOR A MALE)

"I'm 38, my husband is very successful. I've got pretty much everything: a swimming pool, two terrific, accomplishing children, and my husband loves me. I used to have a knockout body—you can still tell, even with fifteen extra pounds. Our social life is very active, we're invited to good parties. But I'll tell you, I'm unhappy and I feel like a bitch. I want to go back to work."

During the last year, Virginia became interested first in a university extension course in money management, then a university degree program in social work, then a design program, and then a job with a talent agency. Each time she was asked to make a commitment, she withdrew. What old childhood reality was lurking in the wings? Why was Virginia afraid?

"It's dangerous out there. I might not make it. My children still need me. . . . I'm too old to start at the bottom. . . . Now it's easy to criticize my husband's work, I can feel superior. If I work, I'm sure to feel inferior. We'll be in direct competition for the first time, but I'm just starting out. Of course, if I do make it out there, he'll fall apart. And let's face it, no man loves a successful, independent, ambitious woman."

This litany of untested assumptions prevents Virginia from taking the next step. If she really wants to progress, she can go slowly and probe carefully. Her husband and children support her work interest. Even if they change their minds later, Virginia still will have many decision points along the way to change her mind. She has ample time left to negotiate with her family; she has the time, as well, to explore other family and career combinations. Yet some internal prohibition—a fear of demonic reality lurking "out there" in the world—makes these untested assumptions seem valid objections, even in the face of the contradictions.

"I picture myself working seven days a week, twenty hours a day, becoming president of a company, having no time for my husband or children and no contact with my own feelings or connections with people."

Clearly, Virginia's fear of failure masked a deeper fear that she was too powerful for those around her, that once her power was loosed through work, she would drive away everyone who loved her and be left alone. Virginia's fantasy grew out of her pent-up resentment of all those years her husband had worked too hard, too long, and kept her at home feeling small, inferior, only an adjunct to him, and completely subservient to his needs.

Work was misinterpreted as her childhood revenge against her parents for overcontrolling her—a longed-for revenge come alive in the present. To work out of a desire for revenge is not a means to satisfaction or an opportunity to exercise talent; it is purely a destructive act, an immature child's uncontrolled fury. Such a motivation would ultimately destroy Virginia's femininity and softness, cause pain to those around her, and leave her isolated, cut off, living only on the corrosive energy of hostility.

In the wings, then, was an old, forgotten childhood fear of a terribly hostile world. Given this demonic reality, it was perfectly rational for Virginia to back away from her work interest. By protecting herself against the return of demonic reality, Virginia inhibited the full development of her talents.

1. Origins of Childhood Demons

Love is a shadow.
How you lie and cry after it.
Listen: these are its hooves: it has gone off, like
a horse.

—Sylvia Plath,
from "Elm"

Children are incurable romantics. Brimful of romance and tragedy, we whirl through childhood hopelessly in love with our parents. In our epic imaginations, we love and are loved with a passion so natural and innocent we may never know its like as adults.

But at times our parents leave us bitterly alone. In our young minds, they steal our love and gallop away. Overcome by sadness, we are envious of their bigness and power. We sit alone, humiliatingly small and angry. *Even if our parents loved us with perfect empathy and understanding, we all feel let down in some way and bear the scars to prove it.*

The intense emotional power of this deep childhood anger originates in our insatiable biological drive to have the total attention of the person we need. Intense disappointment is inevitable because no mother can be with her child at every moment.

But the drive has another unrealizable component that creates the demonic images. Sometimes when we are scared, tired or frustrated, we want to be someone else: to be our parents, or to be inside them somehow. We want either to own them or to have all their powers, prerogatives and skills, to invade their private lives and private adult spaces.

Understandably, our parents experience our expressions of

22

this powerful need as an intrusion into their lives. They see us as jealous, as stubborn siblings or as demanding, controlling or clinging little monsters.

During these critical moments of passion, our intense need and our parents' intense frustration with us conflict—and the demonic image is born. We learn to suppress the behavior, but we never forget the experience. Deep down, something powerful and destructive sleeps in the dark interior of our minds. If it wakes, we believe, we'll become dangerous and out of control.

As children, the pain is too hot for us to handle, so we push it out of our minds—but we can't destroy it. Somehow, we have to keep our demons buried or disguised at all costs. We express this in childhood as the fear of monsters, either inside us or located "out there," somewhere in the dark. Like the witches and goblins in fairy tales, our demons can scare us out of our wits, as this typical dream from a perfectly normal child illustrates. The child told her father:

"The toothpaste I spit out kept getting more and more yellow. It turned into yellow blobs and began to grow. They became horrible, shaking living things sitting on the ledge around the sink. They were like ducks, snails, chickens and eggy, jello-y stuff with hairy antenna on their heads and horrible big brown eyes that stared right back at me. I couldn't breathe or cry for help 'cause they might try to force their way out of me, up my throat, and come out like already-made monsters. I would never know how many I had in me or when they were done coming out."

With monsters like these inside, no wonder we suppress the intensity we feel. This child was so blocked up by her monsters, she could not even talk about them, as indicated in the dream by her inability to breathe or cry for help.

As adults, as long as we continue to harbor a monster deep within us, we're cut off from our core; we have something to hide, and so don't have a full set of human rights.

What triggers the demonic images in adult life?

23

Our demonic anger is aroused, both as children and as adults, every time we encounter a *separation situation*. But a separation situation is different for adults than it is for children. When we were very young children, a physical separation was interpreted as a violation of our inalienable rights and aroused demonic anger, often in the form of a temper tantrum. As we grew older, the withdrawal of love, whether that meant being misunderstood, mislabeled or slighted, became the separation situation we responded to. A love gap took the place of a physical gap.

While we were helpless children, our response to these separation situations took the following form: we felt impotent, controlled and humiliated, hurt without reason; our trust had been violated. Parents became vampires who grew big by keeping their children small. So the angry monster deep inside us grew stronger; we could feel big too. If control and humiliation was our parents' game, we could play too. The childhood demons born in separation situations live on in angry memories of ourselves and our parents as unloving, withholding, controlling, hateful creatures.

As adults we still remain sensitive to any signs of the loss of love, but we don't usually respond with this primitive demonic anger—over the years, we've learned to deal with the imperfections of love with an adult perspective. Occasionally we lose that perspective and blow up, but we then recover and attempt to repair the damage of our overreaction. Of course, in love or authority crises, the demonic view of reality can visit the adult present with a power so intense that the demons feel almost real and current. We are then faced with two realities: *current reality*—the reality of adult consciousness, the way we actually experience events and each other now; and *demonic reality*—the childhood consciousness reality, the intrusion into adult life of painful childhood states.

There is one separation situation in adulthood that regularly triggers the demonic images of childhood consciousness, and few of us have entirely mastered this test. It is the separation situation caused by our self-initiated attempts to change. This is a separation situation because we are attempting to separate from our outgrown definition of ourselves. When we change, we reformulate certain internal standards and transgress our own previously accepted prohibitions. For instance, Virginia was trying to break out of a definition of herself as one who couldn't have a career. Raymond was trying to break out of a self-definition that required him to be totally subservient to the one he loved.

In ways that will be explained in the next chapter, "Protective Devices," each rule that we follow and that we define ourselves by is derived from our relationship with our parents. Therefore, even though it is we who initiate the change, the demonic response is triggered because a love gap is created between us and our parents and a separation situation occurs.

We've now established a basic principle of this book: *By striving for a fuller, more independent adult consciousness, we trigger the angry demons of childhood consciousness. Growing and reformulating our self-definition becomes a dangerous act. It is the act of transformation.*

Adult consciousness progresses between ages 16 and 50 by our mastering childhood fear, by learning to leash and modulate the childhood anger released by change. As we strive to live up to our full adult potential, we confront layer after layer of buried childhood pain. Adult consciousness, then, evolves through a series of confrontations with our own primitive past. Finally, as adults we can begin to master demonic reality and rework the irrationalities of childhood.

As children, we couldn't confront the demonic, so we kept it at bay through *protective devices. Protective devices overcome our feelings of total vulnerability to the demonic and seem to guarantee our complete safety.* But the cure is as costly as the disease: like the demonic they shield us from, protective devices exact a tremendous toll from adult life, because they impose arbitrary outgrown rules of behavior and thinking on us and thereby limit our concept of who we can be.

2. Protective Devices: A Childhood Armor and Adult Barrier

Protective devices are like dependable old warriors. We drag them out to protect us when childhood pain threatens our current life. We choose safe archaic remedies for familiar archaic ills. Protective devices are born in early childhood. By thinking ourselves omnipotent and believing in the omnipotence of parents, we protect ourselves from our anger and hurt.

Omnipotent Thoughts/Fantasies

Children create a fantasy world, a kind of wishful thinking to erase the dread of unbearable separation or disappointment. At that age we become kings, queens, supermen and -women. We construct a future life of blissful marriage, extraordinary success and achievement. We make life exactly what we want it to be and endow it temporarily with the illusion of reality.

DIGGING FOR A PRINCESS
CHRIS: I hate women!
TEACHER: Why do you say that, Chris?
CHRIS: Because when ya marry them ya hafta get your blood
     tested.
TEACHER: What else do you think about women, Chris?
CHRIS: I think they're kookie! I think I'm gonna marry a
     princess . . . because they're better—they're prettier.
JIM: Yeah, because they have jewels and gold—and they have
     crowns!

OLIVIA (*comes over to the boys*): What are you doing?

JIM and CHRIS: We're digging and looking for princesses.

OLIVIA: Well, I have a bride dress at home.

CHRIS: Aw, who cares about that!

JIM: Yeah, ya need a princess suit. (To teacher) Don't tell her we're gonna marry a princess.

CHRIS: Princesses have to wear their princess suits all the time or else they'll be stripped of their beauty.

OLIVIA (*to teacher*): What means "stripped of their beauty"?

CHRIS: Aw, go away! We hafta keep diggin'.

TEACHER: Digging for what?

CHRIS: Digging for a princess, of course.

JIM: Yeah, ya don't find them in New York. We're digging our way to find one.

CHRIS: Well, ya just don't marry one like the regular way. Ya hafta save one first. Princesses fall in love with princes. *Did ya ever eat a princess?*

JIM: *No!* (*They dig for a while silently.*) I dream about army things.

CHRIS: Well, I dream about that I'm a lieutenant with a lovely princess.

OLIVIA: Boys! Boys! I just found a real live earring from a princess. (*She hands them a piece of crumpled paper.*)

JIM and CHRIS: Get out of here! (*They chase her away.*)

CHRIS (*running around the hole he has dug*): Romance! (*Running full circle again.*) Princesses! (*Running full circle a third time.*) Jewels! Let's get digging for those princesses!

JIM: No, we don't really want them. We hafta wait till we're grown up for that.

CHRIS: Yeah, till we're twenty-one!

JIM: Yeah.

CHRIS: And then we can buy a real drill and shovel and a pick.

JIM: And a whole car—and one of those things that go *Rrr-rrr-rrr*.

TEACHER: You mean a pneumatic drill?

JIM: Yeah.

CHRIS: But I wanna dig for princesses.

Child Studies Through Fantasy,
Rosalind Gould, Ph.D.

In adult life we experience these fantasies as an acute pressure to make things turn out right. We push and strain to fit a pre-ordained mold. We manipulate people into place. We squeeze the facts into a pattern they don't quite fit. We insist on rules of conduct we don't quite believe in any more. We determine what must happen so that we won't be crushed. Each disappointment is a blow to our powers. We still have to be the most beautiful or have the highest status or be the superior one, the above-it-all one; because as children, being king or queen kept us from feeling small and humiliated. In our fantasy world, we would never be left alone or slighted.

As adults we impose scripts upon our lives, imperatives that become both goals and restrictions. We must never be without a current girlfriend or boyfriend. We must be booked up every evening; at all costs, we must avoid everlasting, helpless aloneness, those separation situations that may trigger the demonic.

Omnipotence of Parents

Our parents' world is a safe world. If we follow their rules exactly, we will be protected absolutely from any harm. We must submit to their will and adopt their methods, and as long as we do, we will be safe. When our temper tantrums betray our uncontrolled anger, our parents will be our auxiliary control.

The adult expression of this childhood consciousness is manifest in the irrational rules we impose upon our lives—anything from cleaning the toilet bowl three times a week to paying all bills a week in advance. We must be carbon copies of our parents, never go beyond their identity limits. If mother didn't work outside the house, neither can some daughters. Some young men must follow their father's occupation. Our life style and values must not contradict those of our parents.

We live within an invisible set of rules. If we break them, we will suffer the humiliation of a small child. Our badness will be exposed and we will be excoriated just as if we were children again. We remain safe only inside the invisible network of our protective rules, which become rigid components of our self-definition.

Childhood protective devices are the extra clothing we wear into adulthood. The fantasy dramas, expectations of our own omnipotence, and adherence to the rigid rules and inflexible roles of omnipotent parents form the basic protective devices which we embroider with new variations tailored for each situation.

Virginia had to protect herself against her childish fear of unleashing such demons from within herself that no one would love her, so she stalled her return to work. Raymond sniped at Pat to protect himself against the feeling that, like his mother, she owned and controlled him. But protective devices cost Virginia gratification through work, and Raymond an easygoing, comfortable love. Protective devices are unnecessary in adult life. The mythic, demonic dangers they guard against *can* be mastered—by contrasting our adult experience in life (which we have clearly coped with so far) with the intensity of those powerful, childish fears.

3. Mastery: An Adult Opportunity and Childhood Impossibility

As adults we can resolve issues that bewilder children. Our capacities to control and interpret have developed over the years, allowing us to master the dangerous anger that plagued our childhood and hangs over our adult lives. We no longer need react to disappointment with feelings of overwhelming frustration. We now accept a reality beyond our self-centered wishes.

As children, when a toy was taken from us or we were put to bed or mother left the house without us, we erupted in tantrums. Our parents violated our inalienable rights and we owed them proper punishment. They in turn saw us as willful monsters.

The Concept of Fairness

Gradually we learned the adult concept of *fairness: We do not always have a right to have what we want when we want it. Our rights are limited. Other people also have rights*. We may feel frustrated, but we cannot be vengeful. No one deserves punishment. No score is left unsettled.

The Rule of Necessary Limitations

We have also learned the rule of *necessary limitations*. We understand now that as children, *we often wanted more than it was possible to have*. Our greed caused our disappointment.

As adults we expect disappointments from time to time. Instead of an automatic angry, self-centered response, we ask, "Was I treated unfairly or fairly? Was I expecting too much?" If we were treated unfairly, we may wait for the next round to get retribution; if we were treated fairly, we have to accept the disappointment; if we were greedy, we must reassess our demands.

Not all adults are so discriminating. For many people, someone else is *always* at fault and *deserves* punishment. They're never greedy. Fairness to others does not exist in their picture of the world. They take all disappointments personally and live in a constant state of cold war with the world.

The two rules of adult consciousness—fairness and necessary limitations—can help us achieve a more favorable self-image. When we can say to ourselves, "I was greedy last Monday," we gain more inner space to live. Our "total badness" is reduced to an isolated act of bad behavior. Having been greedy last Monday is far superior to being a fundamentally bad person. The monster inside is demystified.

In intimate situations, however, the adult consciousness rules of fairness or necessary limitations are often tossed aside. In the heat of passionate argument with a loved one, it's difficult to remember, "I can't always get what I want." Or, "It's fine that you disagree; I don't hate you for it."

The rules of adult consciousness are also easily abandoned when we are under stress or when we are undergoing rapid personal or social change. But even in times of stress, we can regain our perspective on reality by forcing ourselves to apply the adult rules and by engaging ourselves in the seven-step inner dialogue I will explain below. With these tools we can overcome the rage of the imperial child; we can weather disappointment and live without fearing that any of the dreaded demons of childhood will reemerge to plague our adult life. Each time we master dangerous, angry childhood consciousness, we shed our protective devices and strengthen our adult consciousness. We come to know what we want now, as adults.

The Seven-Step Inner Dialogue for Mastering Childhood Demons

A child's world is confusing, frightening and filled with struggles over power. But we've never admitted before that we have carried that same confusion, fear and anger with us into our adult lives. Now that we recognize that we have been suppressing our own demonic anger and felt its destructive hand on our adult lives, it's time to ask "How do we master demonic misinterpretations in everyday life?" An everyday example should prove illustrative.

Ever try to act natural in front of a menacing authority figure? It's no mean task. One syllable indicating annoyance, a faint tick of irritation for His (Her) Highness and—*flash!*—I'm cornered, afraid for my life. My heart shoots out reinforcements to my outmanned muscles. My back gets tense enough to be a tight-rope. I've got intuitive radar in every pore—anything moves and I'll know before it happens. My palms self-lubricate. Everything's ready. I'm all set for a humiliating spanking. "Don't hit me! Don't hit me!"

The corner we're cowering in is found in childhood bedrooms and adult offices alike. Sometimes we can't tell the rooms apart, and we react as if both situations—facing a spanking father or a powerful boss—are the same. We're all kids again, waiting for Daddy's angry hand to strike.

At the same time, we see things in their present context. "This guy's certainly not my father. Double-knits, no hair—all wrong. I'm no helpless kid, I'm an adult."

In short, we have two contradictory perceptions about the same event. It's a crisis of decision. Which reality do we choose? If pressed, most of us would admit we didn't exactly choose; we sort of "muddled through."

"How can I choose between two realities? By definition they're both real. This is Aristotelian America, the Western world, one reality is all we get. Period."

We are making progress. So far we have completed two important steps in the mastery of demonic misinterpretation of everyday situations: We've recognized our confusion. We've superficially understood that we respond to two contradictory realities.

What next? We'll experiment. Let's ditch adult reality and go full steam with demonic childhood reality.

"Let's say this guy's my father and I'm due for a wallop. What do I do? I sign right up for every anti-parent, anti-child-abuse kid-lib group in town. Or maybe I'm a little more of a coward and decide to do battle with my bladder instead."

At this critical moment, we have completed another step: We have given full intensity to the childhood reality.

"Now, even if I buy this childhood reality and I'm standing there, a scared kid with no options, sooner or later the idea'll snap out of some uninhibited neuron somewhere and I'll know—this guy is not my father, and he is not about to spank me! I'm an adult. I may be scared, but I have options!"

That's great. Another step; both realities exist simultaneously with deeper emotional intensity.

"OK, I'm ready. I'll gather up my courage (from where?) and find out who this guy really is. But how? I know. I'll ask a question, one that needs to be asked (not 'Are you going to spank me?'). About work or whatever. Or I'll make a statement, let him know I have my own point of view. Wait. Even better, I'll *tell* him I want to go ahead with the recommendations of my report despite his reservations.

That's another step: Test reality. Take a risk that discriminates one view of reality from the other.

"If I challenge him, he'll know I'm an adult, and maybe I will too. Of course, even if he isn't my father, he might have a terrible temper or something, which will burst out as soon as I ask the first question. Maybe he'll throw a tantrum and treat me like a child anyway. Well, let's find out."

That's yet another step: Fight off the strong urge to retreat just when we're about to find out what the *real* truth about this situation is.

"What the hell. A little wrath from the boss is a piece of cake compared to a spanking from my old man. I mean, this guy may yell a little, but he's not going to destroy me—I'm an adult."

Congratulations! The final step: We now have an integrated, trustworthy view of a small section of reality unencumbered by the demonic past.

These are the seven steps necessary to master demonic childhood reality when it intrudes on our adult life. Using these steps on important issues may take a lifetime to learn. For less fundamental concerns, it may take only a few moments. But all issues interconnect—work on one issue is always work on all, even if indirectly. Rarely will our seven-step mastery process follow the pure linear sequence described. Instead, we stop and start, go backward, sideways and forward, breaking through one moment and retreating the next. But we still muddle through, and whether we realize it or not, these are the seven steps of the inner dialogue we all go through to free ourselves from the demons of the past. To sum up, we have to:

1. Recognize our tension and confusion.

2. Understand that we respond to two contradictory realities.

3. Give full intensity to the childhood reality; that is, let it be real.

4. Realize that both contradictory realities still exist. We're not sure which one is real. Confusion again, but more intense and better defined.

5. Test reality. Take a risk that discriminates one view from another.

6. Fight off the strong urge to retreat just on the edge of discovery.

7. Reach an integrated, trustworthy view of a section of reality unencumbered by the demonic past.

THE SEVEN-STEP DIALOGUE IN EVERYDAY LIFE

EDNA

Edna, 48, and her husband maintained regular but inhibited sexual contact during their first twenty years of marriage. For the past eight years, they haven't touched each other. When she came for help, Edna complained bitterly, "This is ruining my life."

The best approach to a major problem is not necessarily the most direct. For Edna, using the seven-step process to work on a minor but symptomatic problem seemed a more effective way to attack her major sexual problem.

Edna is back in graduate school. At 48, she still enjoys an active social life with her younger colleagues. She frequents student parties and entertains regularly in her home. Edna comes from stern stock, and her father obsessively emphasized quiet in the house.

In the school library, as her father did at home, Edna requires total quiet. At the slightest whisper, she boils into an almost uncontrollable rage. Vituperative moral indignation races through her mind, but she dare not speak to the offending students. "I won't make a fool of myself." Her intense desire to punish and humiliate the noisy students far exceeds the crime, and Edna knows it. The rush of intense hatred makes her feel misanthropic and overly critical, a person unworthy of the friendship she receives. Her inappropriate anger deserves to be punished, she feels, even though "I'm certainly right about the noise."

Often Edna wants to whisper in the library, but she can't quite do it—even if no one else is there to disturb. She feels mousey, weak, indecisive and socially ill at ease. "I just don't fit. They're so young and flexible. I'm a stiff old goat." She is also childishly afraid of criticism and the authorities.

Edna flip-flops between two childhood realities: she becomes both the tyrannical father who enforces quiet and the child who cringes and cowers in front of him. She brings the quietness issue home from the library. When Edna putters around the house while her husband naps upstairs, she feels forced into quiet, as if he is restraining the free exercise of her daily activity. She feels victimized and then vengeful, as impotent in her marriage generally as she is in her sex life.

Let's follow Edna through the seven-step dialogue:

Step 1. *Recognize our tension and confusion.*

Edna felt angry and misanthropic when she wanted to feel loving. Her tension and confusion were obvious.

Step 2. *Understand that we respond to two contradictory realities.*

Edna maintained two views of quiet. The childhood view—her father's rule of absolute quiet—and the reasonable view that normal everyday sound, even whispering, need not intrude on anyone's space.

Edna maintained two views of her husband as well. She saw him simultaneously as tyrannical and controlling, and helpful and kind. She felt powerful, superior and disdainful one moment and weak and vengeful the next. When Edna went back to school, she began striving for a fuller, more independent adult consciousness and thus brought new intensity and awareness to her tensions.

Step 3. *Give full intensity to the childhood reality.*

Edna refrained from using the protective device of acting superior to her husband and allowed the demonic feeling of the victimized child to develop. She also violated the rule of quiet at home and at the library and felt less cramped but scared, as if punishment would come at any time.

Step 4. *Realize that both contradictory realities still exist.*

Edna brought the two contradictory views of reality into one moment of consciousness. She doggedly reminded herself of the contradictions until she was not sure what was real. She felt victimized and controlled by her husband despite indications that he was actually being a good friend.

Step 5. *Take a risk that discriminates one view from another.*

When her husband came down from a nap, Edna was caught between reason and anger. She didn't know whether to choose the archaic or the adult view. Somehow she took a stand. Edna contained her petty annoyance and questioned her husband but without accusing him. He replied, "I'm a sound sleeper. There are two doors between the downstairs and the bedroom, and short of blasting music, I don't think anything you did could wake me. But if there's a problem, I'll try to work it out with you."

Edna's reasonable tone allowed her to probe openly without forcing her husband to be defensive. If she had been angry and her husband's tone resentful, no matter how conciliatory his words or her questions, no progress would have been made. Edna would have misinterpreted him as a tyrant hiding behind reasonable language.

Step 6. *Fight off the strong urge to retreat just on the edge of discovery.*

Edna had to convince herself that the probe could continue without the monsters taking control. After all, she might lash out at her husband for years of having to sneak around her own house, and he might tear at her for daring to question his divine rule of quiet.

Step 7. *Reach an integrated, trustworthy view of reality unencumbered by the demonic past.*

Edna's new integrated view emerged. She broke the stalemate in their marriage and ended eight years of sexual abstinence. Edna became a person with options again; she could act differently in the library and at home. Now she was free to talk and think about matters she had considered closed for the rest of her life.

Edna overcame an inhibiting piece of childhood consciousness and opened herself to an enlarged adult consciousness. Even if her husband had been in fact a rigid tyrant, Edna would have accomplished just as much through the seven-step process, for an adult woman with a rigid tyrant husband has options that are not available to a child with a rigid tyrant father.

The Evolution of Adult Consciousness: 16–50

Mental life seems to have an unconscious goal—the elimination of the distortions of childhood consciousness and its demons and protective devices that restrict our life. We can approximate this goal through constant, dynamic use of the seven-step process. We can master childhood demons and gradually loosen our protective devices.

As our life experience builds, ideally we abandon unwarranted expectations, rigid rules and inflexible roles. We come to be the owners of our own selves, with a fuller, more independent adult consciousness. We live by a world view generated out of personal experience, not one dictated by our need for protection. As we feel more "adult," we correct our excessive infant demands and abandon the need for complete control and ownership of the loving mother. We come to accept that we own only ourselves. No one else owes us love, attention, admiration or anything else. We are no longer dependent, powerless children, and we can now view life from the independent vista of adulthood. This view evolves slowly for most of us, in four phases over the ages 16 to 50.

4. The Four Major False Assumptions

Illusory Safety to Adult Self

The protective devices we dismantle over the ages 16 to 50 include not only the irrational acts, the rigidly interpreted rules of childhood, and the fantasies we impose upon life, but also a whole network of untested false assumptions (like the assumptions Virginia made about work or those I once made about eventually returning to Milwaukee) that help protect our important illusion of absolute safety. When we are young children, this illusion is maintained by our belief in *four major false assumptions:*

1. We'll always live with our parents and be their child.
2. They'll always be there to help when we can't do something on our own.
3. Their simplified version of our complicated inner reality is correct, as when they turn the light on in our bedroom to prove there are no ghosts.
4. There is no real death or evil in the world.

By the time we enter adulthood, at the end of high school, we know that these assumptions are factually incorrect, yet they retain hidden control of our adult experience until significant events reveal them as emotional as well as intellectual fallacies. We come to trust our own adult thinking and judgment as the real and only source of safety, and then we can gradually afford to replace these false assumptions and surrender the illusion of absolute safety we once found so necessary. The periodic shedding of false assumptions marks our gradual shift from childhood consciousness into adult consciousness over the range of decades.

The first assumption is "I'll always belong to my parents and believe in their world." This assumption is challenged in minor ways before the end of high school but in more significant ways during the ages 18 to 22, when events such as living away from home or joining in a protest march bring the assumption into question. As this first major tie to childhood is shed, we feel a great sense of liberation along with a potent new fear.

The second assumption is "Doing it their way, with will power and perseverence, will bring results. But when I become too frustrated, confused or tired or am simply unable to cope, they will step in and show me the right way." This assumption is most powerfully challenged during our twenties, when we are setting up an independent life and making major decisions that nobody else can make for us, such as marriage, pregnancy or career choices. When this assumption falls, we drop another piece of illusory safety and add to our identity a new sense of fundamental strength and independence built on the solid rock of proven competence.

The third assumption is "Life is simple and controllable. There are no significant coexisting contradictory forces within me." This assumption is most powerfully challenged in our late twenties and early thirties, when most of the simple rules and supposed-to-be's about life prove ineffectual in the complicated real world. Once we have mastered the task of the twenties and become competent and independent in the external world, we can try to get in touch again with the feared inner world.

The fourth assumption is "There is no evil or death in the world. The sinister has been destroyed." This is most effectively challenged during our late thirties and throughout our forties, when time pressures mount, others die, parents become peripheral and children are ready to graduate from the home. At this time we must dig deep inside, where the monsters are supposed to live. We must touch our own inner core to release the power that will rescue us from stagnation without destroying the valuable and dear parts of our life.

This book is organized around these four assumptions and the four major phases of adulthood between the ages of 16 and 50.

These phases of life are determined to some extent by age-linked cultural roles dictated by our society and by the individual evolutionary work each one of us has accomplished in the preceding phase of his or her own life. Therefore, in each particular subculture in this country, there will be a particular mix of forces at work to move the timetable of potential challenges forward or backward. Although the ages given for the four phases are approximate, they fit a very large segment of the population.

We are concerned here primarily with changes in consciousness, with the different ways people interpret events in their lives at different ages. The events themselves—love, work, marriage, dealing with our parents and our children—occupy center stage in everyone's life. But because of changes in consciousness, events are experienced differently at different stages. For example, separation and divorce have entirely different meanings in our twenties, thirties and forties, as do major changes in work, the death of a parent or disappointment with a child. Even though we may predict events in our future with some degree of accuracy, such as when our children will be leaving home to start their own life, we have no way of predicting how we are going to interpret these events. There is no way of sampling a consciousness of the future; at best, we can recapture a sample consciousness of the past.

We are talking, then, about an individual's change of consciousness, which is determined by the individual's own starting point and rate of change. The outcome of change is determined by how successfully we resolve the assumption being challenged. The rate is determined by how capable and efficient an individual is at processing psychological material—in particular, how willing that individual is to abandon the irrational protective devices and reexperience childhood anger and hurt in order to reach inner freedom.

If we cling too tenaciously to the childhood illusion of absolute safety, the assumptions will go unchallenged and we will have to live at the command of others, as if we were still children. We can't be alone when we are defined only by others and exist only as they witness and endorse us. Neither can we tolerate being too close to others, because we become claustrophobic trying to squeeze ourself into their definition of us. We have a hostile dependency on those who control our safety, because we can't freely see, feel or act in a way *we* believe is correct. We can't afford to form judgments that contradict divine rules, just as one does not contradict a god if that god is one's only protector. Because we're afraid of our core, we have no access to heightened passions. There is no inner unfolding of our life, and we feel somewhat bored by the reruns of old realities. We are stuck with a view of ourself that has to be replayed over and over again. We are afraid of our natural impulses, frozen in childhood morality, with our parents' vision of good and bad. We can't trust our intuition, so we lose certain nuances in life and impoverish our interpersonal relationships. We can't trust our own assessments of reality, because we constantly need endorsement from someone who is bigger. In short, if we tie ourselves too closely to the illusion of absolute safety and do not take the risks necessary to emancipate ourselves from childhood consciousness, we live a dull life without full adult consciousness.

As an alternative, we can risk enough to keep growing and moving. When we do this, we progress at our own maximum rate, alternately advancing and retreating, in our own dialectic. We move from dependent little ones afraid of our demons and totally subservient to our parents to independent adults who can think about everything and form reliable judgments. As adults we can replace the illusion of parental protection; we can take calculated risks in order to be free. We can control our own life from deep inside us. Instead of requiring inseparability from a loved one, we can learn to enjoy the benefits of separateness. We can discard the old roles, rules, concepts and clichés that we've previously accepted unquestioningly. We can recoup our rich inner life and allow it to lead us into a new life filled with mystery, compassion, thought and deep intuitive wisdom.

In the remainder of this book, we'll follow the steps and stages in this transformation process in greater detail—our adult dilemma of choice, safety and self.

Section II
16–22
Leaving Our Parents' World

I kept listening for a sign of myself, for some mention of me.

—Jimmy Porter in John Osborne's
Look Back in Anger

Major False Assumption
to Be Challenged:

"I'LL ALWAYS BELONG TO MY PARENTS AND
BELIEVE IN THEIR WORLD."

ROBERT'S DREAM
"I felt like Flash Gordon. Everywhere I went, the 'Invincible Foe' stayed right on my tail. He wouldn't let me do anything. . . . This one time, he was hanging on to me, and I started whaling on him with a club, trying to knock him off me. I didn't want to kill him, though, 'cause I knew he couldn't hurt me. Only, what I was trying to do . . .

"I had my escape all figured out. I became a special CIA agent with a pass, just like the letters of transit in *Casablanca*. Nobody could question it. I could go anywhere and do anything I wanted.

"I got on board my escape plane—I had lost him for sure this time—and we take off. Then the stewardess says I have to show my credentials to the copilot; he wants to check them out. I head up to the cabin, whip my credentials out . . . suddenly the copilot turns around, and it's the 'Invincible Foe'!''

ROBERT'S STATEMENT

"I told my father to get fucked. I said, 'You *can't* be happy doing what you do!' Whew! Was he pissed! . . . Sometimes I wish my father was dead so I could be free to be what I want to be.''

At other times, notably when he walks through his grand campus alone, Robert feels "I'd really like to do right by him, to make him happy, to be what he wants me to be.''

Robert is 19 and in limbo; no longer a boy, he is not yet a man. This dilemma begins typically at age 16 and extends until about age 22. Like Robert, at this age we stop being exclusively our parents' child and start constructing an adult identity.

Robert, like Raymond in Section I, believes that someone is holding him back, keeping him in childhood: for him it's his father. He doesn't really want his father to die; he just wants his need to please his father to die so that he can feel free to please himself.

Robert has already begun to see himself as an adult, so that while there is a "foe" who appears in his dream, he is only a *co*pilot, not the pilot. The completely adult Robert would be his own pilot and fly without a copilot, according to his own directions. On the other hand, if Robert were still completely a child, his "Invincible Foe" (his father) would be the *pilot* and Robert his submissive passenger. With his father as copilot, Robert is clearly still forging his new identity: while trying to cut loose from his parents, Robert has not abandoned the need to please his father.

At each age up to now, Robert has mastered the tasks presented by the culture. He's an A student, athletic and popular and very active in politics. Robert knows he is potentially a competent, self-reliant adult, yet he feels unsure of his ability to handle adult life.

With most of us, as with Robert, the doubt comes less from realistic self-assessment than from an uncertainty about our *right* to take care of ourselves. Until now our parents have been the producers, directors and scriptwriters of our lives while we've been the lowly actors, with limited opportunity for improvisation. Though we are developing an adult consciousness, our childhood consciousness still determines our concept of our rights.

To accept our right to become adults, we must successfully challenge the first major false assumption that allows us to believe in the illusion of absolute safety: "I'll always belong to my parents and believe in their world."

Work on this major assumption takes over our psychological space between ages 16 and 22. For some, the struggle is immense, while others—about 10 percent according to some studies—seem to breeze right through. For a very few, this period is a long and catastrophic nightmare ending in vivid psychosis as demonic childhood anger returns to dominate the adult consciousness. The highest rate of first hospitalization for psychosis occurs in this age bracket.

The irrational fears of our childhood reemerge as we challenge this first assumption of childhood consciousness: we feel painfully vulnerable and are overly sensitive to all authority figures, particularly to our parents. According to one young man, his parents' harsh words can "feel like dumdum bullets that expand inside me and tear me up."

Our parents' influence, while powerful throughout our life, weighs heaviest on us at this age, at the beginning of our adult life. Robert's father not only is his "foe" but is invincible as well. His views are solid and supported by the entire socioeconomic and cultural structure. Robert's fledgling view is often contradictory and terrifying, and he has only his friends for support.

Like Robert, all of us at this age feel unprepared to contest world views with our parents. Even a diplomatically expressed opinion from them can overwhelm our fragile sense of self. Sometimes we feel that if we are definite and unyielding and firm in our position and strident enough in our presentation, we can overwhelm our parents. We hope that our passion will triumph over their solid-as-bedrock view.

As adult perspectives begin to replace those of childhood, eventually we come to see our parents as people, not just as our parents. Seeing them as fallible, typically well-meaning but confused people, we may be drawn closer to them. The dynamics of their mutual power plays take on a new clarity. It is like Dorothy discovering that the Wizard of Oz is only a man behind the curtain. We knew our parents didn't always talk straight; now we learn that they may have been going through difficulty in their relationship with each other at those times.

Once we have analyzed what's going on, we want our parents to admit that they see it too. Our motive may be to help them; but we also want them to acknowledge our perceptions and our right to have these views. What we are asking is formidable: what we see may be real, but to our parents it is their secret that has survived at least twenty years of daily collusion and silence. Just by acknowledging our new view of the family's reality, our parents will have begun to change the only life they've ever known. Change for them is threatening and difficult, yet we feel we must try; for deep inside us, we know what every family therapist knows: the problems between the parents become the problems within the children. At this point in our lives, we still hope to cure their problems and thereby our own.

If they are unwilling to be "honest," we may blast them verbally. Our strong, direct criticism is often just an attempt to goad them into an angry or defensive response. Or we may use more subtle methods. If they claim, "We don't want to run your life," we become passive or mildly self-destructive and wait, our patient trap set. Soon the controlling parent will be drawn out for all to see.

In our pious, tortured logic, we believe that because they have let us know what they want for us, they must be controlling us. The only way to have our freedom in that system of thought is to stop them from wanting anything from us or for us.

But we can control them by causing them pain, by defying their wants and expectations. We gain power at their expense, and then we hate them for being weak and vulnerable. We tempt our mothers and fathers to reassert their dwindling roles by telling them, in minute detail, about the turmoil of our life. We push them into ridiculous authoritarian positions, then scoff at their folly. Though rationally we see their pain, we can't stop ourselves. All we see emotionally is a world of power plays, hostility, deception and self-deception.

Daniel, 20 years old, agonized endlessly one afternoon over whether to go out for dinner with a friend or to accept his mother's offer to make him dinner. If he refused her offer, she might be hurt. On the other hand, if he accepted, he would feel she was controlling him. His choice was to feel guilty or angry—two bad feelings, both caused by her. What should he use as a guide? Does he really feel like going out with his friend, or is it just an excuse for hurting his mother? Are his feelings reliable?

When the childhood consciousness released by a major separation point like this dominates, we suspect psychological violence at every turn. We can perceive only two possible motives—direct hostility or muted hostility. Our belief in goodwill is gone; our faith in love is eaten up by corrosive anger. But this view is too bleak. As a blueprint for future life, this consciousness is much too ugly. We're desperate for a new view. We must develop a more adult consciousness or self-destruct in some childish indulgence, perhaps alcohol or drugs or petty vandalism and crime.

When childhood consciousness dominates, this angry world view is easily triggered. But fortunately, for most of us, the demonic rules our consciousness only in periodic bursts. For the better part of youth, adventure and exuberance prevail.

Five Component Assumptions

Challenging the first major false assumption of childhood consciousness—"I'll always belong to my parents and believe in their world"—usually breaks down into five component battles. Although we may fight on all fronts simultaneously, most of us pick a favorite "belief" and deploy our main forces there.

The five component false assumptions that make up the first major assumption are:

1. If I get any more independent, it will be a disaster.
2. I can see the world only through my parents' assumptions.
3. Only my parents can guarantee my safety.
4. My parents must be my only family.
5. I don't own my own body.

1. Component Assumption 1

"IF I GET ANY MORE INDEPENDENT, IT WILL BE A DISASTER."

This first component assumption is a vague notion that is expressed as one of various specific fears, such as:

I don't have all the necessary tools to be an adult.

If I leave the nest, my parents will fall apart, because I hold them together.

If I show my unacceptable uniqueness, no one will ever love me again.

It's always painful to leave those you love. At 16, 17 or 18, our work to take on some of our parents' power, to become independent of their world view, is painful and traumatic; we feel alone and unsupported. In short, the conflict of this age is that while we want to become independent adults, we don't want to feel the pain of separation. So like some Joseph Heller character caught in a maddening bind, we fight hard, but often on the wrong battlefield.

PETER: "I DON'T HAVE ALL THE NECESSARY TOOLS
TO BE AN ADULT."

Peter is a failure, or so he believes. He left home and now he's back, having suffered an obvious and ignominious defeat. Peter was fine in high school; he and his friends had been together since grade school. But at high school's end, it was time to leave the comfort of years of common experience, of shared gripes about teachers, rules and parents. Peter would have to make it socially on his own merits. Potential new friends would judge him not as a former sixth-grade pal but according to the Peter they met now, in the present.

His parents' home was Peter's prison. He was desperate to

escape and yet afraid to leave. If only they were dead, he would be forced to leave. But that fantasy made him feel guilty. He had to get away, but where should he go?

Some of his friends went to Santa Barbara, so Peter went along, but his sense of initiative vanished. After three months, he came home. Peter had left home physically, but mentally he was still a dependent child. At school he felt "freaky and spaced out." He drifted too much and studied too little. New friends were hard to come by, and he was so lonely he couldn't bear it. Now home again, he feels humiliated, passive, shamed by his own weakness. His future looks bleak.

Peter tries to fit his feelings into the inadequate vocabulary we have all used to describe our inner life. He says, "I feel as if a part of me is missing." When Peter expresses that thought, he's living under the control of the childhood assumption "I don't have all the necessary tools to be an adult."

The way Peter thinks and talks about the problem is unfortunate. For if a "part" of him is missing, then "it" is geographically separated from him, and someone else may have "it." He may need a new "one" from someone else, or he must passively await "its" return. Peter's metaphor makes him *absolutely* dependent on someone else. It says, "I am passive and am an incomplete human being; I am too defective to live without someone taking care of me."

When asked, "What is it you can't *do*?" Peter begins to realize that his current description of himself as a person with an important part missing is not a permanent self-description. He can change. His feeling of missing a part becomes only one of the contradictory messages about himself, his powers and his capacities. As Peter's web of self-distortion unravels, it permits him insights common to his age: he's afraid to leave home but not incapable; he's just tempted to continue *acting* incapable to put off the day of leaving.

Actually, Peter feels intellectually superior to his parents and more "with it." But he is afraid to demonstrate his competence because they will expect him to continue taking responsibility for his own life. He is sure that his parents, overshadowed by his skill and envious of his youth, will hate him. But if he's unhappy or unsuccessful, they have no reason to be envious.

Peter is being controlled by two other variations of the component assumption "If I get any more independent, it will be a disaster." These variations are "If I leave the nest, my parents will fall apart, because I hold them together" and "If I show my unacceptable uniqueness, no one will ever love me again."

Unchallenged, the demons who guard these false assumptions make it seem dangerous and destructive for Peter to live up to his full potential, to be his fully evolved adult self.

Through hard and thoughtful work, Peter unearths many contradictions. He sees that he's been relating to his friends in part as if they are his mother and father. In this way, Peter could leave home physically and still be with his parents in his mind.

For instance, the girls he dates must carry the conversation to put him at ease and then coax him into continuing contact with them. After all, his mother always seeks him out. When his girlfriend Mary does not do what his mother does, Peter is angry. A strange paradox dawns on him: he resents his mother when she babies him; he resents Mary when she *doesn't* baby him!

Peter's social life is filled with self-defeating expectations. "I'm not a very good conversationalist." So Mary ought to carry his part of the work. It's an unreasonable expectation, and Peter realizes he must pull his own weight. *When he sees he's been wrong, Peter sheds a bit of psychic debris;* that is, he replaces elements of childhood consciousness with pieces of adult consciousness.

Peter observes that he has a similar problem with his father and his friend Tom. If either expresses a strong opinion, Peter feels he must submit. A smirk on his face betrays his inner discomfort, and he feels himself shrivel inside. While Tom and his father are merely expressing their own views, Peter *experiences* being controlled and dominated. Whenever his father and Tom actually *do* try to force their views, Peter becomes so perturbed that he also becomes strong and resistant and is not dominated.

Peter's earlier feeling that he always surrendered his opinion, or was overwhelmed, crumbles as he discovers that he is really making a positive decision not to hurt Tom. He actually thinks Tom can't bear to be wrong. So while Peter describes Tom as powerful and domineering, he actually thinks of him as frail, fragile and immature. Again, when Peter discovers *from his own observation* that he has been wrong, he sheds more psychic debris (childhood consciousness) and grows another step.

Peter realizes that even if Tom actually behaves in the dominating manner he fears, it won't be the end of the world, because he can just speak up. He concludes that differences of opinion are allowable and that he can begin to express himself. Encouraged and confident, Peter initiates experimental dialogues with his father.

Some months later, before going East to school, Peter plans to sell his pickup truck for a Volkswagen convertible. After a thorough examination of costs and trade-offs, Peter informs his parents of the plan. His father says, "You're going to buy a car on impulse, like you always do, and be dissatisfied later on and want to sell it."

In response, Peter goes through the following sequence. At first, he feels hurt and damaged; his self-confidence is destroyed. Then, enraged, he storms into the kitchen and announces to his mother, "I hate that man." On a long, thoughtful walk, Peter decides that he knows what he is doing and that his father is wrong. More important, he realizes that it's all right for them to have different opinions. He won't even try to convince his father that he's right. Peter feels all right about himself—strong again and no longer damaged. He's disappointed that his father avoided the real question: "Since it is cold in the East, do you think a VW convertible is the right car?" He wonders, "Why did my father have to attack me like that—saying 'I'm just a kid who never learns'?" He concludes that his view is superior to his father's on some subjects and inferior on other subjects. He need not feel completely inferior or completely superior any longer.

Later that same evening, his father recants after talking to a visitor from the East who supports Peter's position. Though it feels good, Peter is sorry that his father recanted. In his mind, even the good feeling means that his father's approval is still important to him. Peter does not want his father to have *any* effect on him. He wants to be his own pilot and achieve pure independence.

Peter ended treatment at the beginning of summer vacation. That fall, he went to a new school across the country. He felt good about himself and his future. He was ecstatic that at Christmas he would see his parents at his place. He would have enough time to get established and could greet them in his world.

Achieving a fuller, more independent adult consciousness can take other forms besides Peter's anguished to-and-fro movements. Just before high school graduation, some of us soak up love as if storing it against the impending pain of leaving home; in so doing, we disprove the popular idea that adolescence has to be a period of hostility to our families.

At the other extreme, bitter family warfare can occur, usually when we turn our fear of unknown territory into the slogan "I can't wait to get out of here." We provoke confrontations to prove that we stay in this "prison" only because our parents won't let us go. We totally deny that we want a childhood sanctuary where someone will always care for, protect and soothe us and keep life at bay when we need a respite. Leaving childhood does mean bearing our own sadness and fear.

Pounding away at our parents for the tough time they have letting us go helps us avoid dealing with the end of this era. When our terror drowns our thoughts and feelings, it becomes more difficult to sort out the origins of our fears. Then we're caught in a vicious cycle: if we can't think clearly, we have good reason to fear being on our own—the belief "I don't have all the necessary tools to be an adult" appears confirmed.

A reality of past failures or economic or educational deprivation can seem to confirm the idea that we are unprepared for the future. But these real disadvantages can also generate a drive to achieve that the more privileged often lack. Having a privileged key to the world is good fortune, but it can lead to the crippling belief that not much is ever going to be expected of us. We find ourselves living, psychologically, at a subsistence level.

Another false belief, "My parents will fall apart if I don't hold them together," may be reinforced by another reality—that of too dependent parents. Whether we are the first or the last child to leave, parents may hold on too tight. They may even fall apart temporarily if we get our own apartment, move too far away or deviate too far from their future plans for us. But reality changes; an emotionally crippled parent often springs back to life when that becomes necessary to keep our love.

The childhood consciousness belief that "If I show my unacceptable uniqueness, no one will ever love me again" may be based on reality too, but it is an unhealthy reality that we must overcome. Our parents may greet our uniqueness with limited empathy: throughout our childhood, they may have insisted that a meaningful connection with them could be based only on certain behaviors, which made us suppress our true inner selves. For example, we may be energetic and verbal, but they may reward only docility and silence. Even if our parents did insist on rigid rules of behavior when we were children, we can now teach our parents that new aspects of ourselves are just as worthy of love as those they so carefully nurtured when we were small.

On the other hand, we may fear our uniqueness as a powerful sadistic streak that will show if we aren't careful. We're especially worried because we know that our meanness is targeted at the ones who love us (but who never love us enough). This is just the childhood consciousness fear of demons inside ourselves. But this childhood reality, too, can be transformed into adult reality through the seven-step inner-dialogue mastering process described earlier.

Though "reality" might seem to confirm the false assumptions of our childhood consciousness, we must remember that there are always two realities competing to dominate our world view. The "reality" of childhood consciousness is transformed as our perceptions become more adult. We must work to free ourselves of the three false assumptions that prevent us from exercising our adult independence. We must feel that we contain limitless internal resources (have all the tools), that we are engaged in a productive, not destructive, venture into life ("I'm not destroying my parents' or anyone else's life by leaving the nest"), and we must be eager to find and expand our uniqueness, with the confidence that we will be most loved for just that.

Once we rid ourselves of these three false beliefs, we live without limits; we question every axiom of life. We want to, and often do, break every rule of moderation; we throw ourselves into wild adventures and take extraordinary risks; we test the tolerance of our bodies for sleeplessness, hard work and ecstatic sensations. We hurl ourselves into new activities with great intensity and switch violently in midstream from one interest to another. We raise our heroes up to the sky and bury our foes in the mud. We have great loves and tragic disappointments. In short, we are condensed energy waiting for a direction.

When we find a focus, we pursue it with single-minded dedication and confidence until we reach a dead end. Then we pick another direction and enthusiastically explore that path. In this way, we probe life outside the family and test our capacities, interests and passions. We take risks and often fall flat on our faces. We may feel foolishly wrong or so disillusioned and depressed that we're not sure our capacity to believe and risk will ever again return.

We constantly push out, with all of our might, to find the new boundaries. Where are the limits, we ask? When do we crash into the brick wall of reality?

That's just it. Our independence is not complete and total. In our more reflective moods, a very disturbing feeling emerges. We're not free at all. It's just a temporary game. In the end we'll become just what our parents designed us to be. Despite all our struggles, some guidance system within us will lead us in the direction they have planned. Between these two equally false opposing realities—that we are completely controlled or can be completely free—we live out the years between release from childhood and commitment to adulthood. It is a kind of moratorium, during which we take inventory of our talents and develop a dream of our own life.

2. Component Assumption 2

"I CAN SEE THE WORLD ONLY THROUGH MY
PARENTS' ASSUMPTIONS."

One of childhood's most tenacious and harmful falsehoods is the belief that people must be identical in order for love to continue and hatred to be avoided. Stated another way, it is the conviction that differences inevitably lead to antipathy and abandonment. This fallacy can cause us to imitate those we love and can make us fear that our individuality must be sacrificed as we begin to get close to someone.

It is also expressed as "the myth of family one-mindedness." Therefore, for ourselves and our parents we must establish that people can love one another very much despite great differences. The myth of a single family mind dies hard. As differences emerge and inevitable arguments occur, someone or everyone in the family will attack those disagreements to preserve the idea of the single mind.

This is especially apparent if we return for a visit after living on our own. In anticipation of the visit, we feel a combination of dread and eagerness, an unmistakable sign that we've changed but that the issue over differences has not evaporated.

The eagerness is easy enough to explain—the desire to see old friends and the family that loves us, to be back with the familiar, to luxuriate in being taken care of, and generally to escape the pressures of the new life. But we usually hide the dread from our parents because we don't want to hurt them. They're expecting a good visit, full of fun and love, and—most significantly—the return of their child. And that is our dread: that we'll give up our gains in independence and agree to be theirs again. After all, it's easier to be their child again for a short visit. But the compromises are self-defeating. We feel cowardly. Can our adult consciousness gains be real if they are so easily wiped out?

On the other hand, if we refuse to compromise at all and each small difference becomes a *cause célèbre*, we may keep our independence, but not without a lot of overkill and negative feelings.

A special kind of argument takes place during these visits. The substance isn't relevant, but the form of the argument is. Sometime during the visit, we'll brand parents as tyrants. "You're trying to squash me. You're not even willing to tolerate my opinion."

We usually have good evidence for that accusation, for our parents feel the same tension we do. Intellectually they may agree that we have a right to our own opinion, but emotionally they can't resist the temptation to exercise their waning power. Buried in their arsenal, the atom bomb awaits for a particularly bitter dispute. Their nuclear punch is often delivered something like this. "You're making the same old mistake again. We already know what will happen. You haven't learned anything." What can we do? When we were children, they *did* predict the future. Didn't they tell us we would get hurt if we didn't stop roughhousing?

But sometimes we won't sanction a different opinion. Katie and her mother argue over the issue of sex with love versus sex as recreational activity. When her mother says quite calmly, "Look, we are of two different generations; you do it your way, I'll do it my way," Katie sees red, as if she'll have to give up her position if she can't change her mother's.

The same kinds of arguments happen over fundamental life issues—money, politics and values—or the most trivial family matters. We have to be right. We have to demonstrate that we can think for ourselves, and we also want our parents to acquiesce, to validate our opinions. If we can be of one mind with our parents, if they will agree with us, we don't have to bear the full burden of sadness and uncertainty that comes when we are separated from them and their ideas.

So after or during each argument with our parents, we must present the "tyrant of the day" award, a medal we sometimes must pin on ourselves. When we've identified the tyrant, we're in a better position to assess the real argument and decide what to do about it.

Generally, there are four possible explanations for the arguments of this era, and any one or all four of them may underlie a specific incident.

1. Our parents really are tuned in to a weakness in us that we're avoiding.

2. Our parents are jealous of our energies and freedom of choice because they are so overcommitted and locked into position.

3. Our parents are threatened by their loss of power over us and by the dissolution of the family that our independence confirms.

4. We provoke the tension because of *our* separation worries and our disturbing fear that, no matter how we struggle, we're predestined to become what they want us to be.

If they've zeroed in on a weakness we've been avoiding, we must recognize it and do something about it. But if any of the other explanations are behind the argument, only a thorough and ongoing dialogue can help. It is to be hoped that both parties will eventually see the same reality.

We each challenge our parents' world view in different ways. Some of us who are expected to go to college refuse to go. Even if we go to a school our parents choose, we find ways to question their assumptions. Janice, a girl with racist parents, went to a small Southern school and promptly made friends with a black man; Kent, the son of a highly successful professional man, brought home a rigorous Marxist friend from his father's alma mater. Some of us pursue an education though our parents assume that book learning is irrelevant; or we are preoccupied with self-concern to counter our parents' inability to control their lives.

We keep a sharp eye out for their hypocrisies and contradictions. If they're fundamentally wrong about some issue, we feel intensely irritated with them. We feel as if they did something quite destructive to us. In our eyes they have no right to be so wrong.

If we go to college, our questioning of assumptions gets institutional support. The value system of the university demands that we think critically, begin a dialogue with the great thinkers and theories of past and present. Also, life in a university community is flexible, affording us an opportunity to experiment with different values and ideas. We would not have that freedom in most jobs. In that way, the university is *the* institution of the moratorium between the end of childhood and the shouldering of adult responsibilities. It gives us permission to challenge—in fact, it *demands* that we challenge—what we believed as children.

Of course, college does not guarantee that we will rethink our parents' assumptions. College may be merely an extension of middle-class life style. Some of us, whether working at a job or at college, actively avoid the growth made possible by experiencing new and different views. We surround ourselves with a remnant of high school friends and stay too close to home, literally and figuratively. We make only lateral moves in our lives, sometimes wandering a bit and often becoming prey to depression. We have still not overcome the false belief that becoming more independent means disaster for us.

The solution is a commitment to a lifetime of learning (formal or informal), to expanding ourselves and crossing barriers. Whether or not we go to college, we have to create our own college of the world. If we fail, we breathe the stale air of old, tired ideas. During these years, ages 16 to 22, free thinking and free speech are more than precious rights; they are vital to our immediate growth and to the future outcome of our lives.

The deep questioning of parental assumptions is more than adolescent play: it's a deadly serious business.

3. Component Assumption 3

"ONLY MY PARENTS CAN GUARANTEE MY SAFETY."

As teenagers we tested our share of parents' safety rules, but our little trials were tempered by their constant presence, by the fact that we saw them every day.

Until we challenge the childhood consciousness belief "Only my parents can guarantee my safety," we have to live out our parents' ideas of prudence. We have to accept their version of a safe career, a safe person to love, and a prudent life style lived in a prudent place. Females have an added burden because our culture supports the idea that they're fragile and must be protected at all times. "I feel you're in safe hands now" is an often stated, and bitterly remembered, remark when a parent approves of a daughter's future husband.

If we were all coolly unemotional, we'd probe our parents' safety rules step by step, with solid-as-brickwork logic. But being emotional people, we test by embracing the opposite. Instead of saying, "I'm not so frail," we usually say, "I am invulnerable."

Most of us are lucky. We escape disastrous results: we don't get pregnant even when we buck the odds, our canoe doesn't flip over when the calm river suddenly flows into rapids, and our car doesn't go out of control when we race too fast around a sharp curve. The trauma of near-misses and almost-consequences usually brings us to our senses. We finally come down someplace between our parents' safety advice, which underestimates our ability, and our own unreasonable disregard for safety, which is our childlike wish for invulnerability. Our definition of acceptable risk becomes a product of our own experience.

4. Component Assumption 4

"MY PARENTS MUST BE MY ONLY FAMILY."

The very nature of the family calls for lifelong loyalty. We exist today only because our parents nurtured us and gave us life. Despite our complaints or their harmful inadequacies, we owe them our survival.

As we gradually transfer feelings of "family" to other people who are important to us, we suffer great conflicts of loyalty. For instance, when our new love visits home for the first time, we desperately want our family and the "outsider" to like each other; in fact, we want them to love each other instantly, intensely and forever. If the outsider blends immediately, our loyalty conflict is resolved. Of course, it doesn't usually work out that way. The situation is often quite difficult, and being judged sets up defensiveness and sometimes offensiveness. If our love and family don't like each other, we have a head-on collision with the false belief "My parents must be my only family." If we break with our new love, we deeply resent our family. If we defy our family, we're poisoned with guilt and blame our new love for causing the rift.

We run into the same problem between our friends and our parents. We need our friends to support our new view of the world, to fill in the holes of loneliness, to confirm our belief in our new future, to even out our moods, to curtail us from extreme acts, and to provide an occasional respite from the pain of growing away from our parents.

We belong to small informal groups that constantly change and exchange members. Every group maintains its particular world view and tolerates only so much deviance; if we go beyond that boundary, we are cut out, to wander off alone until we find a group that shares our new, deviant view. Group support is necessary to integrate new beliefs as part of ourselves. The more important the new belief, the more potent our sense of group affiliation and loyalty (at least for a time) and the more intense our feelings of disloyalty to our family.

Friendship during these years is a mixture of "the friendship of equals" with "the friendship of unequals." The friendship of unequals is the old form of the family. The friendship of equals is the new form of the community of adults. Our self-centeredness and self-probing during this period force our friendships into the new form: we won't give our friends more than they have coming as equals, because without give-and-take, we would feel used. They do the same for us. Every time they are selfish, every time they refuse to be self-sacrificing for us, they teach us that we are no longer in the old family form of relationship.

In dozens of ways, we carry parental dependencies in our expectations of friends. When we're sick and away from home, we all think of the classic line "You never care for me like my mother did." The long, wrenching talks with friends when we try to sort out who hurt whom are an essential part of our growth. Without friends close enough to disappoint and be disappointed by, the hidden dependencies we carry continue unchallenged and distort all future relationships. Our excessive expectations—what we believe others are supposed to do—make us too demanding and controlling. We harm those foolish enough to stay with us, and we repel others whether we want to or not.

Eventually our central group of intimates and our small galaxy of satellite groups grow constant and become the rival to the family back home. Without the new family's essential support, we might capitulate to our parents' world view. But the new family can also persuade us to take positions we don't fully believe in, so, like a Ping-Pong ball, we bounce back and forth between central group and family, family and satellite groups. The more divergence we encounter during these moratorium years, the more distinctive our own personal philosophy will be by the time we have to choose a way of life.

5. Component Assumption 5

"I DON'T OWN MY OWN BODY."

The false belief of our childhood consciousness that we don't own our body is successfully challenged when we finally give in to the urge to have intercourse. We take full title to our body, wresting it from our diapering and feeding parents, when we decide to act against authority and in favor of intimacy.

The world of intercourse is hazardous; our capacity for pleasure now is coupled with an equally passionate potential for hate. Sex, for most, remains the weak spot in our characters; because of its mystery, it can become the vehicle through which the childhood demonic returns to disturb our developing adult consciousness. A jealous child is evil, but a jealous spouse is quite acceptable. Revenge against a husband or wife can show spunk or guts. Intercourse opens the door to all our passions for exclusivity that were denied by our parents' closed bedroom door.

Of course, intercourse is just the beginning of adult sexuality. Some evidence suggests that our sexuality becomes increasingly intense as life goes on. Step by step, inhibitions get peeled away. We reach sexual contentment, then become restless to move into the unknown, to always gain a little more. We are striving to regain a natural sensuality remembered from our movements within the womb and from infancy, when we felt as one with our parents. Intimacy requires emotional confidence and represents an important step toward a more developed individuality. If our recent independence from the family is still in jeopardy, becoming close with an "outsider" may be difficult. Only when we accept our separateness and uniqueness can we *allow* ourselves full intimacy.

Our parents' sex life and our fantasy about their sex life are equally important to the development of our sex life. If they enjoy sensual intimacy despite lip service to a strict religious line, we will know it and will have little problem enjoying our own living intimacy when the time comes. However, if their sexual attitudes conflict, our response may lead to defiant sex or constrained, "holding back" relationships; to fully enjoy a close, pleasurable sexual intimacy, we'll have to dare to be different from our parents.

Today, the predominant cultural sexual values support the full ownership of our body. But this permissiveness can backfire: for some people, the demand for instant "emancipating" sexual activity may come before they are ready for even the first step, separation.

Intercourse should yield comfort and pleasure—yet it can be so difficult and so powerfully disruptive. The battle over sex is not really a battle with our parents. Certainly parents can cause us difficulty on this issue, but battling with them, no matter which technique we use (secrecy, flaunting, provocation, setting them up, agreeing with them), may just be a way of generating enough defiance to push us over the line. Finally, even if everyone important in our world said, "It's OK and necessary," having intercourse would still be a big step.

Children perceive intercourse and sleeping together as a single parental activity. Our adult rule against intercourse, then, grows out of our childhood confusion at our parents' sleeping together. Alone in a dark, scary world, it seems strange to us as children that our big strong parents huddle together for comfort each night. Why should they sleep together while we're left alone with the terrors and mysterious demonic images flashing brilliant in our lonely, immature minds?

At an early age, we learned to fight our deep longing to snuggle with them in their bed. We had to be forced out of our bedtime tricks: "Can I stay up a little longer?" . . . "Tell me just one more story." . . . "I want a glass of water." . . . "Mommy, come quick, there's something scary in my room!" The tricks that won our entry into their bedroom eventually had to end.

As we slowly gave up access to our parents, we denied an extremely powerful urge to be between them in bed. We learned to oppose our natural urge to cultivate intimacy and safety. We must unlearn that opposition before we can have intercourse. The desire for pleasurable intercourse conflicts with an unknown demonic dread. If we go ahead, something deep and psychic and irrevocable is going to happen, and we are plagued by physical fears and humiliating fantasies from our childhood consciousness.

Romance and Expectations

When a romantic sexual relationship finally blossoms, we confuse our new friendship of equals with the old friendship of unequals we had with our parents. Our old dependencies and expectations, while inappropriate with friends, take control again as soon as someone loves us. Back in the old form, we have a right to expect our loved one to be devoted to us, to be selfless in their regard for us, to care about our sensitivities, to like everything about us, to understand us when we are unclear; in turn, the loved one has every right to expect the same of us.

In short, we are reliving the special kind of love we had with our parents. Our fledgling independence is being risked in another intimate relationship even while our parents still copilot our lives. The notion that "I'm still young and need time to find myself before I settle down or make lifelong commitments" usually prevents us from straying too far, although we do suffer from mistakes along the way.

Afraid of loneliness and wanting to remain in the family envelope forever, we look hopefully to our new intimacy as a magnificent compromise that may free us from our parents without sacrificing our sense of safety and belonging. At worst, this view leads to ill-conceived premature marriages. As the statistics for the survival of teenage marriage indicate, failure is built in.

The decision to marry at this age may seem to be a claim to independence or an act of defiance, but it's really an expression of a secret fear that we need a partner to escape our parents' influence. Friends are not enough; we feel we need to be part of a permanent couple to counterbalance the two of "them." In an early marriage we expect our spouse to emancipate us, because we are afraid we can't do it ourself. It's an impossible task, and our disappointment is severe and predictable. When both partners marry for this reason, the relationship is doomed to bitterness and frustration—instead of freedom with safety, we get dependence with disappointment. Our new love just can't match our parents' devotion.

Identity Formation

Identity formation is a label for the evolution of self during the ages 16 to 22. While busily preparing our career, we're engaged in evolving a fuller, more independent adult consciousness.

We challenge the assumptions of our parents' world and develop our own beliefs and values; we gain our independence, then share it with a group or lose it in a forced agreement with an intimate; we feel big and solid away from our parents and threatened when we return; we sample intimacies for the proper combination of closeness and freedom; we fight for the right to our own bodily pleasures; and we learn the difference between friends and intimates and our own parents.

As we make our first important adult decisions, we are certain that we're not in the least bit like our parents, and we resent our friends' or relatives' pointing out similarities in sensitive areas.

I WILL NOT BE LIKE MY PARENTS

JULIE

Julie wants to be a musician. Her parents want her to become a doctor, which she regards as "an obviously middle-class trip to make me dull like them." A pretty, smart, highly verbal sophomore at the University of Chicago, Julie has a deep, rich voice and a strong interest in drama and music, and she refuses to be scholarly.

She drops out of school and goes to California with only two hundred dollars, the name of a boy her parents disapproved of—and a dream.

Two months later, broke, depressed, lonely and unsure of herself, she is living in squalor, not sleeping for days, and eating old french fries pocketed from free dinners after recording sessions. She becomes sick, begins coughing and is terribly tired. Fifteen auditions have yielded invitations from the worst groups and rejections from the best. She has often spent four hours a day waiting for buses. Her musician boyfriend is out of town with another woman, gone perhaps forever.

But Julie is not about to return to her luxurious home. "At least I am finally starting to get into my own life. I'm no longer going through the motions of school in order to get grades, graduate and follow the rest of a programmed life."

Julie is afraid she'll be scooped up and locked into a worn-out, parent-determined life if she doesn't take powerful action to confirm that part of herself that's *not like* her parents—even if it means denying the part of her that is exactly like her parents. She hates to admit that the security, predictability and material comfort she grew up with have any value to her. Choosing to sleep on strange floors, living by her wits, disregarding her health, and romanticizing poverty may appear foolish to others, but for Julie it's a vital necessity.

We're sculpting a self during these years: the form's not final, but it's a start. At this age, of course, we must borrow a few ideas, a few imitations of our parents' traits and values. But eventually, with great ingenuity, we rework their old fragments and keep only what we want.

I DON'T HAVE TO BE LIKE MY PARENTS

RANNY

Ranny replaced her alcoholic, sexually promiscuous mother as the responsible one in the family. She was her highly moral father's favorite, and before she left for college, they had long intellectual discussions.

During her first year in college, Ranny was a serious, dedicated science student. The next year, she acquired a reputation as a brilliant but erratic student, one who almost failed courses but always rescued herself at the last moment. She was known as a drinking "party girl" who dated only athletes; she pretended to be promiscuous, although she graduated still a virgin. Finally, in her senior year, Ranny became a serious student in a useful but not especially intellectual field. And she kept her fun-loving personality.

During her first year in college, Ranny slavishly imitated her father. In the next few years, she blindly mimicked her mother by living out a "party" life. But throughout she remained true to some inner voice and pulled it all together in her final year.

We form our adult consciousness slowly during these years. Step by step we abandon our parents as models and begin to construct our own identities. By about age 22 we have to leave the half-child, half-adult world in which we can be *anyone* and settle into being *someone*. Each time we replace a piece of childhood consciousness with adult consciousness, we become our own *someone*. The process is painful but also exciting and rewarding.

Peter, who was discussed earlier, wrote me this letter after several months at college:

Dear Roger—
What brings this letter about now—as opposed to any other time—is the occurrence of what I consider a spectacular event. I fought off a migraine for the first time in my life. . . .
Before school started, I was doing really well meeting people—I felt I was open. And being open was the key. . . . Then school started and the fight began. It was so hard. . . . Either I was in or I was out. I could tell if upon arriving at class I would avert my eye from another's glance or if I would feel comfortable, free to talk, investigate others, by myself. OK, I could have some degree of control over these states. Yet sometimes when I knew I could turn the tide I would instead indulge in my self-conscious shell.
Migraine incident: Last night I was at school at the Red and

White party. I hadn't gone in yet and was standing out in front talking to an acquaintance with a huge sea-lion face and perpetual sleep in his eyes and two girls I had never met.

I felt fine—yapping away. Thinking how pretty one of the girls looked and generally having a good time. Knowing how much I hate parties, when the suggestion of going to a bar came up, I was hip to it. So off we went, having a good time in a fairly ridiculous bar. All of a sudden I began to have primary migraine symptoms. OH SHIT!!! So instead of indulging as I usually do, I did my best to relate as usual—gave my drink away and—in between jokes—talked to myself about how stupid it was to ruin myself when I was doing so well. It was kind of like Julie S.'s behavior of crying for Mommy when she caught herself having too much fun. So on the way back to school I realized my visual symptoms were clearing up unusually rapidly and uncharacteristically were not being succeeded by numbness in my left fingers. Wow. As time goes on we grow. My situation now excites me. I got over the first hump and am sliding into the yet to be known.

Section III
22–28
I'm Nobody's Baby Now

Major False Assumption to Be Challenged:

"DOING THINGS MY PARENTS' WAY, WITH
WILLPOWER AND PERSEVERANCE, WILL BRING
RESULTS. BUT IF I BECOME TOO FRUSTRATED,
CONFUSED OR TIRED OR AM SIMPLY UNABLE TO
COPE, THEY WILL STEP IN AND SHOW ME THE RIGHT
WAY."

"In college, my friends and I spent a great deal of time clamoring for freedom of choice on the gut issues in our lives. Once I was out of college, however, I discovered a surprising thing . . . that choice was intellectually appealing, but in other ways it was a bit fearsome. Somehow, it had never occurred to me that the freedom to straighten out your life was also the freedom to mess it up. The realization was a heavy one, and there are still times when I'd like to hand the reins of my life over to someone else and say, 'Here, you drive for a while.' "

This is it! No more Linus blanket to cover our fear. We can huff and puff but we can't blow our terror away. No matter how we strut or bluster, the world still smacks us right in the face, and it is up to us to react, to find a way to cope with that. We can deny that we are now really responsible for our own lives, try to cede

71

our responsibilities to others and limp ahead half child and half adult. But the critical issue of our twenties is that we must build our own lives in the complex, unpredictable real adult world. Either we use our skills and do all that's necessary to sustain ourselves (with a little help from others) or we don't.

Between ages 16 and 22 we began to move away from our parents' view, but now we must move toward our own view. The major experiences of adulthood—work, marriage and family—await our decisions. They are subtle, deeply personal, profoundly important choices certain to confuse and harass us. Though we may want to throw in the towel and live by someone else's rules or decisions, we are the best and only judges of our future. We must make up our own minds.

The major false assumption which must be challenged during this era of life is "Doing things my parents' way, with willpower and perseverance, will bring results. But when I become too frustrated, confused or tired or am simply unable to cope, they will step in and show me the right way."

When we achieve an adult consciousness view of this false assumption, we learn that our parents' way will bring us results in some instances but not all. We learn that if we're frustrated, we can call for help, but we can't let anybody else take over. As the adult architects of our own existence, we must accept the new reality and the full responsibility. This is yet another stage of relinquishing the childhood consciousness illusion of absolute safety provided by omnipotent parents. The material, practical world grabs our attention. We become engrossed in our "doings" and set our sights on doing better. We want to master what is out there, and we gradually shy away from the endless meanderings and explorations of our interior world. Rigid, unyielding schedules absorb our time, and we feel somewhat narrowed, concentrated and focused compared with the way we felt in previous years.

The demands and limitations of each job or our new careers (including, for some, starting a marriage or a family) become the borders of our new life. Out of a vast impersonal world we create a manageable personal space to become important in. We define an area in which, if we devote our energies to it, we can definitely prove ourselves as adults beyond our parents' long reach.

In many ways, life becomes simpler. We have more reason for self-confidence. We are expected to solve only a finite number of problems within a limited range of possible solutions. Tasks can actually be accomplished by interaction, work and perseverance; processes are shared and knowable. It's a mental vacation compared with figuring out who we are, what we believe, what we're going to do with our talents, how we're going to solve the social problems of the globe, what form of government our country ideally should have, and what the perfect way to raise our children will be. Because the self-imposed tasks of the previous years had no end point, they afforded no opportunity to gain self-confidence based on performance (aside from grades and school tasks, which were no longer novel in college) or completion of tasks.

Finally, the extreme self-centeredness of the 16-to-22 age period is broken up as we attend to people and things apart from us. What a great relief to spend time out of that shadowy world of self-scrutiny and constant minor dissatisfaction and to live in a clearly marked world of events and programs not so easily personalized and overvalued.

The kind of thinking we use every day changes, and our methods for success change with it. Between ages 16 and 22, self-reflection and constant meditation on the passion and romance of life temporarily suspended our critical thinking, and we "let things bubble up." In our twenties we must shift to a mode more suitable to the world of things. Thinking must become critical, analytical, sequential, experimental and goal-oriented. Instead of flashes of insight, we must learn to value perseverance, willpower and common sense and tolerate being wrong in order to learn how to be right.

For those of us who accept the challenge of these years and put our will and energy into worthwhile and necessary tasks, daily successes will accumulate and provide a solid base of confidence built on real competence. As we meet each novel experience or tackle each larger task, our sense that everything can be accomplished grows. Fantasy powers are replaced by real powers. A feeling of movement and growth replaces the fear that we will always be small and appendages of our parents. As our confidence, our competence, and our sense of being adult increase, the mocking voices within us grow silent.

Denial of Our New Adulthood

On the other hand, we must master the false assumption of this era; we cannot deny the new reality of our adulthood and decline total responsibility for ourself. If we wait for someone to rescue us, we cannot build self-confidence or come to feel solidly independent.

Those of us who choose this dependent response are miserably unhappy: we feel not only passive but chronically incompetent. As a special dispensation from reality, we want someone stronger to shoulder our psychological work and share our misery because they love us that much—in short, a not-so-subtly-disguised parent. This demand—that our parents exercise their powers on our behalf—binds us to them and grants them or their substitute an *equally* powerful claim on us. Thus entwined, we expend our aggression responding to real or imagined disappointments with parents and substitutes.

The psychological work of this period, then, is to recommit our aggression to adult work so that we become truly competent. This is our only workable strategy for gaining real adult independence; it replaces the childhood consciousness strategy of trying to become independent by making our parents admit we're independent.

If we deny the new reality of our twenties—that we really are on our own—the world seems an unfriendly place. No one does enough for us. We're always disappointed. Even a job with great potential is a disappointment, because its challenges are seen not as opportunities but as unfair and unnecessary demands. In this impossible position, all bosses are parents, all our friends are siblings. No job has any future. We're blind to the future because we are facing backward.

Living under the childhood consciousness false assumption creates the self-defeating attitude that we should not have to put ourself out or curtail our pleasures or force ourself to do anything we don't want to do. We may end up doing things because we have no choice, but then we feel we've done a favor for someone, who owes us something in return. If we are not treated accordingly, we will spoil the atmosphere or refuse to participate any further. We demand, by our visible resentment, to be treated in a special way.

When we're not getting what we want, our disappointment comes through in snide remarks, sarcasm, guilt-provoking looks or helpless postures. Others recognize our disgruntled response, since they've wrestled with the same issues and had to face the tasks we want to avoid.

In the grip of this childhood consciousness fallacy, we constantly anticipate failure and rejection. At best, we view successes as flukes and, at worst, as temptations to raise our hopes so high that the next failure can be devastating. Why use willpower or self-denial if no growth or change is really possible? Everything will always be the same for us! When we're still living with the false assumption of this period, no one cares enough; opportunities for growth are only opportunities to be humiliated again. We will probably fail, but if we succeed we will surely not be properly appreciated or acknowledged.

No one lives entirely within this kind of self-pitying delusion. Sometimes we do see the world as a place of boundless promise, but then in the face of accumulated frustration, parental deliverance can seem the only hope. Also, we function unevenly in the major adult enterprises. We may have an extraordinary capacity for intimacy but be totally ineffective in our career, or vice versa. We may be competent parents yet function like children with our own parents. We may function 90 percent of the time with full acceptance of the new reality, only to regress when we feel unappreciated or disappointed by someone important to us.

Four Component Assumptions

A careful look at our own behavior and thoughts while reading the sections that follow will convince us that we often deal with the world under the influence of the major false assumption being challenged during these years. This major false assumption can be broken down into four component assumptions:

1. Rewards will come automatically if we do what we are supposed to do.

2. There is only one right way to do things.

3. Those in a special relationship with us can do for us what we haven't been able to do for ourself.

4. Rationality, commitment and effort will always prevail over all other forces.

1. Component Assumption 1

"REWARDS WILL COME AUTOMATICALLY IF WE DO
WHAT WE'RE SUPPOSED TO DO."

When we assume that rewards follow "correct" behavior, we
are willing to sacrifice for success. We expect that if we do our
part, life will pay off accordingly. Our dreams will come true.
People will respond to us the way loving and decent people
ought to respond; fair play is guaranteed, and we will be com-
pensated for our efforts. When we find out that life doesn't always operate this way, we're ready to sue for breach of contract. Disappointed, we come once again under the sway of the
major false assumption and wait angrily for someone to rescue
us.

Steven had a rough three months when he came back from a
tour of duty with the Marines in Vietnam; he couldn't get a job
to support his family. A minor car accident kept him at home for
two months with a bad back; then for another month afterward,
he refused to get up and look for a job. He was brooding about
the broken contract with life: he had done his duty; where was
his fair reward—how come it was so hard for him to find a job?
Although Steven had a legitimate grievance—the treatment of
Vietnam vets has been disgraceful—when his wife finally lost
patience and demanded that he pound the pavement again, he
took responsibility for himself and found a job.

After we dig ourself out of one of these holes and deal with
reality, we usually don't amend our expectations. We're drawn
by the optimism inherent in the basic psychological tendency of
our twenties: to face the world and respond to its challenges
with as much energy as the terror of failing and the pleasure of
succeeding can mobilize. And the hope that our dreams will automatically be fulfilled helps keep us facing outward to reap the

very real rewards of our optimism. We don't see another way to fulfill our dreams until the end of our twenties.

Life Dreams

The dreams of life constructed in our twenties come in many shapes. Gerald had a clear-cut dream: he was to become a high-paid graphic designer. He committed himself to a straight course, no distractions allowed; all emotional relationships were a waste of time and energy that would only delay him.

Sharon also had a clear-cut dream: like her mother, she would marry young. She would always look beautiful, prepare beautiful meals, make beautiful love for her handsome dream husband.

Steven's vision wasn't so clear, but he knew he wanted to work outdoors, help people in trouble, and have substantial leisure time with his family.

Karen committed her extraordinary intelligence to medicine; she planned to save marriage until two to three years after she became a doctor. She was open to marrying and having children sooner if she didn't have to sacrifice her career.

The dream of life that surfaces in all of us to guide our decisions during our twenties actually began to form out of the stock male and female role models offered to us early in our lives. As boys we understood that if we did our work well, there would be an end to our smallness, our fear of bullies, and the rest of the terrors and everyday humiliations of childhood. We would become powerful adults through our jobs. Girls could end the powerless state of childhood by becoming wives and mothers, just as little girls become fantasy (often tyrannical) mothers of their dolls. Some people go far beyond these stock gender roles when they discover that they have particular talents. We also gain inspiration from new heroes. In our late teens and early twenties we package, as best we can, our initial adult dream of life.

All too frequently, though, this process of modification seems to stop in our twenties. Gerald lived out his original dream during his twenties. By the age of 27 he had become a famous designer, but he "arrived" with a drinking problem, three arrests for going ninety miles per hour on the freeway, great loneliness, one divorce and a morbid fear of women. He was unhappy, but he overrode his unhappiness by willpower. He needed to drive ahead, for built into his work dream was compensation for his relationship with his mother. He always felt so guilty around her that he had to do or be anything he thought she wanted. In his early teens he learned to feel in charge of himself by being cold, aloof and isolated around his mother and the girls at school. He rose above them all by mastering his willpower (he was able to hold his hand in a candle flame for thirty seconds). He felt unable to love a woman without becoming her vassal, so he masked his defect with an air of superiority. He mastered the work component of his dream, but somehow it didn't satisfy his family needs. He was living out the belief that if he developed his talents, his weaknesses would go away automatically. Self-destructive drinking, gambling and reckless driving became dramatic reminders that half his life was a failure. When the signs became flagrant, he finally recognized the dissatisfaction he had tried to will away.

Sharon also had a rigid, unmodified dream. For as long as she could remember, she'd been waiting to spend all her energies loving and being loved by a man forever after. She had no vision of life aside from some vague romantic notion of effortless family bliss. She was committed to the notion that marriage brings surcease from the struggle of living. At 24, while working as an assistant in a land-brokerage firm, Sharon was just becoming keenly aware that she had a talent for business when she met and married her dream man. Even though they needed her income, she quit her job to set up a dream house. She would take baths in the middle of the afternoon so that she would be sweet, fresh and ready when her husband returned. No more than two months into this idyll she began to get symptoms of disturbance for the first time in her life. Her image of herself as the perfect vivacious girl was attacked by stomachaches and sudden waves of terror that required her husband to come home in the middle of the day. Soon she had a driving phobia. Her husband's work became the object of her anger; his business sense was not as keen as hers. Her savings were used to supplement his income.

Years later Sharon learned that her dream was her way of never leaving her mother. She was going to be the perfect wife as she had been the perfect daughter. In that way, she could keep buried her anger and resentment. To repair the trauma she'd felt at age 4, when her parents divorced and her mother went to work and left her with strangers, she would be a perfect little-girl wife, with an inseparable husband. In addition to suppressing her anger at that old hurt, this dream allowed Sharon to enjoy sex. A perfect daughter could have intercourse only while in love and during marriage. She was the squarest person in her high school class, but as a beautiful single woman living in Los Angeles in the 1970s, she violated that credo with several different men before she married. Each time after intercourse, she found herself desperately in love, even though she wasn't really the least bit interested in marrying that particular man. They all turned out to be "bastards" in her eyes, for they continued to treat her as a date or a special friend and not as the adored "wife" she needed to be to keep from feeling guilty.

While Sharon and Gerald lived out their dream scripts and found themselves with symptoms, Karen and Steven lived out their dream scripts and found themselves quite happy. While an intern, Karen married a man with quiet strength, the kind of man who had never attracted her before. She has put off having children until both of their careers settle down, which she expects will be in her early thirties. Steven, at 27, is a married policeman who works with juveniles and spends almost every weekend with his brothers, their wives and his parents. They barbecue, play poker, go camping, go fishing and laugh a lot. He became a policeman after first being a Marine, then an auto mechanic, then a probation officer.

Beneath the surface of the conscious life dream lies an insatiable older, deeper dream of an ideal state where all the hurts and pains of childhood are permanently effaced. Like an iceberg, the part below the surface is treacherous to our navigation. The more our dream of life is composed of this deeper dream, the more it becomes a rigid, unrealizable mandate of the future rather than a useful, flexible guide. Sharon and Gerald are living off the older, deeper dream, influenced by the component assumption that "if we do what we're supposed to do, rewards will come automatically." But reality clashes vigorously against this belief, causing symptoms of illness. They must become more flexible, like Karen and Steven, to break the lock of this assumption and survive happily in the real world. Caught up in the older dream, we're trying to correct the pains of the 4-year-old rather than living in response to our own unfolding talents.

All of us have some of this deeper dream beneath our conscious dream. The status system patently tells us as men that if we can get enough power, money or fame, we'll reach the magical ideal state of bigness. The status system is a validation, if not the source, of our deeper dream. Even though novels and movies portray high-powered executives with wrecked personal lives and the counterculture has convinced many of us that status is an evil fiction, the myth that power brings bliss remains a potent illusion, for it appeals directly to our most cherished hopes in life. For women, the myth that marriage brings bliss and surcease from the struggles of living remains an equally potent illusion for the same reason, despite the important inroads made by the women's liberation movement and despite every woman's direct experience as a child—marriage didn't bring surcease to her mother's struggles; it added a new struggle.

Forming a Life Out of Our Talents

But the combination of seductive social myths and our deepest wish to find a pain-free ideal state is not the only reason we live out a childhood consciousness script in which life pays off automatically. The alternative, living off our talents, is very difficult. First of all, it's hard to identify what our talents are. The obvious talents in the arts, music or athletics are but a small fraction of identifiable talents. Some of us have the capacity to make things happen or to inspire trust or to hustle or to grasp the center of a problem or to expend great, concentrated efforts or to bring grace or laughter into the world. To fit these talents to roles available in the world is a difficult and consuming task, particularly since no role fits exactly our glossary of talents and since most careers really are a mixture of roles.

Even after we've identified our talents, put them into action and are enjoying great satisfaction, a new set of talents may emerge and upset the life system we've set up.

MARY

By 26, Mary had made several moves in life, from relationships with different men to graduate school to jobs, believing that only change could make her dream of life come true. Each move was made without bitterness and with only a minimum of separation pain and depressive mourning.

Mary is a psychologist, with a master's degree in school counseling. She has a burning desire for social action. Her dream is to combine these elements into a career, and at 26 she is working with a group of dedicated and enthusiastic teachers in a ghetto school on an exciting, productive model project. The work is demanding, consuming and clearly meaningful. After a short time, she is elevated to an administrative position that lets her make use of her graduate-school training within the project. Her future as a school psychologist is bright, and her dream seems on the verge of fulfillment. For the first year, she tells her friends about the job with enthusiasm, yet she is nagged by an inexplicable, vague private reservation. She feels this way for a year, then begins to have physical symptoms: headaches, insomnia and chronic indigestion.

Only when Mary stepped out of counseling to work on a political campaign, and years later, in law school, did she recognize her fear that she was going to spend her life as a psychologist if she continued with that almost perfect job. It was such a close fit that the job might have smothered that part of her headed for social action and politics through law. Getting into a social movement through counseling was a compromise made in college that grew out of a conflict with her intellectually ambitious father and overly traditional, nonintellectual mother. Being active in sociopolitical movements had always been her particular drive, but she discovered that doing it through law was more her own way.

The pathway to satisfaction is fraught with missteps and brings us frequently to critical junctures, lonely periods and unconventional decisions. But, like Mary, if we have the courage to trust our feelings, we can end up in the position that is right for us.

HOLDING ONESELF BACK
BETTY

At 23, Betty has gained the courage to move across country and start her nursing career in a strange town. However, in her daily life, she acts passive and frail. She is unable to show initiative and must not be expected to live up to her obvious competence. She feels disappointed in herself, but she is internally prohibited from acting in any other way. During her twenties she gradually overcomes these inhibitions. She claims her competence by finally deciding to go on an interview for a job that requires initiative and aggressiveness. No hiding place in this job—her presence and decisions would seriously affect the lives of many people. The night before the job interview, she dreams she will be interviewed by three women (her mother and two sisters). The two younger women give her wrong directions and she loses her sight and her beauty along the way, but she manages somehow to get to the interview. When the older woman asks her a question, Betty's teeth begin to chatter uncontrollably; piece by piece, all the dental work falls out of her mouth. The mother interviewer advises her to withdraw her application for the job; instead, she is to marry a doctor. She wakes from this dream in terror. It is the worst nightmare of her adult life.

At first Betty felt timid, as if her success would cause so much envy in her mother and sisters that all inner connection with them would be lost, just as she lost her inner fillings (feelings) in the dream. After all, she already was the youngest and prettiest. What would happen if she also became the most promising professionally? The timidity gave way to her first real adult rage at her mother, and all the fears about the job that had terrified her the day before vanished. Rage lived in every memory of her mother's implication that she was only husband bait—and more rage that marrying a doctor was her obligatory role in life. The extensive rage and the subsequent fear of going on were caused by her continuing partial belief that it is a crime to be other than what her parents want her to be and that the relationship with her parents never changes.

Several days later, in another dream, she carefully moved through the dangerous waters of life past a mother sea lion. Then she became a beached whale, saved from exhaustion and exposure by a hand-fed diet of raw fish. In telling the dream, she inadvertently substituted albatross for whale: "I mean whale—I think of an albatross as heavy like a whale, but I know albatrosses can fly." The job offer and her anger at her mother made Betty feel big. But with her new size, was she now free to fly, or was she destined to become more helpless? Was the albatross a symbol of her newfound freedom or a sign of everlasting enslavement to her mother?

So as we focus on our career, we also have a very full psychological agenda to master. While preoccupied with getting a raise, a higher-paying job, more training, promoting better working conditions, learning new skills, confronting the hypocrisies at work, subverting office politics, or proposing a better organizational plan, we also have to figure out how we fit with the job we're in. We must identify our talents and have the courage and foresight to move on when our inner needs dictate.

Instead of misreading our growth actions as oedipal crimes, we have to win internal permission to be what we find ourself becoming. Society's seductive myths and our ancient dreams of a perfect repair for past hurts must not lead us to follow rigid roles that don't fit our unfolding disposition.

To work through our old dream of life and be true to our developing talents, we must overcome the tempting idea of automatic rewards for "correct" behavior.

Jeff wanted to be a cabinetmaker and his father wanted him to learn the jewelry business, so he worked for his father during the day and in his own garage at night. By 27 he was a full-time cabinetmaker-entrepreneur, with three employees and a well-equipped shop, customizing camper vans.

Unlike Jeff, who took responsibility for his own adult dream, some of us wait for the design of our life to show itself magically—and we lose vital flexibility. We're prey to the illusion that whatever career line we start with will be our final choice, not just the first in a series of choices. Work life is seen as another family situation; we are "theirs" again, doing or being only what our employers want. With this childhood consciousness attitude, we may adopt the same attitude in love. Still seeing ourselves as late adolescents, we expect those in our work and love world to act like parents who will treat us specially but who won't let us leave; it is up to them to dictate our destiny.

It is often painfully difficult to follow our own star even when we know the time has come to move on, as Jill found out at 25.

Jill is a soft-spoken, softly contoured, handsome blonde who has an easy, nonthreatening way with both men and women. For the last three years, she has been a technical writer for a bank. The excitement of getting a paycheck and setting up a way of life carried through the first two years. During the last year, she felt stagnant, dull, trapped. Now she knows she must break out of her life and all its limitations. She is in the wrong place and feels she is also living with the wrong man. She drifted toward both the job and the man because she had nowhere else to go at the time. Both the man and her coworkers treat her as if she were something special, someone above them; she is worried that she is too dependent on them.

Her job does not fit her at all. She is a talented pianist, an English-literature major interested in beautiful prose. She has no interest in banking. Her writing tasks at the bank are like an endless series of dull college term papers emphasizing proper form and good grammar.

In one impulsive and uncharacteristically dramatic gesture, she goes off with a Colorado River boatman for a week, leaving her employer and her boyfriend wondering where she is.

When her boyfriend takes her back, she does her best to get him to kick her out. When that doesn't work, she leaves him, because that's what she needs to do for herself.

She quits the bank and assumes that her resignation has canceled her unemployment rights. When the woman in Personnel tells her to "follow your heart," she "flips." She can return whenever she wants and is eligible for unemployment benefits.

Jill *knows* that the bank job is not for her, yet she feels self-indulgent, idealistic and immature even to want a meaningful and interesting job. Shouldn't a true adult settle for what she has and make the best of it? If you try hard enough, can't you make any work interesting?

Believing the first component false assumption of this age group, "Rewards will come automatically if we do what we are supposed to do," Jill does not perceive her right to change a job or a man that does not fit her life; she feels that she doesn't deserve the change. She thinks that since she fooled the people at the bank and her boyfriend with her winning ways and received their special treatment, she is indebted to them. She assumes that they will not let her leave because they feel she is important to them, and so she must "break out" by ruining her image in their eyes.

Though Jill began her maneuverings under the influence of the old component false assumption, in a roundabout way she still ended up in a new position: "I will do what is necessary to make my dream come true in time." The next time Jill requires a change in her life, perhaps she will no longer feel that an adult must settle for what he or she is given and "make the best of it" in order to be rewarded with self-satisfaction and confidence. In the future, when Jill embraces the right to pursue her own life, she will not have to suddenly destroy her image in another's eyes in order to change. She will no longer be leaving constricting parents who are enemies to her future.

It's often difficult for women like Jill not to expect automatic payoffs. Jill is beautiful and, in fact, payoffs do come her way automatically just for looking the way women in the society are "supposed" to look. Factors other than beauty can make it particularly hard for a woman to overcome the assumption of automatic payoffs. By virtue of her biology a woman can bear children, a kind of creativity that humbles most male achievements. Secondarily, women have not been socialized to be as directly competitive and combative as men or as self-sufficient. True independence for a woman is still foreign to many people's concept of femininity. All these factors can make it more difficult for women to challenge the idea of automatic payoffs for "correct" behavior.

All the people mentioned in this chapter—Jill, Steven, Karen, Gerald, Sharon, Mary, Betty and Jeff—had to wrestle with the component false assumption "Rewards will come automatically if we do what we're supposed to do" before they could release themselves to do whatever was necessary to make their dream come true—to take control of their life. Though it's easier for some of us, all of us have had to do it.

2. Component Assumption 2

"THERE IS ONLY ONE RIGHT WAY TO DO THINGS."

Once again, the *major* false assumption challenged during our twenties is "Doing things my parents' way will bring results or they'll step in to help me." The *second* component assumption and the subject of this section is "There is only one right way to do things."

In childhood we were convinced that our parents' way was the only way to be; any violation of that "right way" on our part was considered a transgression. Doing things that "right way" becomes part of our self-definition, and when we begin to outgrow that narrow self-definition, we experience a powerful internal prohibition against giving up that part of ourself. Throughout this chapter we must remember that the false assumptions and beliefs we're discussing are powerfully reinforced, so that we only slowly change those aspects of ourself.

The idea that there is only one right way, that we can find a magic key to the complex processes of reality, is a lifelong hope as we try to guarantee our future and erase our terror of the unknown.

During our twenties, once we've passed through the previous half-child, half-adult phase and have decided to commit ourself to becoming a "true" adult, the "one right way" assumption enjoys a powerful resurgence. Childish concepts of what an adult really is become the criteria by which we judge ourself and others. As individuals we act toward the new adulthood the way sociologists tell us new waves of immigrants acted on becoming Americans: we adopt the host culture's values in an exaggerated and rigid fashion until we can rethink them and make them our own. Our idea of what adults are and what we're supposed to be is composed of outdated childhood concepts brought forward.

The child thinks that adults are people who work terribly hard and don't have time for fun. Adults know all the right answers automatically without having to learn any more. Adults are very moral and their standards are absolute, so they never have any doubts, never are confused by fuzzy thinking. Adults are omnipotent sources of safety. Adults can always soothe children if they want to. Adults don't want things for themselves as children do. Adults are never greedy, envious, jealous or out of control. Adults are not afraid of anything. Adults handle misfortune easily and face everything with equanimity. Adults are not even afraid to die.

A child's version of an adult is impossible to live up to. Yet these childhood concepts become the filter through which we interpret all our experiences. When, as young adults, we don't fit the ridiculous criteria, we interpret ourselves as inadequate or counterfeit adults. Therefore, we feel, we should not enjoy the full privileges of adult rank.

These criteria for adulthood generated by our mind when we are children confine us and guide our behavior in new situations. We don't just rid ourselves of these concepts. We modify, reformulate and rework them in the same way that we rework all other "divine rules" from childhood consciousness. We do this by the seven-step resolution process, which is set in motion either by a collision between rule and reality or in an attempt to free ourself from an internal prohibition.

Ann is 27, one of those mothers who read everything they can find on the subject of mothering. Despite her intellectual conviction that it's quite all right for her to be angry at her child, emotionally she lives by another rule: that she will be a bad person if she is ever less than perfectly loving. She's had to do some fancy rationalization to convince herself that some of her reactions are pure love. At three o'clock one morning, when she is exhausted and her husband is out of town, her son wakes her for the third time demanding a glass of water, and her fury and a desire to beat him break through her defenses.

Ann's persisting childhood view of proper motherhood, a protective device, was challenged by the collision with an inevitable experience. She was forced to consider herself—temporarily, at least—a bad mother, a monstrous mother. However, enough repetitions of similar incidents, enough talking with other mothers about their feelings, fed the seven-stage mastery process, until she came to an integrated, trustworthy view of reality that all experienced mothers eventually come to: "I love my child, but at times he infuriates me. And that doesn't make me a bad mother—just a real person." The childhood consciousness rule "I must always love my child" was jettisoned as a protective device that was no longer necessary.

The modified childhood criteria become dependable adult values; they must be our own creations, standards that we can live by. If we don't truly modify childhood concepts, either we capitulate to them and rationalize our resentment or we rebel and they become the sensitive spots in our interpersonal relations with our peers, our parents, our children and our spouses.

New Rules with New Roles

With each new role comes a set of rules, the new criteria for judging ourself again as if there is only one right way to do things. When we get our first job or live with someone for the first time or set up a married life or have our first child, we do this within a subculture that seems to dictate how it's supposed to be done. Though we may not do things the way our parents wanted us to, we almost always do it our peers' way. During our twenties we are by no means independent and autonomous. We live according to labels. And we don't just passively accept the labels; we feed our friends the information they need to label us. We're the swinger or the married one or the good Catholic girl or the Italian macho guy or the IBM man or the Jewish kid from the Bronx. We dress and act the part, whether banker or artist. Each of these labels has appended to it a set of regulations about how things should be done. The peer pressure is real and strong, not imaginary, so to break out of some draining, overconfining role prescription, we must take a real risk. Those pioneers who have broken the stereotypes of role relating in marriage, dress code, sexual attitudes and work have given us all more room. To live truly adult lives, we must work to challenge the role formulas that we accepted initially with enthusiasm but subsequently have outgrown. We must work to find that gray area between chronic adolescent rebelliousness and a proper regard for human freedom.

The most rapidly changing role during our twenties, our role as children to our parents, shifts dramatically from the sensitive teenage time to a more relaxed relationship by the end of our twenties. As we get more competent and truly modify childhood rules, we meet our parents with a relatively stable set of values and a firm set of boundaries. In the background, however, our parents are always looking over our shoulder, ready to point out failures that occurred because we broke some rule or program or because we abandoned the "one right way." Each time we hit a low spot, we are vulnerable; we wonder whether they are correct, whether we should follow their rules more and venture out less. Every time we're feeling secure and adult, we are relatively invulnerable to their criticisms, though we resent them nonetheless. We see the criticism as an attack upon our good feelings; we read it as a hidden message from our parents saying that we're allowed to succeed only by doing things their way.

Every time they support and compliment us for following a certain path, our glow of acceptance is singed with resentment. Are we following a freely chosen course in life that happens to coincide with their values, or have we capitulated and continued to be good boys and girls? We're just not sure.

As described in Section II, "Leaving Our Parents' World," both children and parents can cause arguments over the issues of separation and the expression of legitimate differences; we may not tolerate their legitimate differences any more than they tolerate ours. Parents come in all kinds and colors, from those who are excessively critical and intrude into our lives and refuse to let go to those at the other extreme who seem to lose all interest in us after we leave home. How much they intrude or how rigid they are may determine what we do to distance ourself from them during our twenties. One man cut himself off from his parents completely because they were rigid, authoritarian religious people from a small town. "I was raised in an iron fist," he said, "and there's no way to stay half inside that system. Either you are one of them or you leave entirely. If you are successful in the outside world, your success is not accepted." Rigid parents are particularly intrusive concerning our choice of job and spouse and our methods of child rearing.

Somewhere between the overly intrusive parent and the parent who forgets about us after we're out of the house is an ideally empathetic parent who recognizes the relativity of choice, the errors of his or her own way, and our need to find our own way and who can stay with us at a respectful distance while we do it. Reports of such parents are rare, but I suspect that in a national survey, we would find that the bulk of parents fit somewhere in this middle ground.

When we get married we gain an ally against intrusive parents. The marriage acts as a shield from our own parents but frequently makes us quite vulnerable to our in-laws. We may resent our in-laws' idea of what the only right way to do things is—it may be completely foreign to the rules we've grown up with. We become hypersensitive, and in some cases we capitulate to please them. One woman gave up her stylish way of dressing in order to dress, as her mother-in-law suggested, the way a dentist's wife should dress. She interpreted that to mean nonsexy and very conservative. Some years later her husband complained that she dressed like a grandmother. In this instance the mother-in-law's suggestion coincided with her own self-imposed rule—a married woman is not allowed to be sexy any more.

Sometimes we adopt traits that are the rigid opposites of our parents' in response to qualities we do not like about them. Having a passive father who appears totally controlled by our mother, we adopt the other rigidity and never meet our wife halfway for fear of capitulating. If our mother was hypochondriacal and martyrish, we adopt the stance of becoming a superwoman who never complains, who never takes care of any aches or pains for fear that we would be totally identified with our parent. In dozens of other ways, we take rigid positions and measure others by the same standards.

Despite the conflicts, our twenties seem marked by a relaxation of tension in our relationship with our parents and in the way we conduct our personal lives. But if we have children, the tension often moves into that area, either with our parents directly or with our spouse. When we become parents, we jump back to our own childhood, and each of us is tempted to replicate the image of our parents or of the parents we wanted to have when we were children.

Parent philosophy is not a trustworthy guide to parenting. When the childhood memories of twenty to twenty-five years ago intrude and the past and present are meshed suddenly by the stimulus of the child, all previous parenting philosophy becomes pallid and a useful abstraction at best. We have to learn to tolerate each other's style of child rearing and understand it as an attempt to integrate an adult's current value system with a complicated reworking of leftover childhood values.

Masculine/Feminine

Traditionally, the "one right way" rule has had its greatest effect in defining sex roles. Now, however, the only rule on sex roles still operating is that everything is in total confusion and flux. Actually, this allows great latitude for experimentation for those now in their twenties, experimentation that is necessary if two-career marriages are ever to work out. Those parents who accepted the traditional sex-role definition as an absolute in their twenties are astonished at the confusion that reigns today, but it may be necessary to society in the long run.

I'm firmly convinced that except for childbearing, the biological differences between men and women are insignificant in terms of social roles and mental abilities. Men *can* be as nurturing and intuitive as women, and women *can* be as aggressive and goal-oriented as men. No doubt, long periods of socialization have created virulent internal prohibitions on these issues that are difficult to overcome, but it can be done!

MEN

RICHARD

" 'In a Dark House Somewhere in the World,' that's what the sequence is called. . . . It's near the end of the film, Bergman's *Scenes from a Marriage*. . . . That sequence haunted me—I couldn't sleep for a week, and I dreamt about it often for six months. The main male character . . . he's been aggressive, assertive, ambitious and directed throughout the film—a man fighting for his dream of greatness and importance (even if his woman colleague didn't like his poetry). Well, in this sequence, he's older, softer, and for the first time in the film really, he's sympathetic. He never got to Cleveland, he never published anything that made him famous. I mean, he had a solid career, but he never did anything to distinguish himself. Now, and this is what tore me up, I *thought,* well, this guy has finally made peace with himself. He's calm, warm, attentive. He and his wife love each other more now than when they were married, he's finally accepted himself and grown up, he's a giving person, for the first time. He no longer seems selfish or loutish, and I finally like him. That's what I *thought*—here's what I *felt!* He's a broken man, he gave up his dream of greatness, he's a pitiful shell of what he was and what he wanted to be. He's so mediocre— he's just given up, surrendered, let life beat him down. If I were him, I'd rather die. I just couldn't shake the fear that I would wind up a sniveling forty-year-old living in a rented room feeling mediocre and unimportant.''

Richard is caught in a very contemporary middle-class contradiction. The new ethic calls for men to be gentle, nurturing, loving and only minimally aggressive and competitive (after all, someone has to stand up to the new woman). Yet all of us, including Richard, still live in a hierarchical, money- and status-oriented world, where men are socialized to compete for mastery.

Richard feels mediocre because he remains a boy in competition with his father. He hasn't been admitted to the club of men, and he's still full of aggressive, "I'll show you yet" spirit. Because the man in the film has given up the fight (Richard's fight), Richard fears that he too will give up before he's won, before he's become a "big" man. He may be humiliatingly small (mediocre) forever.

At the same time, he *knows* that Bergman's character, though existentially troubled, is also content and peaceful, that he has shed his oppressive need to be a powerful figure. Richard's dilemma is a clash between old socialization and new possibilities.

Traditionally, men are socialized to be protectors and to suppress their need for protection. Their only remaining source of legitimated childhood gratification is to be taken care of by women. Before the recent push for women's equality, this pact worked well for many middle-class men in their twenties, despite the pressure to perform and the burden of responsibility it put on men. The "study, get ahead, kill" taunt of the 1960s antiwar activists not only rejected service to the war machine, but, at a deeper level, spurned the rigid school-to-career track system that prevented young men from finding a fuller, less restrictive way to live.

Women's independence has allowed middle-class men to be less aggressive and less protective. As women direct more of their own lives, men are freed to be more nurturing and more expressive of their own need for protection. Working-class men don't get quite the same break.

The protective ethos is stronger among uneducated working-class men. They don't have the same freedom of inquiry, nor do they enjoy as prolonged a period of experimentation before the world of work closes in on them forever. They are socialized to feel a great need to be protectors, but they find it more difficult to actually protect or provide for their families because of their inferior economic position. A working-class man works extremely hard and comes home tired, wanting wifely (motherly) care. Yet often, to make ends meet, his wife must also work; she's stuck in the dual role of wife and coprovider and feels unappreciated. He feels inadequate as a protector and angry at her divided attention. The anger, hurt and alienation run deep. As the new sex-role ethic increasingly reaches working-class couples, men may learn to escape the pressure to protect, and women may learn to demand more equality.

WOMEN

Women, particularly in middle-class families, are often raised as frail creatures in need of protection by fathers and brothers. Typically the mothers devote their energies and talents to the family, and daughters are rewarded for similar behavior. Because of a girl's alleged frailty (despite the biological fact that girl babies have a higher survival rate), she is denied freedom and privilege. She is taught to perform for the pleasure of others, and she is rewarded not because she is competent, but because she is a "good girl"—unlike boys, who are encouraged to master the world around them. But today many little girls are also being encouraged to go out in the world and compete. No longer is the domestic role the only model for a growing girl. A woman in her twenties today must work to resolve this mixed choice of roles for herself, at least for the present.

In working-class families, the wife-mother role still usually receives the strongest support. A "career" for working-class women usually turns out to be something like clerical work—a "job" rather than a glamorous or rewarding lifelong occupation. Moreover, the economic demands on working-class women often mean that such women must satisfy some of both roles: they must maintain a much needed job as well as nurture the family.

In more privileged families, the contradiction between roles is sharper because there is more opportunity for choice. Independence and career plans are encouraged, but so are marriage and motherhood.

Whatever her choice, a woman must make it out of a sense of her own capacities and not become a victim of the myth that she is frail or unable to pursue her own ambitions.

The significant decision for middle-class women faced with a choice between a domestic career and a career outside the home (or various combinations of the two) is not whether to work, but *whether or not to have children*. If a woman decides not to have children (or to postpone having them), then, like a man, her dominant concerns will be work and satisfying her ambition. This is as true for a woman who is part of a couple as it is for a single woman.

If a woman decides to have children, her life will most likely be organized to a dramatic degree around the child's world. Even if she works, the child will draw attention and energy away from her work. Even in relationships in which child care is shared by father and mother, obviously the woman carries, delivers and nurses the baby, and most often she continues to bear the greatest burden of child rearing. Of course, both a husband willing to share responsibilities and adequate child-care services will help a woman who wants a career as well as a family, but deciding to have a child is still about the most impactful decision a woman makes.

The most important guide to self-satisfaction in choosing between a domestic or an outside career is whether that choice emanates from an adult consciousness view of self or a childhood consciousness view. If a childhood consciousness view is dominant, a woman may stop herself from doing what she really wants. The choice *must* come from her adult assessment of her goals and talents.

Career Outside the Home

A woman who *chooses freely* to live out her talents enjoys great support in the educated middle class. She enjoys the benefits of greater financial freedom, whether she spends her money on herself or, if married, on her family. She also enjoys the prestige of having clearly demonstrable skills, whether those of doctor, lawyer, boutique owner or teacher. But life becomes especially demanding on a *married* career woman, particularly a mother. Then she is constantly having to work out the same home/job trade-offs that men have been coping with all these years. But if the choice to pursue a career has been made with a truly adult consciousness that trade-offs are always necessary in this imperfect world, then she can be one of the women who have experienced *great* satisfaction in meeting these challenges.

A woman who chooses a career because of social pressure or because *she is stopping herself* from becoming a mother will not be happy in a career. Such a woman may really want to be a mother but is childishly afraid that she will automatically lose her independence and her adulthood if she takes on the same role her mother did. She thinks that having a job will somehow magically dispel all her childhood anxieties about gaining adult competence, about getting love and approval. She doesn't understand how much of a test maintaining a job can be and that a career comes with no guarantees of happiness. Rather than positively choosing *for* a career, with all its stresses and rewards, she thinks she is warding off the bitterness, dependence and unhappiness her mother experienced.

Women who are in jobs because they are trying to escape a childhood fear of marriage and motherhood usually manifest a heedless, driven quality in their careers. Rather than the quiet confidence and humor that come from freely choosing a path, the woman still in the grip of childhood consciousness exhibits conflict and a blustery arrogance that announces, "My way is the only way." Such a woman becomes frantic and overreacts when a personal relationship begins to exert increased demands or when things go wrong on the job, because she really believes that if she leaves the world of work, demonic forces will reduce her to the status of a child again.

Domestic Career

A career of raising a family is a reasonable choice for many women. As Sally, a middle-class woman in her late twenties who has two children, explains, "I won't work ever again if I don't have to. I like staying home. I sew and take care of the house and kids. I go shopping. I'm my own boss. I like that."

A woman who believes that being a wife and mother necessarily means that she must stop working outside the home, no matter how much satisfaction she's been getting from her career or how hard she's worked to get where she is, never gives her talents a real chance. She may try to be satisfied by life at home, but if she has given up a great deal to become a homemaker, she may always feel cheated or that she's wasting her time. If so, she will feel like a second-class citizen or will judge herself to be cowardly or defective. "I don't have what it takes to make use of my talent."

Whether she chooses a career in or out of the home, a woman who chooses freely will worry less about making the "right" choice. A woman who stops herself from making the career choice she really wants because of a childhood consciousness fear of the results of taking that other road must live with the tension caused by her denial. Even so, initial career choices usually remain workable despite the tension until a woman reaches her late twenties or early thirties.

Women who strike reasonable compromises between a career at home and an outside career are still pulled constantly in first one direction, then another. They are forced to juggle both careers, and in many cases they end up feeling cheated of both domestic and outside satisfaction.

Having a Child: Effects on Images of Maleness and Femaleness

In any case, the decision to have children, whether freely chosen or not, inevitably brings about unanticipated consequences that draw women into becoming selfless and completely devoted to the care of others, "the way women are supposed to be."

Childbearing leads many women into stereotyped roles. To have a child, a woman must in some measure rely on her husband to take care of her while she takes care of the child. In a normal, healthy relationship, the woman allows herself to be taken care of without losing her own sense of self—her boundaries, options and essential ability to take care of herself. She experiences her role as part of a mutual family contract and not a humiliating surrender to her husband. He, in turn, cares for and nurtures her without presenting a bill for services rendered.

Couples share one world on the weekends; in a relationship where the woman does not have a career outside the home, from Monday to Friday they are in two different worlds. Though men may resent going to work on Monday mornings, the traditional woman's world is more difficult psychologically—it affords her little opportunity to exercise control over her own destiny.

In her daily experience with a child, a mother's time is not her own. She has to respond constantly to unclear verbal and pre-verbal demands from her child. Often she has no idea what to do; many times no good solution is available, so she'll suffer guilt and anxiety no matter what she does. The child constantly explores the boundaries of her patience and power. When the child's control lapses, her own control is required. She must consider using force on a helpless human being who sometimes invades her bodily privacy and psychological integrity like a monstrous, consuming enemy. She deals with the world of child rearing, where hundreds of experts give contradictory advice; the outcome can't be measured for fifteen to twenty years. She has to process this advice through her intuition and a constant stream of her own childhood memories dredged up by her child's dilemmas. And she must do all this with others—mother, mother-in-law, neighbors and schoolteachers—looking over her shoulder, marking her report card, measuring her against their own standards. Though it would be a relief to give up and follow some set of packaged rules, she must dare to be different—the fate of her child depends on her decisions. Besides, no set of rules seems exactly right.

People with careers outside the home live in a relatively crystalline world. Each job or organization has some set of discoverable rules; outcomes are immediate; and although the hierarchy may finally determine any exchange, the everyday dialogue usually consists of clearly expressed verbal contracts between free adults.

These two different experiences pull men and women with outside careers apart from women in domestic careers during their twenties.

As outside-career people, our confidence increases as we gain competence and buy into the finite, orderly world we are mastering. We become more and more involved in that world as it rewards us with recognition of our abilities and promise. We narrow our vista and focus more intently on a detailed understanding of that world, which soon becomes our whole world. If we are going someplace in that world, we find it hard to question its assumptions.

A child's chaotic and disorderly passions require a woman who chooses a domestic career to become expert in the intuitive, phenomenological world if she is to produce a viable and mentally healthy human being. While a domestic woman develops the expertise needed to work at an unending task, she forfeits the confidence she could have gained from mastering a finite, orderly world. Gradually she comes to question her ability to master the world "outside," and her feeling of independence begins to slip away.

There is another psychological consequence of having a child that pulls men and women in two different directions. Becoming a mother diminishes a woman's freedom to champion her own legitimate self-concerns and thus unbalances a marriage of equals.

After giving birth, women experience the child as part of their psychological self. They merge with it and develop an uncanny ability to respond to its changes. It is a deep connection that no man can really share, just as no man can experience a live child growing within his body and being nourished by the nutrients that are carried in his blood. A child is part of the mother's flesh and blood even outside her body.

This normal and necessary symbiosis of early motherhood rekindles a woman's unconscious symbiotic experience with her own mother. Her earliest and most enduring love attachments were with her mother. Having a baby expresses more than a biological urge or love of a husband or a desire to create; it is a bedrock tie to a woman's femaleness—and to the mother who gave birth to her.

A girl's childhood model of the ideal mother becomes her operating criterion for being a good mother in adulthood. The ideal mother met all of her needs and wishes, was always there to comfort her, never let her be in danger, saw to it that she had every pleasure, and never left her out by choosing to be with friends or husband. The ideal mother was *selfless,* devoted to the child's welfare and ease of living, and had no life of her own; or if she did, she would abandon it without a moment's hesitation when the child wanted something.

All children are thoroughly self-centered. Our own poor mother is a disappointment in comparison with the ideal mother our self-centeredness demands. We are angry when she doesn't live up to our impossible model.

As an adult mother, a woman carries the disappointing memories of these early experiences in her head even if she doesn't remember. When her child goes through the same changes she went through, that segment of her early experience is refreshed. The childhood images of the ideal mother and the unsatisfying mother are within her emotions but are buried in the archaic language of childhood consciousness. If she wants to be a good mother, she must give herself totally to the child's life. If she keeps some of her own life for herself, the anger she felt at her mother for not always being selfless will be transformed into the feeling she is doing something wrong. Her child owns and controls her time. The child is the center of the world, and she is just a satellite. She is owned, controlled by unseen inner mandates; hence she is drawn back into childhood consciousness, even though it is a child who owns her rather than a parent.

This impossible emotional mandate, "Abandon your own life totally to another's life," is essentially manufactured during a woman's early childhood and becomes, without examination, a powerful rule by which she lives her life. The rule, enforced by the powerful rewards and punishments of maternal purity and maternal badness, feels right even though it is contradicted by the experience of living. Over and over again, her own direct experience teaches a woman that when she does enough for herself, she feels better and better about her child. When she does too much for too long for her child, she feels harassed and drained. But over and over again, she lapses into doing too much. Tired of constantly trying to correct the balance herself, a young mother hopes someone else will appreciate her distress and insist she take more time for herself. At this point, a sensitive husband, parent or friend really helps.

A young mother tries to establish a new, adult consciousness rule for her life that has as much authority as the rule she manufactured in childhood. Today, a young mother has more help from society than her mother did twenty-five years ago in her struggle to get away from being too selfless, but it is still not enough. Though current social values endorse a woman's right to legitimate self-concern before she has a baby, society's message is still ambiguous once a woman becomes a mother.

Most experts agree that a child's basic character and temperament are formed during the first years and that the most important addition to the biological constitution of the child is the quality and continuity of caretaking. And in our society today that means the mother. "Quality and continuity" calls for an empathic mother capable of suspending her own needs for the fragile but passionate needs of the child. A degree of selflessness and merging is essential to good mothering, but all young mothers are under tremendous pressure to sacrifice their own development to the physical and emotional needs of their children. Consequently, a young mother may feel that her child and husband are eating up her life. She may feel that she deserves some form of special love from her husband in return. If she doesn't get enough special attention from her husband, the false assumption of the twenties—"Someone is stopping me from growing by not rescuing me"—is rekindled, along with a demand for compensation. A promissory note for the future will be written.

Women must grow and gain direction for their lives to minimize the effects of selfless motherhood. For a woman this sense of growth comes only through continual effort, while her husband gains it automatically with his career. When his career growth is blocked, he too feels misused, stagnant, unhappy, preoccupied and quite resentful of added family demands.

In our earliest years, we men also imitated our mother and emerged from the matrix of her personality. But growing up in this culture, we learned to renounce the desire to be like her, at least consciously. We adopted our father (and other male figures) as our basic model. I want to emphasize that the goal is to be like our father in ways that connect us to our own talents yet differentiate us from him as a model. In our twenties, using our mother as a model is much too threatening to our maleness, so it is quite ruthlessly repressed and does not become in any way an acceptable alternative until our forties. Only after our maleness is largely confirmed in the world can we psychologically dare to open up to our "female" potential.

The cultural message to us as young men is that "we must make it in this world." The future for us and our new family depends on our work output and our ability to create a place for ourself in the world. This is true even for those of us with guaranteed income or position through inheritance of family name, wealth or business. We still must make it. We can't conceive of trading places with our wife, because it is too threateningly close to the mother-woman part of ourself we ruthlessly repress. But our envy of her position comes out in many ways: the ubiquitous question "What did you do today?"—insinuating that she did nothing but stroll through the day while we worked—is part of our repertoire in the earliest years of marriage. We can't comprehend how her time can be eaten up by the necessities and emotional pull of young children because we envy her exemption from "making it" and are afraid of being in her place. We usually can't understand why she is not as efficient and productive during her day as we are during ours. However, after a weekend with small children, we are secretly glad to go back to work, where life is not so disorganized and there are no small irrational creatures to flout the rules of self-control. We know she resents being left for the long week with the children, but we resent being treated as if the pressures of our world are simple compared with hers.

But we also want our wife to be selfless and disprove our fear that she is really envious of us—that really she wants to destroy our good life outside the home. Three factors contribute to our fear of her envy and to our compensatory drive to make her a mother, selflessly devoted to her family. (1) We are feeling better about ourself and more confident. We are actually enjoying the work world despite our complaints, while she at times seems to be going in the other direction. Work has become a sore point between us, separating us into two worlds with different rewards. (2) This real difference is multiplied tenfold in our mind by our own repressed envy of her womanly-motherly self. Instead of recognizing our own envy directly, something which is almost impossible in our twenties, we project our envy onto her. Our repressed envy causes us to believe she is a dangerously envious person. (3) Because of our repressed envy, it is difficult to be sensitive to the pressures in her life. When we feel pressured and tired of pushing ourself against the world out there, we feel we are putting more into the partnership than she is. We deserve to be coddled, taken care of and made to feel important. It's "only right" that someone should make it easier for us, at least at home.

When we harbor this view, we believe our life is more important and our mind is more capable than hers. We undermine our wife's mind, in part, because we want her to be selfless—after all, we can't admit our envy of her womanly position and capacities. We also attack because she sees through our main blind spot—work. Work is our vehicle to the success we dreamed about. When a woman presents her view that our work world is narrow, when she challenges our work commitment and hope, we just can't listen.

A wife sees clearly and remembers the hypocrisies of the office and the company management, the dehumanization of the job situation, and the petty misuse of power and status that we are subjected to and complain about.

She may see that we are too ambitious or becoming obsequious and thereby selling out our integrity. She may see that we are too timid and missing opportunities or that we have an exaggerated opinion of ourself or that we don't belong in a particular career but stay in it to please a parent or to prove a point or because we are too proud to admit we were wrong or are too scared to change. She may see all this and much more with her finely honed person-to-person intuitive skills. If we could make use of her knowledge, we could save ourselves great quantities of pain, pressure and anguish and probably would make better and more sophisticated decisions about ourself in the work world.

Usually we're not ready to listen. We parry the thrust of her challenge with a technical argument or by pointing out the impracticality or cost of her suggestion. Out of resentment, we devalue her intuition and cut her down. Years later we may say to our friends in front of her, "You know my wife knew that years ago." But then it will be received with a mixed reaction by her—pleasure in the belated recognition and pain accompanying the refreshed memory of the insult to her self-confidence.

But we also attack her perceptions about our work because we feel that she doesn't understand what success and failure mean to us and why we hold on to illusions so long. She isn't living within the same consciousness; she doesn't know that a failure at some task is not just a temporary setback—it can signal a hidden defect springing out of our past to ruin our whole life.

On the contrary, a success suddenly assures us that our whole future has been written. It is not that we are reassured we will get there, we *are there*. It's like being catapulted into the future. We race ahead in excitement; it's unreal and a bit frightening. It is a tremendous relief when we come down to earth and realize that this was just a starting event in our fantasized trip. It was a real success, but one soon forgotten by everybody; we must continue to perform well to have a good future.

Success can set us up as a target for envy. Success can be read as a triumph over our parents. Failure can be read as capitulation to an internal prohibition against success. It's this part of a man's life that many women, especially those who stay at home, have difficulty fully comprehending.

In a marriage, when the man works outside and the woman works inside the home, all of us are pulled toward certain ideas about manhood and womanhood. Sex-role stereotypes do exist, and the very real dynamic forces brought to bear on every marriage provide the power that keeps them alive. This makes our images of maleness and femaleness the most difficult childhood images to change. All the other too-rigid rules and roles discussed in this section are comparatively easy to overcome— once we understand that there is no "one right way to be."

3. Component Assumption 3

"MY LOVED ONES CAN DO FOR ME WHAT I HAVEN'T
BEEN ABLE TO DO FOR MYSELF."

Coupling

In our twenties, whether we are heterosexual, gay, or bisexual,
we all feel an increasing desire to have someone special and to
be special to someone. By our late twenties, as our friends couple off and spend time with other couples, we feel left out if we
are still single.

Those of us who couple early sometimes feel superior to our
single friends. We have demonstrated our ability to be intimate,
yet in the back of our mind we wonder whether we would have
the guts to bear the loneliness and rejection of life without a
partner.

Those of us who remain single sometimes feel superior to couples because we feel more self-reliant and independent, but in
the back of our mind we wonder whether we are just too
frightened of intimacy and dependency to find a partner.

What's the right formula? Twenty-five years ago the only right
way to live was as a heterosexual married couple planning to
have children. All other life styles were deviant; bachelorhood
was a disease to be cured; most people cured themselves by
marrying in their early twenties. Today our society tolerates not
only bachelorhood but also homosexual bachelorhood and non-
permanent coupling. Some even say marriage is bad for the human soul.

In this heyday of life-style variations and experimentation, a
successful couple knows that when love is good, it is addictive.
The world looks and feels different. A walk in the park with
someone special is no longer just a walk in the park. Our shared

secrets become love bonds, and we feel confirmed as loving, lovable, worthwhile and wanted. Our strength is quadrupled and our confidence is multiplied tenfold.

As a couple, we *strive* for the ideal of two healthy, self-reliant, clear-thinking people sharing a life enriched by each person's contribution. We want to believe we are two independent people forming an interdependent unit—but we *fear* that the other person will siphon off our life energies and crowd out our sunlight.

The challenge of coupling is how to have an intense relationship without losing our self in the depths of the other person. But we can lose our self only if that self is confined by our *own* rigid internal prohibitions, as described in Section I. Therefore, *the only way a mutual relationship can cause us to lose our self is when we blame our partner for our own internal prohibitions*.

Once that mistake has been made, we feel trapped and controlled by our partner; we must persuade, manipulate or cajole him/her to gain permission to grow. At the root of this profoundly important error is a third part of the major false assumption being challenged in our twenties. The major false assumption, once again, is "Doing things my parents' way will bring results or they'll step in to help me." The third component assumption is "My loved ones can do for me what I haven't been able to do for myself."

Forming the Conspiracy

All of us occasionally feel inadequate in some area of our life. "I have no talent" or "I'm not strong enough, loving enough, smart enough, masculine enough or feminine enough" are typical feelings we all share. Although sometimes a feeling of inadequacy reflects a real limitation that we do have to correct or come to terms with, it doesn't always mean that and so can't be taken at face value. Oftentimes a feeling of inadequacy is a message tuning us into an internal prohibition. That is, we are not actually limited in the way we claim but rather we are feeling a strong urge to be what we're capable of but won't let ourself be.

Thus we often feel inadequate in the midst of success or attach obscure feelings of inadequacy to our body, thinking it is ugly at one time and beautiful the next.

When the feeling of inadequacy indicates a buried internal prohibition, it can become an important switching point. We can dig deeper and confront the outgrown concepts and demonic misinterpretations that constrain us and master the trouble spot by beginning the seven-step inner dialogue outlined earlier. Or we can try to get rid of the feelings of inadequacy by the "cure" of love. Being told we are respected and important and cared for can temporarily wash away our feelings of inadequacy. But it also takes us away from the unpleasant starting point of hard psychological work—the very feeling of inadequacy.

All of us need "cures" of love as part of the growth dialectic: we can't always be in the process of change or make growth work the major preoccupation of our life. But when we rely on the "cure" of love too much, we arrest our growth and form an unhealthy conspiracy with those who have a special relationship to us. And the more special the relationship, the more we depend on the other person to help us.

When our temporary dependence on others to reassure us becomes a fixed requirement—that is, when we *expect* others to take *responsibility* for us—we form a *conspiracy* to avoid confronting our disguised childhood demons. In this conspiracy, we don't have to do anything; they, our loved ones, will do all that we can't do for ourself.

When our loved one does a "good job" for us, we idealize him/her. He/she becomes the carrier of all our childhood consciousness beliefs. "What he or she believes is automatically right. I have to live up to all of his or her standards in life."

In this conspiracy, we no longer feel inadequate. Our disguised demonic badness is magically covered up and controlled by our loved one. The problem is that a relationship built on conspiracy must eventually become hostile because of dependency. Although we no longer feel inadequate, we still feel inferior to our partner because he or she is able to do for us what we can't do for ourself.

On the other hand, when our partner does a "bad job," when he or she doesn't reassure us and we still feel inadequate, we feel let down. This person we love so much has such superior powers (like parents) that he or she could have helped us but chose not to. Therefore we feel very hostile.

The conspiracy is a no-win situation. Eventually we feel either hostile or dependent and often both. In any case, our simple pact with our loved one becomes a destructive conspiracy that prevents our developing a fuller, more independent adult consciousness.

MALIGNANT CONSPIRACY

ROSALIND AND RAY

Rosalind and Ray married when they were both 22. She is bright and attractive, wholesome and at the same time mysteriously sensual. She is strong but has never been able to rid herself of the feeling that she's a loser in life—that she'll never quite be able to make good.

Ray has none of these fears. He's tall and strongly built, not nearly as attractive as Rosalind, yet they make a handsome couple. Ray is optimistic about his own future success and is sure he can help Rosalind with her self-doubts. Everyday problems are like food for him. He swallows them up and deals with all difficulties by rational mental effort and concentrated willpower; he feels stronger after every challenge. Ray has banished all helpless feelings from his life.

When they married, they were both in graduate school, he in architecture and she in biology. They cleaned house together every Friday night; he scrubbed the floors while she vacuumed. They shopped and prepared meals together, went over the checkbook together, and considered themselves to be perfectly equal partners. When Rosalind became pregnant during the second year of their marriage, they decided to have the baby and then another one soon after. She was to return to school after the second child was old enough to go to nursery school.

In the meantime, Rosalind poured her energies into becoming

supermother and superwife. She organized a book club, got involved in local politics, ran their joint social life, read widely, thought deeply, and became very knowledgeable about architecture. Ray's successes became her successes.

Though things seemed to be going well on the surface, Rosalind and Ray were simultaneously living a second, unhappy reality. As the perfect wife and the perfect mother, she had become a winning part of his winning life. In her mind he was a winner but she was a winner only as long as she was a part of his life. She was dependent on him because she felt inadequate—internally prohibited from being a winner herself. He had everything; she had nothing if she didn't have him. She was flawed; he was perfect. She needed him; he didn't need her. Despite their equality, Rosalind felt like a stereotyped dependent female; Ray was the stereotyped male looking down on her from his lofty professional life.

Ray had never been able to understand fully Rosalind's lack of self-confidence. He had done things to help her while they were in school, such as insisting that they have identical desks in their study. He encouraged her to study when she suddenly felt sleepy or wanted to go to a movie during exam time. Sometimes it worked: good grades bolstered her self-confidence. But sometimes she told him to stop acting like her father. Ray thought his only concern was for her well-being; he didn't recognize that Rosalind's self-doubt and uncertainty made him feel uncomfortable because they brought to mind his own fear. Ray had banished all self-doubt because it was feminine, weak and paralyzing. When his doubts began to appear, he quickly found a problem to solve or another step to take along a narrow corridor of success. He could afford to be introspective about philosophical matters but not about self-doubts. If he could rid Rosalind of her self-doubts, he could magically keep away his own doubts.

So they each participated in the conspiracy. Rosalind got an illusory cure for her inadequacies: if she could please Ray, she would feel fine. Ray not only helped push away her doubts but, in so doing, was saved from his own doubts while enjoying feeling big and important to Rosalind. The surface reality of the conspiracy was perfect: two equally bright, productive and well-liked individuals sharing a life. But the second reality, the reality beneath the conspiracy, stalked their happiness. Rosalind felt she was an inferior, defective female being carried by her husband. Ray was forced to keep running away from his doubts and fears. Both avoided the seven-step inner dialogue—or any serious introspection—and so neither did the psychological work necessary to master their nagging childhood demons.

The "cure" of real or imagined inadequacies by love and the conspiracy that results is yet another dynamic that pulls us into stereotyped male and female roles during our twenties. For that reason, I consider that kind of relationship a *malignant conspiracy*.

There is another aspect of the marriage conspiracy that Ray and Rosalind demonstrate clearly. Often, among our many reasons for marrying a specific person, we pick someone who has qualities we desire to have ourself but have not developed as fully as our mate. (Rosalind sought the "winner" quality in Ray that she felt prohibited from exercising herself.) *Initially we marry in an effort to achieve wholeness*. We attempt to acquire these qualities for ourself along with acquiring our mate. Our aim is not to work at becoming more like our mate or to learn how to exercise the qualities they possess; rather, we actually consider the other person as a piece of us. This is one part of what we hope to get from the false "cure" of love that is not usually recognized as such during our twenties. But it becomes a problem to be dealt with as the need to individuate within the marriage grows stronger. One partner is seen as clearly the possessor of the desired quality, while the other partner is left with his or her internal prohibition against acquiring that quality and a sense of inferiority exposed. This will be discussed more fully in Chapter 4 of the mid-life section, under the heading "Developmental Envy: Neil and Sheila."

In the typical twenties conspiracy, each partner tries to please the other. Both partners are busy working for the other and measuring themselves by the other's response. It's either "I am not doing enough to please her and that's why she hasn't helped me" or "She is just not doing enough for me and that's why I still feel inadequate."

When couples break up in their twenties, each person usually blames the other for not doing enough to conquer the demons. The message is "You should have been able to make me feel better, but you didn't. I still feel inadequate, so I'm leaving you to fix myself or to find someone who will love me more."

There are many good practical reasons to remain uncoupled during our twenties. There's complete freedom to come and go as we please. It's so much easier to keep our own self-image in mind when it's not being blurred by someone else's constant presence. Being involved with many different people highlights different parts of us. We can make commitments to low-paying public-service or political jobs more easily if only our own living standard is being sacrificed. Jobs requiring extensive traveling and frequent dislocations can be taken. There's no reason to restrict whom we meet for lunch and no reason not to strike up a friendship when there's no potentially jealous partner waiting for a report. Love affairs, which are usually profound learning experiences, can be entered into fully without guilt or a makeshift schedule or a premature ending.

While single life clearly has advantages, there are still many in their twenties who don't want to remain single, yet are unable to couple. If we cannot let new relationships evolve naturally but immediately insist that our new partner become a conspirator with us in a script that covers up our inadequacies and internal prohibitions, this prevents coupling and interferes with intimacy.

Handsome Jack, 26, had a set of specifications that he applied to every date on the first meeting. None of his dates made it. He went with at least twenty girls for about two months each, but the affairs always ended "because they were boring."

Rob, a very handsome man, protested with great pathos that he wanted to get married but couldn't find the right girl. Yet he exclusively dated women he picked up on the street and then proceeded to seduce into bed as rapidly as possible. He practically had a temper tantrum on the spot if they were hesitant or refused. In his mind, women had something he had "to get" from them. Then when he was through getting it, he felt guilty and saw the women as soiled.

Joan, a beautician, was always abandoned early in a new relationship because she unilaterally decided the man was hers for the asking; she became petulant whenever the man continued to date other women.

Linda, a bright young woman, decided she was to be loved only for her brain or not at all, so she made no effort to trim off offensive, sloppy fat. Yet she resented anyone who didn't think she looked attractive.

Robin, a tall, slim beauty who habitually wore Daisy Mae shorts and blouses that bared her midriff, couldn't understand why men didn't want to be just friends. Why did they always make a pass at her? It always ended her interest in them.

The common imperative buried in these patterns is "Those who want me, I don't want. Those who don't want me, I do want, but only until it seems that I can have them." These patterns are all organized by the component assumption "My loved ones can do for me what I haven't been able to do for myself." Like the people in the examples above, we are all waiting for our special demands to be met. We demand a partner with traits that complement our special configuration of traits like a lock and a key. We run prospective partners through an obstacle course; we withdraw love for missteps. Partners expecting to be loved by us end up feeling controlled, criticized and guilty for not being what we decided they should be. Then they leave; or if they stay, they come to resent us.

Though many people unfortunately live out their love lives confined to these neurotic patterns, most of us learn not to place unrealistic expectations and dependence on our loved ones. We begin to have open, evolving relationships that can grow deeper because we are living in the present, not the past.

We all have patterns that continue to interfere with our intimacy, and living with someone brings them out more clearly than just dating. When we believe that our loved ones can do for us what we are unable to do for ourselves, even a temporary partner has the power to hurt or help our self-image.

MARILYN

Marilyn's relationships with the many men she has lived with were all characterized by the same attitude: "I am a crushed little girl who can't bear pain and must be protected from the world by a big strong man." Her soft voice and kittenish ways softened her demanding look: "I am hurt; what are you doing just standing there?" But she left each man after a year or so because he didn't take good enough care of her.

In these relationships, each man put her up on a pedestal, which made her feel quite powerful and superior. She felt contemptuous of the men for letting her get away with her childish demands yet resentful of anyone who didn't let her get away with it. She knew she couldn't grow up unless she learned to relate in a new way, but she couldn't bring herself to give up the indulgences she won by being a "crushed little girl."

Marilyn felt that someone special had to come along and forcibly take away her privileges. So far no such man had apppeared, so she moved from one man to the next when it was convenient for her. She always considered marriage, then left just as the next affair began.

It is while making the decision about marrying Alan that Marilyn finally conquers the assumption that someone special will do for her what she can't do for herself. Marilyn knows she isn't going to marry Alan. However, she prefers to stay with him until a new man comes along, so "I won't have to give up what I want. I still like Alan. I don't want to leave him while I still have feelings. It hurts too much." But she also knows that Alan couldn't stand to lose her to another man.

It's a conflict she has managed to avoid with all the previous men in her life—her desire for a painless, free-floating life versus a friend's right not to be hurt needlessly by her. Her wish to be the powerful baby who is spared pain through the sacrifices made by indulgent parents (Alan is just a substitute) must be reconciled with the fact that she's a 27-year-old adult who is consciously choosing to badly hurt a trusting human being.

Is she going to wait for someone to discipline her, or is she going to discipline herself? "I know I should, but I don't want to" is her first response. She can't convince herself that her intuition is strong about not marrying Alan, nor can she pretend that he won't be hurt unnecessarily if she leaves for another man. She can't ignore the contradiction. She must decide whether she will remain a spoiled, indulged child or whether she will become an adult who accepts her own decisions whether they cause her pain or not.

Marilyn chooses to leave Alan, as her conscience dictates, and after a year of living alone and enjoying her independence, she meets a man who cares for her deeply but won't respond to her demands. "I'm a real danger to you," he says, "because you can't control me; you're going to hate me for being strong, but then you'll love me." And so it is.

For many singles who begin to couple, power and control are the issues. No matter how we disguise it, when we're relating with the assumption that someone special owes us a special feat of magic, we're exercising our childhood desire for omnipotence. We are treating our partner as an actor in our personal drama. Anyone who won't play out the assigned script, we stay away from. Anyone who goes along with us, we feel in control of, even while we're bitterly complaining about being controlled or misused. These dramas are multilayered sadomasochistic games reflecting a basic fear of and anger toward the opposite sex. They are always accompanied by a nonloving sexuality. Women have trouble with orgasms, and men with potency. Underlying Marilyn's demand to be treated as an indulgent child was her certainty that men are selfish exploiters. If they *wanted* to indulge her, she had some insurance against her underlying view of male malice and could then relate to them without too much fear and anger.

We escape these self-imposed traps through the same sequence Marilyn went through in her decision to leave Alan: we must first recognize the pattern, then remain scrupulously honest at a critical decision point, and then have the good fortune or good sense to choose someone who is not vulnerable to our controlling ways.

There's more to learn from living together than just the important lessons of how we interfere with intimacy. When we live with someone, our defenses are penetrated every day, and our deepest personality secrets are exposed along with our bathroom habits. Our lack of confidence comes out through our bravado, our timidity shows through our intimidating postures, our ignorance shows despite our know-it-all attitude, and our dependence pokes through our self-reliance.

If we're lucky, our nakedness will not hurt us badly but will teach us a valuable lesson.

LAURA

After John returned to his wife, Laura reviewed what living with him had taught her during their six months together. Laura learned that pretending to know all the answers didn't work and wasn't necessary. John could see when she was bluffing and called her on it; he convinced her that he didn't think she was stupid if she didn't have encyclopedic knowledge or a well-thought-out opinion on every subject. When she shared her personal feelings, he listened and understood instead of telling her she was "crazy" for not being more conventional.

But it could also have turned out badly. John could have made Laura feel she was odd for having her own views or crazy and stupid for pretending to know it all. She was quite vulnerable, and instead of promoting her self-confidence, he could have worked her over viciously. He could have scared her and turned her away from trust and openness. Had that happened, Laura would have learned a bitter lesson in life—that people can work you over for their own purposes and that people have blind spots that don't allow them to understand you or tolerate your individuality. Laura could have left that six-month relationship wondering for years what was wrong with her before she finally came to see clearly that the problem was not with her, but with him. By allowing John into her special space, Laura gave him some of the same enormous power that our parents had: the power to determine what's "real" about us.

Conspiracy and Forms of Coupling

As stated earlier, the more special the relationship (that is, a love partner is more special than a friend), the more we expect from the other person. In addition, the more intimate the form of the relationship, the greater our fear of it. For example, we are less afraid to date than we are to live together and less afraid to marry than to have children.

Each form of relationship carries its own advantages and disadvantages, its own degree of intimacy or specialness. From single life to marriage-and-parenthood, the more intimate or special the form of the relationship, the greater the threat and the greater our opportunity for deep happiness.

Any form of relationship is ripe for conspiracies during our twenties. Pacts can be made between boss and employee or between two friends. But conspiracies develop in greater numbers and with more intensity as we enter a relationship which is very much like the family in which we grew up. We are most likely to form conspiracies and to believe that "my loved ones will do for me what I am unable to do for myself" when we are in a traditional family in which the husband works outside the home and the wife is a homemaker with children.

We'll look briefly at different forms of relationships—single life; living together; marriages in which both partners work outside the home and have no children, then have children; and finally the traditional marriage. The relationships are ordered from the form least like our childhood family to the one most like our childhood family—that is, from the form least likely to generate conspiracies to the one most likely to do so.

Single Life

The pros and cons of dating or living apart as a couple are well known. As we stated earlier, the primary advantages are freedom and independence and a sense of self undiluted by constant interaction with one other person.

The disadvantages are essentially loneliness and lack of intimacy. As a single we have freedom to move about, but we have little opportunity to move in, to probe ourself and others deeply. Our childhood habits, protective devices and demons are not challenged with the same intensity found in couples living together.

Living Together/Marriage

When a relationship deepens and marriage is considered, we're afraid of being trapped by greater commitment. The latent fears about our partner's long-run potential reach center stage. Is he or she a loser; someone who will be too dependent or too overpowering; or someone who will falter under the pressures of family responsibility? Having lived together is not a reliable guide to future behavior, because that kind of impermanence has different effects on people. It makes some of us miserable. We can't enjoy the relationship even when it's good because we're worrying about when it's going to end. We're afraid to put too much into it for fear we'll end up with nothing. On the other hand, that same impermanence is what allows some of us to join the relationship more fully, for we have an easy escape to allay our fears of being trapped. The partner who was pained by the impermanence is more likely to flourish in the marriage; the one who felt relieved by the impermanence is more likely to feel trapped in marriage.

"I don't understand it; we lived together for two years, but after we married he turned into a stranger. He's become bossy and picky." "Before, she was industrious and optimistic; since we've been married she's become morose and lazy. The only time she became her old self again was when I hurt my back and she had to work and take care of things." "She became dependent and grasping." "He began feeling boxed in and resented coming home, yet he was the one who wanted to get married."

Many of us don't have negative reactions to marrying; we luxuriate in the advantages. There is a great release from the worries of impermanence. Competition is markedly reduced. We're not on the make, looking for a better fit. Fidelity becomes a background concern. There is a calm sense of direction; we can invest in the future by working out our problems in a new way—with the door to escape closed. We face our more intense problems with the understanding that they have to be resolved. With this commitment, we feel more solid in our everyday life.

The Two-Career Marriage Without Children

Much to the chagrin of soap-opera producers, the two-career marriage is on the rise. And no wonder, for without children, a woman in her twenties needs work gratification as much as a man.

When both partners pursue careers outside the home, each may gain a sense of self through mastery and competence in the world. Neither partner needs to depend on the other for status or self-confidence, and both have an opportunity to share two separate worlds of work, thus broadening their scope of ideas and experiences.

But this career-oriented marriage has its own major hazard—competition. When both partners are drawn into the status/power career game, there's a great danger that the partner with the higher-status job will be viewed as superior and the other partner as inferior.

With two careers in one family, inevitably, the question of whose career is more important comes up, usually in terms of a possible move to a new location which will advance one partner's career while slowing down or suspending the other's career. Then there's the fear that our success will come while our partner is down and that his or her identification with and support for us will turn into thinly disguised, bitter jealousy. Should we adjust and slow down to avoid that jealousy? If we do—something women are more likely to consider than men— how will we handle our own resentment?

With the uneven pace of careers, temporary jealousy and competition can cause us to misidentify one of our own internal prohibitions preventing us from success; we may interpret it as a nasty rule our partner is imposing on us whereby he or she is allowed to be "successful" but we are not.

Time can lead to the malignant view that one partner has become "nothing" while the other has become the superior ideal. This feeling of our "nothingness" when our partner is ahead of us is the key to the problem of competition in marriage. If competition in marriage were like competition on the playing field, it would be a useful stimulant. But competition becomes something different in marriage. In marriage we easily lose sight of the fact that we are two individuals, each on his or her own track. We respond to our partner as if there is room for only one at the top, and when our partner is more successful or feels more confident, he or she has the top spot while we plummet to nothingness. It's a terrible feeling and inspires all sorts of compensational hostility. Our only means of repair for this feeling is to allow it to run its course without granting it adult reality status and without holding our partner responsible for our discomfort. If we can learn to do this effectively, we may be able to see competition in the marriage as a stimulant or even be able to transcend the entire competition framework. We may then come to recognize competition as irrelevant to the real source of self-love, which is finding our own particular growth path.

Drs. Ellen Berman, Harold Lief and Sylvia Sacks, in an article entitled "The Two-Professional Marriage: A New Conflict Syndrome," described the problems of several couples who met while in professional school and began having serious trouble two to four years after entering their professions. They estimate that there has been a fifteenfold increase in requests for help from couples like this in the last three years. While sharing the same goals, interests and friends during the arduous training in school, the couples seemed to be compatible and strong. But the conspiracy was just beneath the surface of each marriage. Though bright and attractive, the women felt somewhat unfeminine because they were ambitious, hardworking and directed. The men they married were usually socially more at ease, handsome, comfortable with their masculinity, and comfortable with the concept of a coequal relationship with an ambitious woman. The men made the women feel feminine despite their ambition. That is, the women depended on their husbands to confirm their femininity. Only with this guarantee did they feel able to accept independent careers without jeopardizing their female identities.

When the women ceased to be tense, anxious students and became exciting, attractive, well-traveled professional women, they found themselves surrounded by challenging new admirers. In this way, they were integrating their professional and feminine selves.

Their new self-confidence as masterful professional women made the conspiracies with their husbands unnecessary. The husbands all felt demoted by their wives despite their own substantial career successes. "She doesn't seem interested in me any more." The husbands became possessive and often wanted their wives to settle down and have children, which was interpreted by the wives as an attempt to tie them down, to take away their recent growth. When the husbands became obviously jealous of their jobs, the wives' suspicious interpretation of their husbands' sudden desire for children was corroborated. The husbands became what was holding them back, not their own internal prohibitions.

Drs. Berman, Lief and Sacks conclude that the rapid personal growth of a woman who integrates her professional and feminine identity in her mid to late twenties is not matched by her husband's personal growth rate, and the husband begins to lose self-confidence. At the same time, he becomes more possessive and controlling and begins to idealize his wife precisely while she is deidealizing him. These forces are easily transformed into the familiar irrational polarity of superiority and inferiority—both begin to feel that she has everything and he has nothing.

In these couples the men lost confidence as they saw the women gaining rapidly in self-confidence; it is the reverse of the disease of the traditional marriage, in which women lose confidence as their husbands gain it.

This erosion of our self-confidence is exactly what we men fear when we think about entering a marriage with a coequal. We are afraid that our wives will become too strong for us and discard us as protectors. We are afraid that if we lose that masculine-role prop, our wives will become the towering figures looking over our lives that our mothers once were.

Women have a corresponding fear: that if they are too confident, strong and independent, they *will* be too much for us and thus will lose all claim to being deeply loved, protected and cared for in time of need. They are afraid we'll become little boys and they'll become obligatory mothers.

In order to protect themselves against the danger of being too much for their husbands, women sometimes surrender certain rights they shouldn't. As husbands we conspire to accept these little retreats, but unconsciously we then push the deceptions to resolution by abusing them. This was the case with Betty and Jerry.

Betty is a bright, attractive 28-year-old physician. Jerry, her lawyer husband, frequently comes home tense and irritated from the office and "dumps" all over her. She feels abused and hurt; she knows her growing resentment will one day burst into an ugly scene because he's being so unfair. She is verbal and articulate and not ordinarily hesitant to confront her husband or to be confronted by him. They have an ongoing agreement to be open and discuss everything that is bothering them. Yet for over a year she is excessively patient, kind and understanding during these episodes. She goes out of her way to be soothing. She is disappointed when Jerry doesn't do the same for her, and she feels cheated by the double unfairness.

One day Betty is particularly hurt by Jerry and recognizes her confusion: she is being patient and understanding because she believes that a wife is "supposed" to be patient and understanding when her husband is overburdened. On the other hand, no good is coming of this for her or for him. Her sympathetic response only encourages him to greater excesses, which make her more resentful. She does not deserve to be abused verbally or emotionally when his business pressures make him tense.

Finally, Jerry makes a remark that brings the issue to a head: "You know, it's too bad you are married to me; I wouldn't act this way with a friend."

In the ensuing discussion, Betty sees that she has two views on the subject. One view is a legacy of her childhood consciousness and is a surrender of her rights as a person: always to be kind to her husband when he is burdened, regardless of the conditions for her. Yet that rule has not been working; it has separated them, when it is supposed to bring them closer.

The other view is generated from the experience of her adult consciousness: "While I can and want to understand my husband's problems, I can't and won't tolerate emotional punishment in return for being good to him. He's being a cowardly, complaining little boy."

In a moment of surprise and wonder, it dawns on Betty that her adult view of the situation can supplant the rigid childhood view that is causing her so much trouble. But she also has a chilling sense that she was better off not knowing that. However, she puts her adult view into action the very next day. Her husband understands. He is not a little boy. She becomes more "herself," cheerful and effective. Her strong sense that she is really a little girl living an adult married woman's role falls away dramatically.

Her behavior becomes less rigid and repetitive; she is now open to change, and with it, the second cycle of her resentment is broken. She is no longer disappointed with her husband for not acting toward her as she did toward him, for she now sees she is no longer required to act a martyr's role herself.

Just transforming that unconditional rigid rule—*always* be kind to an overburdened husband—to its conditional form radically improved her marriage. But it also had consequences for her self-image and her relationship with her parents.

Once Betty modified a childhood concept of marriage so that it fit her adult experience, she felt more confident and independent in an overall way. The next time she saw her parents, she was far less sensitive to their subtle denigrations of her competence as an adult. She felt more confident of her ability to see things as they really are and better able to correct problems by her own initiative.

As the situation improved, she was relieved of the resentment that had made her feel mean and unloving and had made her secretly question her ability to love or be kind. She could love and work out a relationship. She didn't have to be selfless when it didn't serve anyone's interests.

Jerry was also relieved when Betty stopped surrendering her right to be treated like a person. He hated her acting like a martyred mother. He knew he "dumped" on her when he was angry at her for her attitude of superiority. Every time he got away with punishing her, he felt guiltier and more like the little boy she thought him to be. That only made his resentment worse. So Betty's demand that he begin acting like an adult man removed the source of the guilt that was reducing him to the status of a small boy.

We've been focusing on the two major problems of the two-career marriage: the rapid growth of the professional woman in her mid to late twenties and the woman's tendency to retreat to avoid the danger of being "too much" for her husband. But two-career marriages are not all problems; in fact, most people in two-career marriages are enthusiastic. They are proud of their ability to work out the difficult logistics and to overcome the hazards of competition and comparison. They each take pride in the other's achievement and status while enjoying the benefit of two salaries. They have two social lives from which to pick and choose friends. Work problems are easier to share because the partner is living through a similar set of problems. Long hours are more excusable when one's partner also has to press at times or has work of his or her own to do. With each combination of careers in a marriage, there is something important to learn from our partner.

A career woman who has no children enjoys certain advantages. Her work life is not interrupted for childbirth. There is no siphoning of energy into caring for a child or managing its care through others, no loss of mobility because of concern for stability in a child's life. A childless career woman enjoys increased self-confidence from work, and she need not worry about financial dependence.

But the pull to have a child, to be like her mother in that way, is relentless for a woman. It can be suppressed, ignored or counteracted by the conviction that the best life is one without children, but it will crop up over and over again. A childless woman experiences periodic doubts about her femaleness, her motivation. She wonders what she has missed and whether she is, in some evil and primitive way, repudiating her mother. Uncertainty about her decision to be childless will wax and wane with the ups and downs of her life without children. While still in her twenties, a woman has sufficient time left in her biological clock to change her mind, but in her thirties, age reopens this issue with new force.

The Two-Career Marriage with Children

"Whose turn is it to pick Jimmy up at school?" "Well, I've got to shop for dinner." "So what! I did the laundry." "Well, I've got an important conference." "No more important than mine." This is the stuff equality is made of. It's a new and difficult path that challenges all the willpower and determination young couples in their twenties can muster.

Two bustling careers or time-consuming jobs overwhelm each day and snap the patience of even the most devoted partners. Add children to this hectic mix and it's a wonder that any couple attempts this new-style family. But the dream of a satisfying life is quite powerful, and despite the headaches and sacrifices, the psychic cost of breaking new ground, this kind of relationship is the promise of the future for a growing segment of the population.

The advantages are manifold. With proper juggling, each partner can enjoy the satisfaction of a career *and* the joys of raising a family. At its best, there is no better life style, for it combines the advantage of childless marriage with the blessings of a traditional marriage. But the "best" is not easily achieved and is even harder to maintain, as the following quote, from an article in *New West* by Mary Murphy, "Love and Hate: How Working Couples Work It Out," illustrates:

"He was proud, . . . but he was also torn and upset by my success. I think it scared him to death. He knew then that I would only stay with him because I loved him, not because he paid the rent—I think most men secretly believe that the only reason women stay is because men pay the rent.

"Instead of telling me he was afraid, instead of talking to me about his fear, . . . he started telling me that I wasn't a good mother, that the house was a mess, that I wasn't a good cook. One unforgettable night he announced that it was all right for him to be liberated in business, but at home he wanted to be king of the cave."

The problem, then, with a two-career marriage is that it's really a three-career marriage, with the women typically holding down two careers. One is outside the home and the other is in front of the stove or the crib. The arrival of a child tends to bend even sharing, equal relationships into the shape of a traditional marriage. This depends to a large degree on the arrangements for child care and the way the child fits into the woman's dream of life. The more she feels ready to have a child as part of the fulfillment of her dream, the less the child is seen as an interference with her career and the less likely the child-care responsibilities will become confused with a prohibition of her growth.

But almost all women feel some pull toward their children and away from work. The pull toward motherhood and away from a career comes from two primary sources: memory—the personal experience of growing up in a traditional family—and the demands of the child.

The need to imitate one's mother is a strong, deep force that few daughters can permanently ignore, as Ms. Murphy also discovered in writing her article:

We've found that most of the women's responsibilities are self-imposed. The husband doesn't feel guilty if dinner isn't on the table, but every woman in a dual-career marriage knows that if her mother came to the house that evening and dinner wasn't being prepared, she wouldn't approve.

With a selfless mother at the center, the ethos of a traditional family is "Give the child everything." Yet a woman remembers that as a child she never got enough of her mother, and she is determined deep down inside to make sure her child gets everything.

The real demand of the child is "Give me everything" all over again. This endless cry pulls a mother toward a traditional selfless attitude. The pull toward motherhood and away from work saps a woman's energy and attention in both areas. Her work concentration is divided, which leaves her at a disadvantage compared with her fully attentive coworkers. This in-between position can cause her to feel like a victim of forces she can't control; this feeling is expressed by the cry "I'm not allowed either motherhood or a career!" The reality of time and energy limitation becomes confused with an internal prohibition (I stop myself). It can also lead to the idea that "he is stopping me." Then the husband is seen as the cause of the prohibition, and that leads to envy, hostility and either breakup or conspiracy.

For a man, the arrival of a child also evokes his childhood memories—except that he remembers his father's role. As the time demands of parenthood begin to pressure him, a man may want to simplify his complicated and hectic schedule by reverting to the traditional roles: he will be the working father and his wife the traditional nonworking mother. After all, as San Diego State professor Jeff Bryson observes, even "liberated couples still accept a man's right to shortchange the family for his career, but not, heaven forbid, a woman's."

If a woman feels that her husband is stopping her career, whether he is or not, her resentment will show, and her husband may say, "Why don't you stay home? You'll be much happier." Her suspicion that he is the source of her prohibition is confirmed. If she agrees to stay home *for him,* their relationship is doomed to unhappiness or breakup because she'll always resent him for stopping her.

Obviously, this new relationship—the two-career marriage with children—is more difficult for the woman. She has no backlog of experience to guide her and few role models to help. In addition, she is bucking a male-dominated, male-oriented view of her life.

Another research team—from the University of Michigan—recently studied the comparative marital happiness and satisfaction of working wives, husbands of working wives, housewives and husbands of housewives and found that "the least happy and satisfied person" of the four was "the working wife, particularly if she had young children."

But there is hope for more flexible marriages with less rigid roles. Slowly, men are accepting a larger share of parental tasks, and more women are learning that they can at least try to keep their job and their baby too. Perhaps economic pressure for two incomes and government support for child care will encourage more attempts to develop equitable, balanced marriages. Soon perhaps more women will claim, as one working mother did, "I'm still the overseer of the household chores, but now Bill and the kids cook, and if the house is dirty it has become our problem instead of my problem."

The Traditional Marriage

The traditional marriage invites the greatest expectations and the deepest forms of conspiracy. With a commitment for the future secured, we often act as if we can now indulge our unsatisfied need for a respite from the struggle of psychological work. Now that he/she is "ours," we are no longer the left out child. The deeply committed marriage fulfills our sense of safety; we feel triumph as long as rivals in the form of children, lovers, and career demands don't intrude.

The traditional marriage segregates the roles of men and women. Men deal with the world outside the family. Women raise the children, run the household and support their husbands' efforts.

The traditional marriage tempts us to form a particularly malignant conspiracy, as illustrated earlier by Rosalind and Ray. The division of labor becomes a division into two alien and mutually exclusive worlds, with a superior, independent-*appearing* male and an inferior, dependent-*appearing* female.

The malignant compact is this: "I am a man, and I will take care of the outside world, because I am able and you are not. You dare not enter my domain; you are to depend on me to carry those skills on your behalf." "I am a woman, and I will take care of all the feeling life of this family, because you can't understand tender, noncompetitive, nurturing relationships; you can't maintain close contact with people. Not only that, but you can't understand or appreciate the arts and the deeper currents of life, so I'll try to educate you, but you'll always be an amateur."

By conspiring to halve the world into inside and outside worlds over which women and men respectively have hegemony, the husbands and wives who join this conspiracy become the real-life prohibitors of their partners' growth.

Men are just as capable as women of being in touch with the deep nurturing currents in life; women are just as capable as men of making a living. When we are *prohibited* (in contradistinction from freely choosing) from carrying out a whole range of behaviors that we're by nature and education quite capable of performing because they are "too male" or "too female" in character, we are deeply split within ourself. And when we're deeply split within ourself, our intimate relationship bears the scars. We envy what the other is allowed to do while we are prohibited from doing it. And envy is love's worst enemy.

There are four major forces in the traditional marriage that draw us toward a malignant conspiracy of male superiority and female inferiority. When all four are present, the pull toward conspiracy is almost irresistible, for the terms and requirements of a traditional marriage are the precise terms on which our conspiracy is based.

1. If a woman enters into a traditional marriage feeling that she is prohibited from having an outside career, her decision, even if uncoerced, does not represent a free, adult choice. She will come to view her role as a stifling, joyless obligation. She will feel incomplete and dependent on her partner—all the basic ingredients for a conspiracy. Most women now in their twenties were reared in traditional families, since the trend toward careers for women is quite recent. Consequently, it is very likely that many now in traditional marriages feel prohibited, internally, from having a career. The society says a career is OK, but their childhood backgrounds tell them otherwise.

2. Our culture has an economically based ranking system for success in life. Housewifery and child rearing are near the bottom, despite their obvious importance. "Man's work" is almost inevitably ranked higher than domestic work, so society seems to confirm a homemaker's feeling that her man is everything and she is nothing. This tendency is increased when the man is ambitious or his job is glamorous or if he is in an occupation with a clearly defined hierarchy that reinforces his magical hope for happiness through work success.

3. Since in our twenties we gain our independence from our parents by self-reliance and competence in the world, work becomes an especially meaningful proof of adulthood. Therefore the partner who works outside the home gets an extra measure of self-regard and a greater feeling of independence. In traditional marriages, that partner is always the man. A woman in a traditional marriage forfeits the improved sense of self that out-

side work can bring; she always wonders whether she's just transferred economic dependency laterally from her parents to her husband. Having had a good job before marriage or before childbearing helps minimize this.

4. The single most important force in this quartet of forces affecting the traditional marriage is the effect of having a child. Nothing more certainly pulls us into stereotyped maleness and femaleness than becoming mothers and fathers, for the reasons discussed in the previous chapter, "There's only one right way to do things."

Having a child is a remarkable accomplishment. Our sense of responsibility increases and our future well-being takes on new importance. Options close as we feel more motherly and fatherly: one eye always remains fixed on the child's whereabouts and safety. Closeness between the two adults as a couple becomes even more important yet harder to maintain as the life of this wonderful, awe-inspiring accomplishment intrudes more and more into the space between us. Jealousy and rivalry with the baby characteristically afflict the man. These feelings start during pregnancy, when the wife turns more into herself and her changing body and away from the life that was theirs together. The man feels rejected, even if he understands. Women also have fears, fears that their husbands will lose interest in them as partners because they're now feeling more interested in being taken care of as their bellies swell and their breasts engorge. Some men get ulcers during this period.

But jealousy and rivalry with the baby emanate also from the mother when she feels that her husband is more solicitous of the baby's comfort than her own. She fears that he loves the baby more purely and with less conflict than he loves her. Either fathers or mothers can see the baby as a rival.

The baby can also bind us closer together as a couple when the "thing" we share becomes human and evolves a personality; eventually it walks, talks, makes funny faces, cuddles, is hilariously funny and has the most preposterous fantasies. In this way we become enmeshed in a network of bonds that resurrect the deep sense of security and brightness about life that we felt as children.

All these feelings and effects of parenthood happen equally to men and women; it is part of the homelife we share, enjoy and work out together. But when the weekend is over, the traditional marriage reasserts those separate worlds again, and even the happiest new mother feels the unpleasant conspiracy of superior male/inferior female take hold. The pull of motherly symbiosis draws a woman whose whole life is at home further into selflessness, with the danger that she will eventually feel terribly unrewarded and unrecognized because her sacrifices bear so little visible fruit.

In short, the net effect of all these forces is magnified in a traditional marriage. The notion that men are superior and women inferior beings is such a malignant conspiracy that only great effort and a constant use of the seven-step inner dialogue can control the demons unleashed by the distortion.

Coupling at any age is extraordinarily complex, but is especially so in our twenties, for then we're carrying out two separate activities at the same time. We're building a partnership for daily and future living, and we're using the relationship to emancipate ourself from the consciousness of childhood. This second activity confounds the first. We form excessive expectations and suffer great disappointments; we idealize our partner at our own expense and get even by unnecessary rivalry; old family scripts are replayed in an attempt at mastery; and conspiracies are formed to cover over the presence of internal prohibitions.

Central to all this is the battle of the sexes. This battle is supposedly ruled out by a committed relationship, but it continues nevertheless, for it is no more than the demonic misinterpretations of childhood power imbalances played out in adult life.

We don't all suffer equally the intrusions of childhood consciousness into our adult love life because of the different degrees of adult perspective we bring to bear. This delicate balance is tilted by the component false assumption of this chapter,

"My loved ones can do for me what I haven't been able to do for myself." The more we operate on this false assumption, the more problems we have with our love relationships.

But no matter how thoroughly we've cleansed ourself of this false idea, the traditional marriage that simulates the family most of us grew up in invites the unwelcome guest of childhood consciousness. This is not an argument against the traditional marriage; it's only a warning against the main hazard of that form of love relationship.

While the traditional marriage can transform real men and women into caricature males and females, the factors contributing to this outcome are known, so to that degree they're controllable. On the other hand, one of the advantages of the traditional marriage is the very fact that the wife is not working for a living. Therefore she can develop and champion the broader and deeper aspects of life and oppose the narrow and lethal definition of life as work. The wife can be an essential balance against the natural tendency of men in their twenties to be co-opted into the value system of their chosen careers.

This advantage of the traditional marriage is the hazard of the two-career marriage. With both partners enmeshed in the work-world value system, the narrowness of the twenties can go unchecked, at the sacrifice of the basic humanity of each partner. On the other hand, the hazard of forming a malignant conspiracy that creates a relative loss of self-confidence in the woman is mitigated. If anything, the problems of competition that are likely to surface in a two-career marriage will probably cause more of a problem for the man.

When deciding between these two life styles, a couple must also consider the value system of the time. If the only life valued as meaningful for men or women is a work life, then the hazards of both the traditional and the two-career marriage are increased. If a meaningful life is defined as one centered around deep human contact, then the hazards of both life styles are minimized. And in a culture where deep human contact is valued, then parenting a child is not idiot's work, but one of the most difficult, challenging, demanding and important tasks in life. Someday this society may recognize the stupidity of giving the lowest status to mothers and teachers while charging them with the future generation.

4. Component Assumption 4

"RATIONALITY, COMMITMENT AND EFFORT WILL
ALWAYS PREVAIL OVER ALL OTHER FORCES."

The fourth and final component false assumption to be challenged during our twenties is "Rationality, commitment and effort will always prevail over all other forces." As we work through our internal prohibitions and the conspiracies they spawn, this false assumption is confronted head-on. If we become an actor in our partner's conspiracy or if we force our partner to join ours, we deaden the relationship. If we refuse to join the conspiracy but have an empathic understanding of our partner's internal prohibitions (incomplete parts of our partner), we deepen the relationship. The trick, of course, is to recognize the conspiracy so deeply placed within the private spaces of the relationship.

CONSPIRACY: BETSY AND DAVID

One of the things Betsy found most appealing about David was the way he handled her moods. He didn't become annoyed or impatient as others had; in fact, he'd join her in long, helpful conversations about her problems. Often he bought her a flower or made a funny face; sometimes he just let her be. She felt very loved, and she loved his sensitivity. David felt very loving and appreciated.

Within six months the first profound shift took place. Every time Betsy was in a bad mood, David felt pressured and Betsy then felt dissatisfied with him. Both had conspired to make David responsible for breaking up Betsy's bad moods.

A second profound shift took place a year later, when Betsy began to complain that David was patronizing her and treating her like a child because he was so preoccupied with her slightest mood shift. It seemed to her that he was focusing on her mood shifts to retain some paternal influence over her and to make himself feel superior. She felt that it was his way of controlling her and keeping her dependent on him. David didn't understand; he felt unfairly attacked and no longer important to Betsy.

Betsy was not a free self. She had not developed the independence of an adult consciousness which would help her modulate her own moods. Therefore, Betsy felt that the only way she could achieve her independence was to declare that David was no longer absolutely necessary to her, that his responsibility for her had to end.

In the prior arrangement, when David helped assuage Betsy's bad moods, he felt important to her. Now he felt small in her eyes. When David continued to feel responsible for her mood changes after she had declared her independence, Betsy concluded that he was the one who all along wanted her to be incomplete and dependent. She was wrong. Betsy and David both conspired to keep her dependent on him. She had stopped herself from assuming complete, adult responsibility for her own moods. When she finally shed the psychic debris that was keeping her dependent, Betsy effectively challenged the component false assumption that a loved one could do for her what she hadn't yet been able to do for herself. She took another major step toward a fuller independent adult consciousness.

This sequence of Betsy's growth in her relationship with David is the model for growth sequences in all coupling relationships. During the conspiracy, our partnership (special relationship) becomes the warehouse for all the unfinished business of our personal growth.

Using the relationship of Betsy and David, we can distinguish three stages in the life of a conspiracy. The first stage was when Betsy appreciated David's sensitive understanding of her moodiness and his help but clearly felt her moodiness was her problem to solve. That was the stage of deepening the relationship by empathic concern from a respectful distance. That is the ideal stage to be nourished, the one to return to from the next two stages.

The second stage was when Betsy and David colluded to make David responsible for her moods—he was to notice them, articulate them, find the source and then cure them. He became an indispensable person. Betsy dictated the terms of the conspiracy, and David accepted them. He became the loved one who could do more for her than she could do for herself.

The third stage was when Betsy took back the powers she had given to David. She was not aware that she had ever given away her powers; she was only aware that he seemed to want to keep her dependent on him and that she would have to recapture the ability and responsibility to modulate her own moods.

Once the second stage of a conspiracy is spotted, a clear line of responsibility must be drawn without a punitive withdrawal of empathy by one partner. David has to say to Betsy, "Every time you get moody, I get a pressured feeling in my gut, as if I either cause your moods or am in some way responsible for getting you out of them. That's bad for both of us. I have my own moods to worry about and resolve; I shouldn't have the burdens of yours too. If I do something that bothers you, tell me. If a mood comes over you that you'd like to talk out, I'd be glad to listen."

We can recognize our collusion in the second stage when we feel "pressured" to perform what seem like impossible and unfair tasks for our partner. If we love or care enough about our partner, we won't have to look very hard before we figure out what we're actually responsible for—to make our partner feel important or loved or worthwhile. Or perhaps he or she wants to feel sexier or more masculine or feminine or successful or satisfied or more like a good parent or a good son or daughter. The one we love may want to be reassured that that explosive temper does not signify that he or she is basically mean or excessively ambitious or deplorably greedy or hopelessly lazy, and so on. We must work through that pressured feeling until we can clearly articulate and discuss the distortion that is happening to us. For each time we conspire to take over a responsibility for our partner, we play out the scripts of past family relationships; we give in to childhood consciousness and freeze our growth.

In the second stage, Betsy lost sight of the unfinished psychological work she needed to do in order to solve the problem of her moods. She was not able to get a perspective on reality to contradict her mood; since she did not know the true source of her irritation, it smoldered and remained unresolved. She had not given up her expectation that things should magically be different from the way they were. Neither had she learned to speak out to the right people at the right time in the right way in response to the real slights she encountered in daily life. None of this essential work could be directly confronted as long as David was responsible for her moodiness. She did not grow in this area until she took over the responsibility for her moods in the third stage of the conspiracy.

When Betsy ceded responsibility for her moods to David, he was just acting the part of her father. For when Betsy was growing up, her father had been the one who always noticed her moods and made her talk endlessly about them; he was the one who cared so much for her happiness that he wouldn't let her be moody for very long. He was the one who really loved her as only a parent can love a child. As long as Betsy could keep David conspiring with her, she had her father with her. She didn't have to be a grown-up. And David was not really David but a composite of David and her father. When David conspired with Betsy, he agreed to participate in her childhood reality even though it meant he was not free to be himself.

It is the third stage that breaks up relationships or causes the biggest scars. By the time we reach the third stage, the original conspiracy has become a sturdy new reality. By the time Betsy started taking back from David the powers she had given him, David had come to accept having those powers as part of himself. He now believed his ability to control her moods was an essential ingredient of their relationship. He liked being the indispensable person; it made him feel important and powerful. It rid him of all his previous fears of rivalry with other men. He was so important to her that she couldn't possibly leave him. It made him feel that he was "good" to be able to help her when she couldn't help herself. Their conversations about her moods became part of what he considered an extraordinary closeness between them and a way of getting to know her more deeply. Controlling her moods became his way of loving her and of being a husband to her.

And now she wants to take all that away from him by taking back his power to help her. She wants to tell him his love is no good. She wants to make him unimportant in her life. She wants to repay him for all his devotion and thoughtfulness with a slap in the face and an attack on his motives and a complete misunderstanding of him as a person. It really makes him mad. She's an ungrateful bitch. David can't see Betsy's struggle for growth. Instead, he sees her as someone trying to take away something that belongs to him.

Betsy sees that David is against her change. She feels that he is just like the internal prohibitor that has kept her incomplete and dependent. David is the internal prohibitor who stops her freedom and growth. David must be fought, and fought hard. He is no longer her husband; he is her enemy.

Arguments during this third stage have a telltale feel about them. During the hours or days preceding an argument, we feel something nagging at us that we can't yet identify. We feel pulled into a mood and a perspective on the world that diminishes our goodwill. We feel angry and hurt, even though we might try to squash it by acting the opposite—sweet, kind, giving or especially considerate.

There is something distorting or stubborn going on, and we are not feeling open at all. We now have a heavy stake in being right, even though we have an equally strong feeling that we are exaggerating or collecting examples to confirm our point of view. Our examples can become evidence for our side only if we distort the context in which they have occurred and make an arbitrary reading of our partner's motivation. We reinterpret what we previously understood to be reality. The generic statement is "Although you appeared one way, you *really* were trying to make me feel bad."

We are preparing for battle, setting up our partner for blame. We discount all of his or her complexity as a human being. We become certain that we know our partner's dangerous secret motivations and intentions. We become more and more innocent and aggrieved. The issue is no longer one of differences or negotiation; it is no longer seen in shades of gray but as black or white, right or wrong. And finally, the past has so thoroughly clouded the present that we once again feel as helpless as a child confronted by a parent. We have now minimized our capacity to create a solution or to resolve the conflict with our partner.

As we prepare for battle, we replace an adult image which allows for goodwill—that we are just two complicated people living together in a complicated world—with a demonic image from our childhood consciousness. The two images compete, and we must choose sides.

No matter what legitimate issue or difference or fault or insensitivity is being focused on, we feel that our loved ones, who could be whatever we need them to be, must not love us enough. They must be quite mean and selfish. We deserve to be loved properly and better. If Betsy really loved David, she'd not be taking something away from him. If David really loved Betsy, he'd not be trying to stop her.

No matter how rational or contractual or fair we try to be, no matter how much willpower, vigilance and sensitivity we exercise, and no matter how loving and devoted we feel, we will be accused of being mean and selfish by the one we love. And no matter how perfect our loved one may be, we will at times experience him or her as being mean and selfish. It is an inevitable part of the third-stage arguments. Any rational defense we put up against the accusations will be weakened by the powerful feeling of hurt in our partner, and we will not be able to stop feeling guilty in some inexplicable way that only our partner can see.

The third stage can't be handled like the second stage. Because we are no longer relatively innocent conspirators, we can't just confront our partner and give back the responsibility we agreed to take temporarily. Now we have an ax to grind, and we don't see things so clearly. We must expose all the complex feeling states and different versions of reality floating around on both sides.

The dialogue must start something like this for Betsy and David. David: "I have this terrible feeling that you are destroying the basis of our relationship because of some misguided ideas about being free of my influence over you. It makes me feel unappreciated and unloved. I can see that something good is happening to you. You are becoming different about your moods, and that is good for both of us. But why do you treat me like an enemy?"

Betsy: "I know what is happening to me is good for me and you, but despite your words, the little things you do make me quite certain that you don't want me to change. You've become used to a certain way of relating to me that is now dead. You seem to interpret my change just the way you stated it in your first sentence—as if I am misguided and taking something away from you, as if I am destroying rather than enhancing the relationship between us. As long as you think that way, you must be against my change." From this starting position, the dialogue must continue through all the twists and turns of constructed realities until an understanding is arrived at that, whatever else, they are just two people growing, changing, experimenting, rearranging and making mistakes. There must be room for false accusations that are partially true. The demonic images must be replaced with goodwill images; we can no longer blame our partner for *our own* internal prohibitions. `

These are the ways the three stages of a conspiratorial compact must be handled to enable the growth of each partner in a love relationship while deepening the relationship between them. Anything less is a compromise that has great costs, since compromises only perpetuate the false, restrictive reality constructed by the conspiratorial compact. By its very nature, the conspiracy is the reinforcer of an internal prohibition. Yet not all the conspiracies set up in the coupling of the twenties are ripe for this kind of direct confrontation. During our twenties, conspiracies serve a purpose. They allow us to perpetuate indirectly certain dependent ties with our parents without undermining our growing sense of self-reliance and independence. The conspiracies that serve to continue our ties with our parents are: (1) Being married to or in a love relationship with someone who has a negative characteristic identical to that of one of our parents. (2) Re-creating a part of our parents' marriage within our own relationship by becoming like one of our parents. (3) Insisting on one-mindedness, which will be discussed later in this chapter. These three types of conspiracy warehouse our future growth; when uncrated, it becomes a source of great disturbance to the relationship and of painful threats to our sense of safety and familiarity.

It's easy to understand why we would choose to couple with someone who has positive qualities like those we cherished in a parent: the feeling of being loved is molded by our earliest experiences, and we become addicted to it. But many people seem to pick partners who have a central characteristic strikingly similar to that of the parent who gave them the most trouble and left them with their greatest self-doubt.

Tina married a man who treated her exactly as her mother did, lavishing praise at one moment and bitter criticism the next. She constantly tried to win the praise and to avoid the criticism, all the time feeling at home, but hating the pressure. Men who didn't treat her that way didn't attract her. When married, she felt a remarkable independence from her mother. When she divorced in her early thirties, Tina felt as if she had been returned to late adolescence. Her mother became a dominating presence in her mind even though she was thousands of miles away. Bob married a woman who was cold, abstract and hated physical affection, just like his mother. He became dependent and virtually had to beg for love. Tom married a woman who was as childlike and insatiable as his mother, hoping to cure her. Alice married a man who was strong and dominating like her mother and father. Nancy married a man who was as self-centered as the mother she could never reach. The list is endless.

144

Each and every one of us pick partners that, in subtle ways at least, help us re-create a partial parent-child relationship that has not yet been mastered. Our separateness from our parents in our twenties is really just a fiction. We work on increasing the separateness directly with our parents and indirectly via our spouse. There are advantages in working over bothersome patterns with a spouse rather than a parent. With a spouse, the balance of power is different. We have new levers and new freedoms. We can argue more candidly, and we can negotiate with affection and sex. We can appeal to fairness and equity. We can figure out our spouse's vulnerabilities without intruding into the privacy of forbidden parental domains. There is a big stake in perpetuating these particular conspiracies. As couples we tend to live out parent-related conspiracies during our twenties. We live off the old dramatic themes of our lives until we build up new ones.

We not only preserve and continue to work out a relationship with a parent through our spouse as substitute parent, but also preserve parental bonds by reenacting the role of one of them; that is, often we attempt to master the leftover problems with a parent by becoming that parent. Most of the time our role playing is well disguised, but an older brother or sister or aunt or uncle can see it plainly: "He's treating her just the way his father treated his mother—he expects her to pick up his socks and cater to him as if he is king and much too grand to do any work around the house." Women tend to replicate their mothers' patterns around the house and men tend to replicate their fathers'. Even those who consciously disavow their parents' ways can't escape reenacting, in part, a form of their parents' marriage.

Shelley vowed she would never be a martyred, dissatisfied wife like her mother. She took great pains to look after her legitimate self-concerns, but she couldn't rid herself of the feeling of being cheated. She hid it well, suppressed the feelings whenever they came up, and was sure it didn't show to her husband, until one day he said to her, "I can't prove it, but I have the strongest feeling that you think you're being cheated all the time and you're doing me some kind of favor for which I'm supposed to be everlastingly in your debt.'' She was shocked but continued to deny her husband's intuition. It couldn't be; it was her mother who felt cheated, not her. Didn't he see the difference!

It is inevitable that we replay some of our parents' realities, but our reenactment doesn't have to dominate our lives. In fact, the more aware we become of our limitations, the less this tendency to replay warps our relationships.

Living through some of the patterns of our parents is essential for a vital relationship, as we can see in the case of Sam and Donna. At 30, Sam and Donna divorced in the most civilized, rational way imaginable. They each came from families in which the parents quarreled constantly and mercilessly, and they both felt poisoned by that experience and quite consciously vowed it would never happen to them. They would settle all their differences together, amicably and rationally. They succeeded.

During their twenties, they considered themselves to be a model couple and were so considered by all their friends. They were attentive and considerate of each other and were constant, good companions. They never argued or even raised their voices, yet they were not passive or retiring in their discussions. They were both well educated, bright and good with words. Their sex life remained on an even keel and was considered entirely adequate by both.

And then, over a six-month period, their vibrant relationship just fell flat. Nothing was there. They were not enemies—in fact, they were good friends—but somehow they had become more like brother and sister than husband and wife. They just drifted apart and separated.

They fulfilled the extreme formula in an attempt to avoid replaying their parents' relationships. Sam and Donna had to suppress their desire to speak up and to explore painful emotional areas. But it is exactly in these emotional areas that we make a passionate connection with our partner—and work through the vital connection with our parents' roles. Only when we reexperience our childhood demons and face them with our adult consciousness can we reset them safely in our memory. Sam and

Donna tried to push their demons out of their current life through sheer willpower, and in so doing they sacrificed the vitality of their relationship.

The third type of conspiracy that preserves parental ties and resists change during the twenties is "one-mindedness." When we're in love, we temporarily lose our self-reliance and independence and value our lover so much that to be with him or her is more important than our work, our friends or our customary leisure activities. We want to touch her or him all the time and be loved and appreciated and understood forever. We constantly strive for a complete meeting of the minds on all issues of importance and seek to eliminate all criticism or expression of differences.

When we are in love, we try to forge one mind out of two. Often, we see our partner as the other half of us. Some of the most painful moments of the relationship come when this wonderful illusion is shattered by rivalry, jealousy or the expression of real and important differences of style, family background and emerging values and beliefs. In love we feel a memorable feeling of safety and well-being which can't be reproduced in any solitary activity. We resent any differences that would destroy this glorious feeling. When we don't see the uniqueness and differences in our loved one, we feel safe. Paradoxically, when our loved one does not recognize our uniqueness and differences, we feel misunderstood and hurt.

If what is valuable and emerging in us is a threat to our partner, we feel curtailed and confused, for we believe that if we are "ourself" we will rupture our treasured new relationship and hence become responsible for destroying the much-prized love and safety we both want. But if we are not "ourself," we violate our self. We feel cowardly, and we build up resentment that will eventually rupture the prized feeling anyway.

Each time we must decide whether to speak up about something or let it pass, we face this dilemma. But there is no easy formula for these decisions, although we do know that the two extreme rules—always speak up or never speak up on loaded issues—do not help us solve the complex conspiracies of our relationship.

Underlying the conspiracy of one-mindedness is a mutual-defense pact. As long as we are of one mind, we are one insep-arable entity. Our childhood consciousness fears of separation are banished while we become as intertwined mentally with our lover as we were with our own parents. We preserve the parent-child feeling that we can never be abandoned.

These three types of conspiracy, though they serve the sense of safety, connectedness and vitality in our relationships, in fact form a serious barrier to completely open dialogue. We have such a vested interest in preserving these three kinds of conspir-acy that we work around them, fit them into our relationship, rationalize their presence, and conspire with our partner to keep them out of view. Yet each of these three conspiracies limits our setting into motion the development of a fuller, more indepen-dent adult consciousness. Someday we must return to a more open dialogue and remove these restrictions upon our growth and our evolving self.

Optimism, determination and confidence in willpower and ra-tional understanding characterize the twenties. This compen-sates temporarily for the open dialogue that we are unable to face at this age. In the thirties, as we will see, a new method evolves as we secure our independence and separateness in the world and can afford to dispense with our hidden dependent ties to our parents and the conspiracies they generate.

Social Class

In the chapters on the twenties, we've focused on the evolution of consciousness resulting from our challenge to the four compo-nents of the major false assumption "Doing things my parents' way will bring results or they will step in to help me." We haven't yet taken into account the enormous variations caused by socioeconomic class. There's no research available which links socioeconomic class with the specific assumptions we've been discussing, so we can only speculate from research that was designed for other purposes. Given the almost infinite number of socioeconomic subcultures in this society and the limitations of the extant research, all we can do is sketch the dimensions of the class issue by contrasting two particular, distinct groups: a blue-collar group and a middle-class professional-managerial group.

In her book *Worlds of Pain,* Lillian B. Rubin reports on fifty "hard living" blue-collar families that she's been studying for the last ten years. Most of the couples married in their late teens; the women delivered their first babies an average of seven months after marriage. Both husbands and wives shared the American dream of having a place of their own, a family, and an increasing number of acquisitions to add to their comfort and leisure. The men were young, unskilled and had trouble keeping a decent-paying job; even when they did keep such a job, there was really not enough money to live much beyond subsistence. Though the women had come from working-class homes, which accustomed them to barely making it financially, they had hoped that somehow it would be different in their own home. It was one thing to be denied a new dress because their mother or father said they couldn't afford it and another thing to handle the money and find out that the choice was between a new dress or paying the rent. Staying home with one or two small children in cramped and plain quarters with no discretionary money to spend became the tedious reality of everyday life that disappointed their dreams, sapped their willpower and turned their enthusiasm into bitterness.

The men found their sudden responsibility to a wife and child to be more confining than they had ever expected. They felt resentful about coming home to a wife's complaints after a hard day at work, and they felt trapped into working at a job they could not afford to leave. Instead of being rewarded for their effort and endurance, they felt that their wives looked down upon them because they could not produce an adequate income. They envied their single friends who worked only when they wanted to and just had to take care of themselves. Though their optimism about the future persisted, it was blunted by circumstances.

The ubiquitous in-law problems of every new marriage were accentuated because the young couple remained in their parents' neighborhood. Often they had to call upon their in-laws to baby-sit—for instance, whenever the wife needed to work. In addition, since both husband and wife generally moved from their parents' home directly into their marital home, a deep involvement with their parents hung over the new marriage. Often the man had been contributing to his own room and board, and his mother felt the financial loss of him to the daughter-in-law in addition to the emotional loss. Both husbands and wives lived in fear that under the pressure of being "dirt poor," their spouse would be transformed into one of their "hardworking," twice- or thrice-divorced, drinking, abandoning, nagging, complaining, yelling mothers or fathers or aunts or uncles.

In the matter of just a few short years, the husbands and wives of this group went through the transitions from teenager to married adult to parent. They had to cope with growing up, the pressures of poverty, an unreliable income and a bleak future, learning how to relate to each other, and taking care of a child all within that short span. Along with their freedom, they had to sacrifice their leisure, their mobility, and many of the opportunities for further education. All this hard work cast a black shadow over the optimism, vigor, enthusiasm and energy that generally characterize the twenties.

The middle-class professional-managerial pattern is in striking contrast to that of the blue-collar group. The transitions are made more leisurely and stretch over five to eight years rather than one or two years. Usually the first transition out of the home is made by going away to college; this transition is fortified by a period of single life lasting at least several years after college. The middle-class future is tied to a career that promises satisfaction and an ever-escalating income. There is enough discretionary income for leisure and vacations. Young adults of the middle class can afford to have an apartment of their own and experiment with various living arrangements and sexual liaisons. Usually there is a geographic separation from their parents and from their in-laws after marriage. Children come later, leaving even more room for individual growth. But even if they marry young and have children early in the marriage, the middle-class group has discretionary money to decompress the cramping effects of having a young child. All these factors facilitate the natural youthful vigor, optimism, enthusiasm and energy of those in their twenties in the middle class.

The contrast of these two groups illustrates not just how different the life styles are, but also how the psychological work of the twenties is done by different groups. Although our focus here has been on socioeconomic class difference, we should not forget that in terms of the painful psychological pilgrimage from childhood to adulthood, we *all* struggle, despite our different situations. There's no reason to believe that the *psychological* work is easier *or* harder in a working-class group than in a more privileged professional group—though the problems of survival and the quality of life are obviously more difficult. Because there has been no research, we still do not know whether hard living is actually detrimental to the evolution of adult consciousness or not.

The challenges to the four component false assumptions discussed in this section peak during our twenties. They must be worked on the rest of our lives, but they are of decreasing concern as we get older. By the end of the twenties, challenges to these four false assumptions gradually fade into the background as we gain some mastery over them. Then the next major false assumption to give us trouble begins to take center stage.

Section IV
28–34
Opening Up to What's Inside

Major False Assumption to Be Challenged

"LIFE IS SIMPLE AND CONTROLLABLE. THERE ARE NO SIGNIFICANT COEXISTING CONTRADICTORY FORCES WITHIN ME."

By our late twenties or early thirties, we've had eight to ten years of experience living outside our parents' home—outside their world of absolute safety. We've established at least the basic ingredients of an independent life, and most of us have become prideful, self-reliant adults in no danger of having to return to our parents' care. Now we're ready to challenge the major false assumption that dominates this age period: "Life is simple and controllable. There are no significant coexisting contradictory forces within me." During our twenties, when we focused all our energy on becoming independent and competent adults, coming to terms with the false assumption that we would always be helpless children needing our parents helped us keep a lid on the confusions of our inner world. But now our adult consciousness is developed enough so that we feel able to turn inward and reexamine ourselves for something other than the narrow limits of independence and competence that seemed so all-important a few years earlier. So it was with philosopher-mathematician Bertrand Russell.

In 1900, Bertrand Russell, then 28, had already made the fundamental breakthroughs in his analysis of the foundations of mathematics which culminated eventually in his *Principles of Mathematics*. He and his wife, Alys, had been living with Alfred North Whitehead and his family. In his autobiography, he described the extraordinary changes that came over him that year; the month of September 1900 was "intellectually the highest point of my life."

It seems to me in retrospect that, through that month, every day was warm and sunny. . . . Every evening the discussion [with Whitehead] ended with some difficulty, and every morning I found that the difficulty of the previous evening had resolved itself while I slept. The time was one of intellectual intoxication. My sensations resembled those one has after climbing a mountain in a mist, when, on reaching the summit, the mist suddenly clears, and the country becomes visible for forty miles in every direction.

In the latter part of the winter, Mrs. Whitehead became increasingly ill and suffered severe attacks of pain owing to heart trouble. One day, they found her in unusually severe pain. Russell writes:

She seemed cut off from everyone and everything by walls of agony and the sense of the solitude of each human soul suddenly overwhelmed me. . . . Suddenly the ground seemed to give way beneath me, and I found myself in quite another region. Within five minutes I went through some such reflections as the following: the loneliness of the human soul is unendurable; nothing can penetrate it except the highest intensity of the sort of love that religious teachers have preached; whatever does not spring from this motive is harmful, or at best useless; it follows that war is wrong, that the use of force is to be deprecated, and that in

154

human relations one should penetrate to the core of loneliness in each person and speak to that.

At the end of those five minutes, I had become a completely different person. For a time, a sort of mystic illumination possessed me. I felt that I knew the innermost thoughts of everybody that I met in the street, and though this was, no doubt, a delusion, I did in actual fact find myself in far closer touch than previously with all my friends, and many of my acquaintances. Having been an imperialist, I became during those five minutes a pro-Boer and a pacifist. Having for years cared for exactness and analysis, I found myself filled with semimystical feelings about beauty, and with an intense interest in children, and with a desire almost as profound as that of the Buddha to find some philosophy which should make human life endurable. A strange excitement possessed me, containing intense pain but also some element of triumph through the fact that I could dominate pain, and make it, as I thought, a gateway to wisdom. The mystic insight which I then imagined myself to possess has largely faded, and the habit of analysis has reasserted itself. But something of what I thought I saw in that moment has remained always with me, causing my attitude during the first war, my interest in children, my indifference to minor misfortunes and a certain emotional tone in all my human relations.

In less dramatic but equally important ways, we discover a new region of our consciousness after we have established ourselves as adults in our own minds. And like Russell, we are likely to find that new region in our late twenties and early thirties, whether we are at the height of our success or experiencing failure and disappointment.

The treasures of our new region are those desires, tendencies, wishes, talents and strengths that we shut out of our lives during our early twenties because they didn't fit or they caused too much conflict or we didn't have time for them or we didn't dare believe we had the right to realize them.

As we tap our treasures, we become deeper and feel more entitled to be closer to our friends, to be "filled with semimystical feelings about beauty," and to act on our desire to discover a philosophy that would "make human life endurable." But along with that spiritual awakening comes the companion reflection that only love can combat "the loneliness of the human soul."

We keep this entire range of feelings out of our lives during our early twenties as we concentrate on "making it" in the world around us. Like Russell, we are unaware of the shake-up about to befall us.

Our "opening up" is not part of a mass movement; it is an intensely private personal feeling. We are individuals realizing truths we've half known before but which for a variety of reasons we've been unable to give their due.

Terry, 29, will soon become a partner in a prestigious law firm. Yet he begins to think more and more about devoting himself to public service or running for office. He is considering a leave of absence that will jeopardize the position he has been working toward for several years.

Beryle, an independent 30-year-old woman who enjoys her single life as a stewardess and prides herself on her good spirits, feels a sudden urgency to marry and have a family, even though it will change her successful life.

Conrad, a man in his early thirties who runs a successful design studio, comes to realize that the homosexuality he has been practicing for the last fifteen years is no longer really satisfying or acceptable to him.

Ralph, a well-to-do sexual athlete/bachelor, decides at 34 that all his relationships with women are unsatisfying and that it's not because Miss Right just hasn't come along. He's doing something wrong himself.

Deborah, just turned 30 and married to a man she loves and respects, living a comfortable middle-class life, finds herself dreaming of running away and becoming anonymous, even though she loves her children and is living exactly the life she set up for herself.

Sam, a devoted radical, suddenly finds himself approaching 33; he decides to marry and work from within the system. He will finish his law degree, perhaps run for office, but as part of the respectable middle class.

Buz, an ex-Marine, tough as nails, a 32-year-old police officer with a good future, begins to have serious doubts about whether he should use or even carry a gun.

Leslie comes in for therapy. She is 28. A burst of sexual passion has confused and frightened her. She thinks she is becoming a nymphomaniac or a prostitute. She realizes that she'd never had an orgasm before, though all along she'd thought she had.

Ned, at 31, doesn't know what is happening; he just knows life is suddenly fuzzy, more complicated. He is less sure of what is right. He just wants to talk to someone professional about it.

The transitions of the late twenties and early thirties are often introduced by depressions. Men who are changing careers or changing within their career often experience depression because they are also changing the values and beliefs that helped them gain their independence from their parents. Similarly, women who are married and have children and then decide to return to work are often depressed before they realize they are moving in the right direction. The same applies to women going from a career toward a family; they also have a transitional depression before they realize their choice reflects their adult consciousness.

Jack, a 31-year-old lawyer, came to see me after thinking about suicide for almost a year. The suicidal thoughts came after he made an error which cost a client an extra year in jail. But that error was only the tip of the iceberg. He's been unable to get rid of an intolerant perfectionist part of himself that resurfaced around his thirtieth birthday.

Jack comes from a small town in Kansas; he was raised in a strict fundamentalist tradition. He kept a "confessional" diary during college which he abandoned as soon as he entered law school, where he developed a strong political ideology.

When his depression began at 30, his political ideology began feeling like the familiar fundamentalist preachings of his youth. Jack even resumed his confessional diary.

The return of late-adolescent conflict, as suggested by Jack's return to his confessional diary, is a familiar theme during the opening-up period of the late twenties and early thirties. Jack first substituted a strong political ideology for his parents' fundamentalist religion; the substitution allowed him to pursue a career different from those normally expected of a farmer's son. Yet while he was different, he was also the same, since the moral structure of his political ideology was the same as his parents' religious ideology.

But now that he's developed as an adult and is no longer a child living under his parents' rules, he can question the whole fundamentalist world view, whether religious or political. He can question whether there is one right way for him to follow. In fact, he is forced to challenge that belief by his own unconscious workings, which make him fight off the idea that there is one right way. It is no longer an issue between him and his parents. It is no longer a reflection of his capacity to be a man. It is a question now of what kind of man he is to be.

In a similar renewal of an adolescent conflict buried during the twenties, Hillary, a 29-year-old woman, suffered a depression that lasted three years.

Her last years at home had been bitter, angry, fighting years. Her father beat her regularly, and her mother periodically threw her out of the house. Her parents wanted her to go right to work after high school, but Hillary wanted to go to college and study art. Nursing school was the compromise, and she went there only because of a scholarship. Hillary married at the end of nursing school, when she was 21, and moved directly from the dorm to a new apartment with her husband. She settled into being a wife and a mother under the protective wing of her husband, who, in contrast to her parents, seemed to worship her and wanted to do everything he could for her. Life was fun, moving and simple during her twenties.

Her depression started one month after a minor car accident. She began to flinch whenever her husband touched her face, and soon she did not want him to touch her at all. She had fantasies that he wanted to hurt her, and she totally abstained from sex. She had no interest in anything outside her home.

Just before the accident, she'd been accepted by a very choosy art teacher for private painting lessons. The week after her car accident, she cancelled her third lesson—in fact, she had her girlfriend cancel it for her—though she was well enough to go. She never made another appointment. She began to slide into a depression.

The conflict with her parents, put aside in her twenties, came back in the form of symptoms acted out upon her husband. Her husband became her father, who was always ready to hit her; she worried that he was going to abandon her and kick her out of the house. He became the brutal man who didn't want her to live out her talents.

Breaking the Outdated Contract of the Twenties

During our twenties, we agree to do what is necessary to pursue our dreams. When we accept that contract, we agree to a series of obligations—to be a certain kind of person, to act a certain way, to see the world a certain way. Then we wait for the pay-off.

In our contract, we are looking for self-satisfaction, happiness and contentment; and we are hoping that some undesirable part of us will go away. By the time we reach the end of our twenties, we come to see that the payoffs of our dream of adult life aren't being delivered.

The young man offered a partnership in a prestigious law firm had his outer dream of life delivered ahead of schedule, but life did not deliver the hidden promise in his contract. He was happy and proud on the one hand, but confused and uncertain on the other hand. He was disillusioned with the office practice of law as a lifetime occupation.

Bertrand Russell's contract may have stipulated that if he remained a productive and brilliant intellectual, he could avoid the pain and loneliness that he knew so well from his own childhood. But that contract was broken, and he had to dedicate his life to easing the world's misery before he could weave his painful personal history into the tapestry of his adult life. When life fails to deliver, we feel a little less sure of ourselves, a bit more edgy, a bit less optimistic, sometimes quite disillusioned and fidgety about what we want to do in the future. We wonder again what this life is all about.

It hurts us to see that life is not what it's supposed to be. But when we see life's opportunities as they are, offering drawbacks of one sort or another with every reward, we are in a better position to make something of them.

Making a New Contract

During this period of unrest, depression, disillusionment, dissatisfaction and questioning, we challenge and modify the rigid rules of our twenties, and a new way of seeing the world is born. Instead of "I will do what I'm supposed to do and my dreams will come true," we arrive at "I will get what I can reasonably expect to get based on what I have done. Dreams don't come true by wishful contracts."

When we accept this new, more adult view, our expectations of magic are seriously diminished. If we want to satisfy a need or desire, we will have to work at it directly. If we want to get someplace, we will have to find the direct path; there is no magic-carpet service. If we want to improve a troubled relationship, we have to abandon our patchwork efforts, repetitive old methods and crossed fingers and look clearly at the painful evidence of what is not working and why.

Our new view of life comes from an adult sense of where we want to go and a more realistic sense of our powers. This gives us a better shot at getting there. Though we may go through a turbulent period and feel desperately shaken and pessimistic, we actually feel some relief that we don't have to wait for the impossible to feel satisfied or happy. Like Russell, though we suffer pain, we also enjoy a strange excitement, an element of triumph because we can finally dominate the pain of growth.

As we shed another layer of childhood consciousness and challenge another false assumption, we get one step closer to being our own person. At the same time, we have opened the door to a rich interior life filled with mystical and universal psychological truths just waiting to be discovered. Like Janus, the guardian of the doorway, we now face in two directions, and life becomes complicated. As we continue to gain greater competence in the outside world, we now listen with rapt attention to the inner stirrings of our soul.

Our competence in the world increases as we accept the limitations of our powers and the complexity of reality. We learn that one bright idea does not make a career, one memo does not shake up a department, one dinner party with the boss does not mean three jumps ahead, and one good lovemaking session does not patch up a marriage.

We come to see that helping a spouse gain self-confidence doesn't lead to undying gratitude but more likely to resentment. Being married is not the solution to life's problems; living with a father or a mother figure no longer comforts us. In short, we come to see that life is not fair.

Up Against the Contradictions

Barbara, 32, came to treatment because over the last two years she had felt progressively unhappier. In the last six weeks she had felt so depressed she could barely function. Two years ago, at 30, she left her work as a successful administrator to go to law school.

During her twenties she lived an interesting single life, had both serious and casual love relationships, traveled abroad extensively and lived in three major cities while following her career. She never had a serious depression and was never quite sure whether she wanted to marry. Although nothing was going wrong in her life, she felt cut off from her feelings, and despite her current painful depression, she doesn't want to return to that state.

During the last two years she has come to see something that

161

disturbs all her personal relationships: she feels intensely alone, even when she is with friends who seem to love her. In retrospect, she discovers the same pattern in her early years, when her parents were having serious marital problems. She saw it again in her twenties, although she didn't recognize it then.

She reacts with automatic violence when she thinks she is not being listened to. Once she "catches" someone not listening to her, her trusting relationship with them is essentially finished. Barbara knows she has no special claim on being listened to; in fact, she herself turns off when she should be listening to her friends.

During the second week of treatment, she asks me whether I have understood what she has told me about the severity and depth of her depressive episodes. I assert that I remember her description and think I understand her experience as well as another person can.

A moment of silence follows during which she is quite upset. Then she wonders aloud whether I have said I understand her to cover up that I was not listening when she told me the first time. She feels like vomiting and doesn't know whether to suppress the violence of her emotions. She fears she may return to the unfeeling state of years before if she holds her feelings in too tight. She is more afraid of not feeling at all than of a flood of unwanted feelings.

Barbara suspects that I had not listened to her the first time. When she is momentarily *convinced* that I have not listened, the threat of vomiting occurs. She reports that she began to suppress her intense physical reaction when the thought occurred to her that maybe I *had* listened.

In that moment of hesitation—during the gap between the doubt and the conviction—a whole new region of consciousness opened up to Barbara. At that instant, the hidden false assumption of the twenties—"If I do what I'm supposed to do, my dreams will come true"—was both exposed *and* challenged. When Barbara's conviction that no one listens becomes a suspicion that perhaps some people listen sometimes, there is room to observe and reflect; to see with me and with others whether her reality, which she feels strongly, still holds true or whether there is another, more adult reality that includes some people who listen.

If her belief that her dreams will necessarily come true in return for her "good behavior" continues unchallenged, every new person will be a disappointment and her loneliness will remain unabated. Even if she manages to force herself to be with someone all the time, the door to any real relationship will remain closed.

Barbara's disillusionment with her contract of the twenties is really a blessing that allows her to confront an incapacitating automatic reaction that cut her off from others. Now she has some confidence that she has mental powers to counteract the strange and hitherto omnipotent inner demonic reaction that she was too afraid to see before.

To continue our growth and open up doors to our future that were shut tight during our twenties, we don't necessarily have to pass through a paralytic depression or a traumatic event.

Most of us don't suddenly fall through a trapdoor into a new consciousness as Russell did, but gradually we edge toward it, open it, take a peek, close it, forget it for a while, open it again and slowly make our way down there. It is rare that a flashbulb suddenly lights up in the new region and gives us a glimpse into the future as it did with Russell. But even if we don't have Russell's condensed and vivid picture, we do have the same general result. What we begin to encounter in our late twenties and early thirties are the interests, parts of ourselves and values that we will develop during the remainder of our lives.

While we are developing, connecting, expanding and refashioning the centers of our psyche according to our changing insights, we continue on with the work of our life. To our casual acquaintances we may appear unchanged, and at times, when our insights have faded somewhat, we may declare ourselves unchanged. But as the years go on, that dimmed inner vision represents itself with ever-increasing intensity until we either pay it heed or must ruthlessly repress it, whether by becoming extremely rigid on this point or by trying to blot it out with alcohol, frantic activity or drugs.

Four Component Assumptions

The process of opening up to ourselves in our thirties, of discovering the substance and mechanisms for change, is the subject of the next four chapters. In each of those chapters, I will discuss one of the four component false assumptions of the major false assumption challenged between the time we are 28 and 34: "Life is simple and controllable. There are no significant coexisting contradictory forces within me."

The four component assumptions, each a variation on this theme, then, are:

1. What I know intellectually, I know emotionally.
2. I am not like my parents in ways I don't want to be.
3. I can see the reality of those close to me quite clearly.
4. Threats to my security aren't real.

1. Component Assumption 1

> *It's life's illusions I recall, I really don't know
> life, at all.* *
>
> —Joni Mitchell, from
> "Both Sides Now"

The Inner Dialectic

As I have just described, people in their thirties experience a
new kind of opening up. The emotional experience of life breaks
through our controlled exteriors, and this eruption of new emotional and psychological processes offers information on possible new directions for our lives. If we ignore these new feelings, we will be cut off from our evolving inner selves. In the
future we will act not out of our own internal needs or sense of
direction, but according to the stereotyped external demands of
society.

Ignoring the complexity of our inner being means that we will
be trying to make do with inadequate, outdated guidelines for
our lives. As they fail to solve the more complex problems we
begin to encounter further along in our lives, keeping our sim-
plistic old standards will actually increase our pressures and
anxieties.

The truth, as best we can know it, must be our goal, no matter
where it leads us. Every self-deception causes erroneous judgments, and bad decisions follow, with unforeseen consequences

* "Both Sides Now" by Joni Mitchell. Copyright © 1967 by Siquomb Pub-
lishing Corp. Used by permission. All rights reserved.

to our lives. But more than that, every protective self-deception is a crevice in our psyche with a little demon lurking in it ready to become an episode of unexplained anxiety when life threatens.

The self-deceptions which are designed to protect us from pain actually end up delivering more pain. We fortify our deceptions to protect them from the natural corrections of daily life. The larger the area of our mind we find it necessary to defend, the more our thinking processes will suffer; we will not allow our mind to roam freely because new information might contradict our self-deceptions. The larger the self-deception, the larger the section of the world we are excluded from. To expand our anxiety-free range in life, we must root out the restricting self-deceptions.

How do we locate our self-deceptions once we have decided to root them out?

If we are coupled, we have a leg up on the problem. Everything our partner says about us that we don't like to hear, that touches the raw nerve of a self-deception, contains a kernel of truth. If we cannot "prove" our mate wrong, we must examine the evidence that our partner is right. A loved one is an excellent source of starting points. For the rest of our life, he or she is going to know about us what we don't want to know.

A second source of starting points is our behavior. If during a conversation we try to change the subject or walk away or stop listening or light a cigarette—if we feel uncomfortable or suddenly lose charge of our ordinary vocabulary or become belligerent, stubborn or anxious—then this is a signal letting us know that self-deception is blocking our efforts to think straight and have an honest, straightforward exchange.

As stray thoughts streak across the screen of our mind and we turn depressed or anxious, we should recognize a self-deception. If we repeatedly have to put certain thoughts out of our mind, we can be sure we have seen our demon. Discounting the stray thought *as only* a stray thought and therefore meaningless is a favorite technique for avoiding our crucial messages. If it was only a stray thought, why did it have such a pronounced effect on our mood?

We must learn to use all this readily available information about ourself instead of letting it pass by. It is a relief to discover what's really bothering us, even though admitting to it may be painful.

Arthur learned that he was not the "pure" intellectual he wished himself to be; he was more like his father at times than he wanted to admit. His attitude toward giving money to his children was *not* pure generosity but an impossible attempt to rewrite his own childhood. Arthur also learned that in his arguments with his wife he was not always right. In fact, he couldn't do a better job of raising the children than she did.

These insights were painful, but Arthur already half knew them. Once he acknowledged the truth there was no reason not to explore the possibility of correcting it or understanding it in a new way. If he was like his father in some ways, that did not make him identical to his father. If he was not a "pure" intellectual, that did not make what he was any less valuable. If he was not superior to his wife in child rearing, what a relief; now he didn't have to feel burdened by her supposed inadequacy.

Michael learned that taking Sally for granted and discounting her feelings as childish and therefore unworthy of attention and response kept him from realizing how important she was to him. It was a self-deception that almost cost him her love.

Because she felt so victimized, so innocent, Sally had blamed Michael for the whole problem. But she learned through pain and disillusionment that she had ceded responsibility for her life to Michael out of fear that she could never think or do well on her own.

It was painful for both of these people to lose their self-deceptive core. But they both became more capable of solving their problems. In subsequent months, they wondered why they had held on to these false views so stubbornly, but by then they were ready to defend a new set of false beliefs.

In the same way, each of us encounters waves of self-deceptions that we must continually purge to stay in touch with our complicated world.

We cling to our self-deceptions for three reasons: our attitude toward pain; our hatred of having been wrong; and our connection with the repressed.

We continue to live with the archaic concept that mental life should be painless, that if there is pain, either it is unfair or there is something wrong with us.

A 30-year-old woman discovered this in the dentist chair when she was starting to panic because she felt some pain after her novocaine shot. Then she noticed that the pain was so slight it was completely bearable. She realized her panic had started only because she believed there should be *no* pain at all; therefore the slightest pain was intensified tenfold because it meant something was terribly wrong.

In mental matters we are not accustomed to making the distinction between necessary and unnecessary pain. We know that our body needs exercise, yet we expect our mental life to take care of itself without the exercise of necessary thinking work or pain. We must learn to *seek out* sources of pain, since they are clear signals of the underlying greater pain of persisting self-deception. Pain tells us what to work on.

The hatred of having been wrong runs deep in all of us because it strikes at the foundation of our sanity. How can we ever act again if what we were so sure was right turns out to have been wrong? How dare we be brave or bold or stand up for our decisions or make a commitment? How can we ever have confidence in ourself again? In fact, we half knew we were wrong all the time. When we think back, often we can find the turning point when we literally chose to deceive ourself because it fit what we wanted to believe at the time.

The connection with the repressed is a spooky issue. We are afraid that if we undo one self-deception, the whole tangle of half-truths and false assumptions in our life will come out as if our mind were Fibber McGee's closet. In a way this is true, since the dismantling of one self-deception does let the next one rise to the surface of our consciousness. However, the self-deceptions of our psyche don't fall out with a bang—they are teased out gradually over the years in quite manageable doses.

If we are to make pain a gateway to wisdom, we must learn to get on friendly terms with it. Pain must be turned from an enemy to a potential friend, a messenger of useful information. C. S. Lewis, in "Of Other Worlds," an essay on children's stories as a reflection of the child's imagination, writes the following about fear:

Different kinds of danger strike different chords from the imagination. Even in real life there are different kinds of fear. There may come a point at which fear is so great that such distinctions vanish, but that is another matter. There is a fear which is twin sister to awe such as a man in war-time feels when he first comes within sound of the guns; there is a fear which is twin sister to disgust such as a man feels on finding a snake or scorpion in his bedroom. There are taut, quivering fears (for one split second hardly distinguishable from a kind of pleasurable thrill) that a man may feel on a dangerous horse or a dangerous sea; and again, dead, squashed, flattened, numbing fears, as when we think we have cancer or cholera. There are also fears which are not dangerous at all: like the fear of some large and hideous though innocuous insect or the fear of a ghost. All this even in real life. But in imagination, where the fear does not rise to abject terror and is not discharged in action, the qualitative difference is much stronger.

During our twenties we were quite intent on controlling our feelings within practical bounds; we practiced methods for their modulation. When we feel a depression beginning, we use one of our favorite techniques to change directions—we buy something, go on vacation, flirt with someone, goof off a bit at work or work extra hard. Often we use drugs or alcohol for the same purpose. We do the same when anger threatens. We may take a cigarette or change the subject or bury ourself in work details. We may start an argument or yell at an innocent or go for a long walk or a fast jog. Each of us has a favorite stable of techniques to bring us back to a steady state.

We must selectively abandon these techniques to allow our emotions to deepen, to decipher our feelings. As with the fears described by Lewis, if we allow our fears and depressions to linger we learn what they are and what they are not. It is important to learn that the depression we feel today is not the same as the one that scared the hell out of us years ago. It is also important, however, to learn that the depression we feel today stems from the fact that yesterday we found out we weren't the way we hoped we were. Often we put feelings of depression out of our mind too soon.

Our greatest fear is that our feelings will pour through in huge quantities and tell us that nothing has really changed inside from the time of our childhood terrors. We fear that we are therefore doomed in the future to choose between terror or total repression of feelings. But each time we deliberately allow fears and depressions to linger in our consciousness, we can use that time of assessment to discriminate between new fears that may be quite manageable if dealt with now and archaic or deceptive fears. Thus we reassure ourself that the adult present and our childhood past are quite different in very substantial ways.

Discovering the Truth of Clichés

One evening, at the end of a lecture given at UCLA, I asked volunteers to come up and share any anecdotes that indicated what they had learned recently about life.

Among the volunteers was Tim, who was 29 years old, had a wife and two children, and was going to school at night to advance his career while holding down a full-time day job. The week before final exams, when his wife insisted on talking to him about something quite disturbing (which he didn't describe in detail), he became very angry and sullen and remained so for days, while carrying on with work, school and preparation for exams. One night, while walking out of class, he suddenly felt relieved and a hundred pounds lighter. He said aloud to himself, "Life is a struggle!" and then chuckled to himself at the inanity of that overworked cliché—yet it was true in a way he had not understood before.

Tim told us he had always assumed that if he was doing the right thing in the right way, everything else would just fall into place; his wife would be happy when he needed her happy, and so would his children and his parents. When he was forced to acknowledge that life is just simply a struggle, Tim saw that he had no inviolate contract agreed to by his wife. If she had disturbed him when he felt it was inappropriate, it was still not the act of a criminal. After his revelation that she had not broken any rule of the universe, but just his private rule, Tim's anger at his wife vanished.

Discovering that "life is a struggle" is like rediscovering the wheel. What our culture knows about life and has already condensed into clichés, each of us has to discover through our own experience. Often when we are trying to explain to a friend some new, almost mystical insight into life which is going to transform both our lives, we end up quite embarrassed. At the end of the conversation, our puzzled friend says something like, "Are you saying we have to be responsible for ourselves?"

We may hem and haw and say, "No, not that exactly," but we can't discover how what we are saying is any different from that old cliché. In the midst of a mystical illumination, Bertrand Russell learned that war is bad, love is good, and there is loneliness in the world. Hardly startling insights for a brilliant philosopher! At 30 years old, I discovered what Thomas Wolfe wrote about before I was born—you can't go home again. Oh well.

As we discover the great truths of life, we feel so much more mature. The world is so much more complicated than we had imagined! We learn that life isn't fair, sometimes we have to make hard decisions, experts don't know all the answers, no one is perfect, and sex is not always romantic. We discover that parents don't fall apart if you cross them, separation and divorce are not the end of the world, a leopard doesn't change its spots, a stitch in time saves nine, experience and hard work do count, and timing is everything in life. Every cliché or aphorism ever written can be transformed into real knowledge during this period when we are assaulted by the facts of life through infidelities, betrayals, separations, divorces, deaths, accidents, ill-nesses and bad luck.

As children we believed that there were absolutes in life and that true adults had a way of knowing what they were. In many ways, that archaic view of life underwrote the way we measured ourself during our twenties and caused us to bluff and act as if, being adults, we "knew." In the long periods of uncertainty, we wondered what was wrong with us. It seemed as if everyone else had their act together like good adults.

As we get to know other people more deeply and over a longer period of time, we see that they share our own most piti-ful thoughts or characteristics. We begin to develop a different kind of self-confidence, based on our similarity to other human beings, as distinguished from a self-confidence built exclusively on the principle of competence—"I am acceptable because I do something well."

"I am acceptable even if I don't do everything well" is the principle we learn during our thirties. Moreover, because of it, we are less likely to dismiss other human beings for their imper-fections. We even apply this to our parents as well!

As we shed some of our prescriptive, confining codes, we feel an urge to be freer, to explore what's "out there." We want to be known more deeply than ever before, and we want to share our insights and see what life is like outside the confines of our usual routines and friends. Simultaneously we have the opposite urge—to settle into the confines of our home and our family. We are pulled in two directions, and it is a powerful struggle.

Work in the Thirties

In the thirties, work means different things to men and women. While men march ahead in their work somewhat blind to distrac-tion, women are pushed and pulled continually by the nagging question "How will I spend my childbearing years?" Even a childless career woman cannot completely overcome the urge to have children, and therefore, unlike her male counterpart, the energy she commits to work will be diffused from time to time.

The work men do substantially determines their world view and self-image. A young man clearly on the way up has a different attitude toward his *career* than does a man already at the peak of his *job*. A man with a job works to live, and often a man with a blossoming career lives to work. Accordingly, my discussion of work in the thirties will be presented along class lines.

Working-class men reach their wage peak by age 35. Their skills are fully developed, and further experience will teach them little more about their job. Though these men *knew* that the American Dream would not become a reality for them, they now *feel* that knowledge emotionally.

Their wages are scarcely adequate to meet the needs of the family month after month, year after year, not to mention "luxuries." The slightest crisis shatters the family's fragile economy, which often can never be put back together.

Typically, working-class wives must work. Both the husband's and the wife's jobs are extremely vulnerable to lay-offs and industry moves; and if the job has any element of danger, the worker risks physical injury or incapacity.

If their jobs still present some challenge or satisfaction or a degree of autonomy, working-class men will continue at them reasonably content. If they have gathered all the satisfaction or challenge they can from work, they will change jobs. The high turnover among auto workers manifests their dissatisfaction with deadening work. But few jobs offer sustaining challenges or satisfaction, so many workers compensate with projects or hobbies at home. Often these projects promote close family contact, but some hobbies may further insulate a dissatisfied man from his family. Similarly, a second job keeps a man from his family and threatens to trap him in monotony and make him permanently withdrawn at home. It is not unusual for young workers in their thirties to move from one physically taxing eight- or even ten-hour shift (plus overtime) to another in the same day, with only a quick sandwich or a peck on the cheek from the wage widow as she chauffeurs him between jobs. To pay the exorbitant physical cost of this schedule, even a young, energetic worker must borrow heavily from his body's future, and finally his health suffers.

Middle-class men don't have the time to worry about the validity of the American Dream; we're too busy trying to make it. For us, work—or, more properly, a career—is connected to a deeper magic dream; in this dream, work will somehow free us forever from the humiliating smallness of our childhood.

As we doggedly pursue our dream, we do not have enough time or emotional energy for our families. We want to be with them and they want to be with us and everyone complains that we don't spend enough time together, but we're really just too busy.

Social life for middle-class men becomes a vehicle for career advance. We join clubs and pursue hobbies (golf, tennis) in part to "make contacts" useful to our work. I once asked a rising young insurance executive why he became an active Republican; his answer: "Because my best clients expect it."

In our early thirties we are usually near the lower end of the money/status ladder, but we can look forward to more of both as our careers mature. It is worth recalling that by his mid-thirties, a working-class man has reached his peak income, while a middle-class man has just begun to climb.

Middle-class men make good money, but it's never enough. We are trapped; we feel guilty because we have so much more than others (even some former close friends) but not yet as much as the "big boys." We are neither at the top nor on the bottom in our career rank. We are not fledgling youngsters, so we are not treated tenderly, but neither are we highly placed enough to be treated deferentially. Yet we often know more than those with higher status. Without fail we are slighted in some way by a higher-up—it may be a dispute over getting the right office, a car allowance, or an invitation to a dinner party or consultation or just an unfriendly exchange. Some friends just jumped ahead two spaces or made an end run into another business or way of life or married a rich girl or the boss's daughter.

One of the boss's relatives or some new whiz kid or a woman is trying for our job.

One day we feel special, our future is at hand, and the next day we feel horribly ordinary. One day work is exciting and stimulating and meaningful, and the next day we're not sure whether any of it makes any sense. We fear dismissal, layoffs. We worry that we won't get the bonus we need, the promotion we were promised or the respect we have coming.

There is never enough money. It gets eaten up by the kids, inflation and a mad-spending wife. She is the one buying the groceries, signing the charge slips, calling up the repairmen. She is the one who notices the sofa is worn or the beds need replacing or the drapes need cleaning.

"She can stay home. I have no choice! I have to be here! Yet often she complains about her life as if I'm responsible for making it better. Let *her* try spending her life working for money to support everyone else and never having enough for herself."

In some large organizations, bosses play on our ambition and greed to make company men out of us. We watch ourself give up more of our self-determination to pay off the monster of future rewards. We find ourself engaged in "group think," pushing and twisting our mind around so that we can end up in agreement with those who have power over us. We have to stifle that part of us that wants to break out and be free again. We convince ourself that we will be able to be ourself in this organization—if not now, at least when we get above a certain level. We know that we are violating ourself, but we don't feel we have a choice, given the world as it is and the responsibilities we bear.

Of course, we may like our work, feel respected and have a genuine opportunity to grow. If so, we are among the fortunate few; but still we are plagued by doubts—about age, about lack of choice, about slights of rank and envy and competition with our friends and acquaintances.

We are keenly aware that we must overcome our own obstacles by ourself, and our load feels heavier than it did during our twenties. At the same time, despite our complaints, we feel quite young and somewhat proud of our ability to shoulder such a heavy load—it's a sign of our manhood. We look forward to what's coming up next even if it appears to make our load heavier. We have not given up the dream of going someplace, and no one can attack our right to dream or suggest we'll never make it.

We enjoy our capacity to do things. We are frequently impressed by our own skills. We know more shortcuts and which rules to follow. We refine and invent our own ways of doing things, and we gain more pleasure from our daily activities. While our career builds slowly, we find intrinsic pleasures in our work and deepen our knowledge about how the world we are locked into works.

Middle-class and working-class women who have no children and work outside the home have experiences similar to their men's—except that women experience the powerful pull of the urge toward childbearing.

In their twenties, women do not necessarily feel a strong urge to have a baby. But as the biological clock ticks away into the thirties, the urge becomes more difficult to resist. According to one study, working women in their thirties talk more about pregnancy and babies than women with children!

For women who *freely chose* a career rather than motherhood in their twenties, the decision is reopened in the thirties. It's a difficult decision, because one can't easily have two careers with equal joy and effectiveness. The choice is most difficult for women with successful careers. The prospect of giving up independence, identity support, work satisfaction and the other perquisites of a career in this time when there is such career concern among women weighs heavily against the decision to bear children. As one successful career woman put it, "My life is too abstract, without any dimension. A child would ground me in a concrete reality."

Women who choose a career because they are internally prohibited (that is, they stop themselves) from having children develop along two basic paths:

1. Some women deny that they ever wanted children; in fact, they feel quite happy committing all their energies to a career.

They seem hard-driving, extremely focused and without a trace of the urge to bear a child. This pattern works quite well until the mid to late thirties, when a new time sense sets in.

2. Some women who stop themselves from having children also stop themselves from making a full commitment to work. They feel that, because they insist on a career, something must be wrong with them. A career "should" be something that a woman does *in addition* to having children, "or so I've been taught." Their fractured, distracted attitude toward work frustrates them, and instead of facing their internal dilemma, they blame their troubles on all sorts of external, even mystical forces. These women must work through their internal prohibitions to make a free choice. Only then can they fully enjoy an outside career or motherhood.

As noted earlier, working women with children really have two careers, one outside the home and a domestic career as well. Most working-class women work for economic reasons alone. This can lead either to resenting the children (raising them is a second, unpaying job) or to treasuring them as the bright spots in an otherwise dismal day.

Because her job typically offers only minimal satisfaction and she could not quit if she wanted to and because she has little help at home to lighten her domestic load, a working-class woman has few options. Of course, improved child care, a more equitable division of domestic responsibilities with her husband, and a broader range of career possibilities would do much to improve her life.

A middle-class woman with two careers has the option to devote more energy to one or the other. She has greater career opportunities than does a working-class woman, so her work may be very attractive to her. In addition, a middle-class woman finds it easier to get help at home either by sharing it with her husband or by hiring cleaning and/or day-care services.

Because her income may not be essential to the family's well-being, a middle-class woman has the option to give up her outside work and concentrate on her domestic career. Given her education and affluence, she will have wider opportunities for interesting part-time jobs, for hobbies and for organizational, political or social activities. As one successful working woman put it, "I'm glad to quit my job—I'm tired of working. I'll go back when the kids are grown."

A woman opts for a domestic career out of three basic positions:

1. Free choice—as an adult, with a developed, independent consciousness, fully enjoying her choice.

2. Minor internal prohibition—which only shadows family life and her self-development but does not cause her to feel selfless or cheated, because on the whole she's doing what she wants.

3. Severe internal prohibition—the low point of a woman's life. She is blocked from any real pleasure by a malignant conspiracy with her husband.

A woman who freely chooses a domestic career fights off the housewife blues and the boredom of housework by constant creative effort and deep personal involvement. She tries to make a life of joy for her family and herself. In small, everyday ways, her energy and concern radiate through the home. She becomes the champion of home values and perhaps plans to expand her family. She learns to enjoy and make good use of the flexibility that being her own boss offers. She develops her talents through hobbies, lessons, volunteer work or minimal part-time jobs. She makes full use of her leisure time and involves herself deeply with all facets of the children's lives. If she has been to school or already had a taste of an outside career and *then* opted for a domestic career, her adjustment to homelife is easier and less conflicted than that of women who choose a domestic career with no other work experience to refresh them.

The subtle, minor internal prohibition does not interfere with a woman's self-confidence or happiness, but it does have an effect on the quality of family life and on her self-development.

SANDY

Sandy, 34, is scared but eager to go out into the world again. Until now she had prided herself on being a supermother, the best her 9-year-old twin boys could have. She provided the right schools, the right neighborhood and the right experiences for her sons. She even plans their spontaneity—and they are, she reports, truly great kids.

On her husband's fortieth birthday, he talks begrudgingly about the money for the private school she had convinced him their son Roy must have. That same money could have bought the car he always wanted. She begins to realize that her experience of being a supermother with superchildren has changed during the last few months. The boys have been more thoughtless, selfish and defiant lately. They didn't even put any special effort into an anniversary gift for their parents—just a plain old card and a poem. Nick didn't even write a thank-you note to his grandparents. She had trained them to be sensitive to others, but they were backsliding.

She feels irritated by their ingratitude, and later she discovers how important it was for her to be supermother. She remembers how it all started. She hadn't planned on being pregnant; it just happened, locking her into a way of life she hadn't expected and didn't like. She salvaged the situation by doing the best job possible, the Perfect Job. But all these years as supermother helped bury her feeling that she was giving up her life not entirely out of free choice. Now her sons' ingratitude, her husband's resistance to sacrifice and her own eagerness to get into *her* life conspire to unearth her buried sets of resentments. She sees how she controls her boys' lives. To maintain her denial of her own needs, she forces rigid rules upon her sons. The normal 9-year-old boy's preference to play on his skateboard rather than write his grandparents an original, thoughtful, sensitive thank-you note is seen by her, and therefore experienced by her son, as a criminally selfish act.

There are three important lessons we can learn from this story. One is about the role of resentment. Resentment is absolutely necessary to break up the rigid family framework, for it supplies much-needed information to Sandy and thus affords everyone more living space. The boys are no longer expected to be trained robots, and their self-assertions are now more tolerable. Her husband has more room to express his contrary views about child rearing and parental sacrifice. He is not met by such a powerful need on her part to have it her way. And, most of all, she is free not to be a perfect mother. Now she can go out into the world without fear that she is unleashing some terrible demonic force on herself and the world. She already knows about her forgotten resentments and the hidden flaws of supermother; nothing terrible will be revealed to her out there.

The second lesson we can learn from Sandy's experience is about the "shoulds." Her rule that the boys are "supposed to be extraordinarily sensitive and sacrificing to other people's needs" indeed becomes the "shoulds" in the heads of her twin boys. They must be perfect, for she is perfect and is able to hide her resentment about sacrificing her time to them. It would be different if she noticed that her sons were characteristically sensitive to others; then her encouragement would be part of the parenting process. In that case, the boys would not end up with the "should" position. Their sensitivity would be just another aspect of their personality. But because she forces them to be sensitive out of her need, they will feel conflict about being sensitive and will have to resolve that problem in the future.

The last lesson is about the origin of Sandy's "supposed to be" in the three-generation cycle. She needs to be sensitive and thoughtful toward her children because she feels her parents did not give enough thought to her growth. To correct her childhood hurts, Sandy has to make her children into what her parents were not, and this becomes a major source of conflict in her children's minds. In that way, multiplied a thousand times, our grandparents become part of the "shoulds" we have to free ourselves from as adults. The unique set of "shoulds" in each of us reflects the social history of our lineage. We are filled with archaeological relics.

Sandy resolved the issue of change which unleashed her resentment by giving more to herself. She began enjoying the leisure time available to her as a mother of 9-year-olds. She took a dance class, lost weight, had long and frequent luncheons and started feeling sexy again.

When other women said she must start a career, she felt, at first, that something was wrong with her for not espousing more "liberated" values and going to work. But she overcame that feeling and decided that she might work eventually but not now.

A woman quoted in Lillian B. Rubin's *Worlds of Pain* said: "I don't know what's the matter with me that I don't appreciate what I've got. I feel guilty all the time and I worry about it a lot. Other women, they seem to be happy with being married and having a house and kids. What's the matter with me?" When a traditional marriage becomes a malignant conspiracy, a woman's life looks bleak. She won't let herself enjoy work outside the home, and she can't feel satisfied by her domestic career. Whatever she does is overwhelmed by the feeling that she is doing something wrong. She feels trapped by her marriage and family and flails around madly in her cage. The illusion of the twenties still grips her consciousness, and she believes that if she pleases her husband and obeys all the wifely rules of selfless devotion, she will be rewarded with automatic happiness. "I should be happy—he should make me happy," she tells herself, but it just doesn't work.

She resents her husband because he is preoccupied with work and doesn't have time or energy for family activities. She envies her husband because he's not prohibited from enjoying his life. She feels inferior and increasingly dependent on him. Soon, she's convinced, he'll leave her for a happier woman, and she is already lonely and rejected. She doesn't want to seem clinging, but she needs reassurance that he loves her. "Dammit, he just won't do his part. He won't make me happy. He must not love me enough. That's it. He keeps me pinned here; he works me to death caring for his children, washing his dirty laundry. No wonder I can't work."

She's not interested in sex much any more; the children are more important. Now she understands her parents better; she has greater appreciation for their misery.

Her husband is bewildered, impatient, dissatisfied. "I do my share. You'd think she'd be happy. Why is she punishing me for her problems?"

He thinks she's still an ungrateful child. She thinks she's a selfless mother and her husband is a selfish, self-indulgent little boy. The air is thick with hostility.

If she breaks out and goes to work at this point, she feels forced into it by an unloving husband. He should have made her dream of becoming a loving wife and a happy mother come true. She resents him now, which sets up a later desire for revenge or separation.

If her husband suggests that she take advantage of her domestic career by enjoying her leisure time or developing a talent, she feels he is acting superior and imposing his solution. If he suggests she go to work, she feels he's only trying to get rid of her instead of giving her more love or attention. In fact, he may be a depriving, withholding husband who won't give the family anything of himself; but that discrimination must be made very carefully, since disappointment of expectations also leads to a feeling of being deprived.

More than likely, he will not be her real enemy, but because she regards him that way, she must find support elsewhere. In situations of this kind, the support of other women (not to mention treatment, of course) can be helpful.

Her only real task is to resolve her internal prohibition. Having done that, she can work without feeling abandoned or forced "out there"; or she can tap some of the satisfaction inherent in a domestic career. Many bright, aggressive women who suppressed their ambition during the early years of their marriage while their children were growing are able to fight through the internal prohibition. They come to understand that they are not breaking any rules by making a life for themselves, and therefore they happily begin a career in their early thirties. In the mid to late thirties, this issue takes on even greater urgency.

As we open up in our early thirties, life is not as simple or as well-ordered or as easily controlled by the mere exercise of our will as we thought. In fact, it is complicated and bewildering. Our disappointment at this information can send us into a tailspin, or we can discard our disillusion and gain a realistic view of what we must do to live as adults. That is, we must become responsible for our own growth and learn to shape our future based on a realistic view of what is inside us and the world around us.

2. Component Assumption 2

"I AM NOT LIKE MY PARENTS IN WAYS I DON'T WANT TO BE."

The major false assumption of the thirties—"Life is simple and controllable. There are no significant coexisting contradictory forces within me"— has a second component assumption: "I am not like my parents in ways I don't want to be." During our twenties, the struggle for adult independence helped us suppress and diminish our awareness of being like our parents in ways we preferred not to admit to. We ignored all the deeper roots of our personality that now need space to grow.

Our internal world is manifested most clearly while we're engaged in the impossible task of parenting. The parent of a growing child faces an unending series of novel challenges, with only a bewildering set of guidelines for help. Because we have to make up the rules as we go along, we are glaringly inconsistent, but we manage to fool our children most of the time. We get our comeuppance when they become smart-ass teenagers and zero in on our inconsistencies like a heat-tracking missile.

In the absence of a clear right way, we have one ever-present set of rules that covers almost every occasion, although we don't always admit its existence—our memory of what our parents did to us at that stage of our life. Occasionally we remember a specific event or an example: When my mother or father did this or that, I didn't like it, but it turned out to be the right thing. Or: I liked it, but it spoiled me; it was wrong because I never learned for myself. It was nasty and wrong of them—and it only hurt me—therefore I will never do it to my child.

More often, though, we don't have an explicit memory; we just have an intuition or a compulsion to act in a certain way with our child. Automatically we follow our parents' pattern.

We essentially become our own parents while parenting our child. Many of us complain about becoming just like our mother or father. We feel it to be a mysterious happening that we didn't choose and can't stop, and we feel terribly "suffocated" in life—as if we are straitjacketed in someone else's form. One woman, Janice, who felt she had the meanest, most rejecting mother of all time, vowed to be the opposite to her children. Despite her conscious effort not to be like her mother, she behaved toward her child exactly as her mother had acted toward her, including humiliating her daughter in front of company. Tony related to his 10-year-old son in a rigid, authoritarian manner that contradicted his self-image. He always thought of himself as orderly but liberal and easygoing. However, his father was rigid and authoritarian.

Parenting philosophy is not an accurate guide to our behavior as parents. Every time we respond to our child or make a decision about our child, we conform to or defy our parents. This surviving unconscious memory of our own childhood is the basis for our empathy with or understanding of our child. It is a marvelously designed system for automatically reproducing the next generation as a replica of the former generation. It probably worked very well when cultural change was slow, but it's not so good in this era of rapid cultural flux.

We want our children to be free of our bad characteristics or hang-ups. Also, we want them to grow up with the adult values we cherish or find meaningful—yet these often differ from our own parents' values.

ARTHUR: A CONFLICT OF VALUES
Arthur is in his early thirties. He was a smart kid, raised in an uneducated but commercially successful family. His parents are shrewd but do not understand or value the world of the printed word. The dollar is their criterion of success and accomplishment. "If you have money, you have status," they preach to Arthur by word and deed. When he proves to be smart with words, they wrap their value system around his talent and push

him to become a highly paid professional—a doctor, lawyer or accountant. He is sent into the world packaged for commercial success.

During college, Arthur's academic interest deepens, and he must choose between a low-paying, low-family-status academic career and a high-paying, high-family-status professional career. He chooses his parents' route but dreams of going back to academia eventually.

During his early twenties, Arthur single-mindedly pursues his professional legal training and dreams alternately of becoming a law-school professor or a rich private practitioner. By the end of his twenties, he has maneuvered his life into a compromise in which he is neither and both. He holds an administrative position in a law school and has the title of professor but no leisure time to study and research as a "real" professor. The job allows a part-time private practice, so he makes more money than a simple professor but less money than a full-time private practitioner. At the end of his twenties, he seems to have the perfect job, and to himself and others he is living a happy, successful professional life.

In his early thirties, his whole solution is undermined by doubts from within. The solution looks good and continues to work in terms of job success, but it doesn't feel right. Arthur yearns to have more time for study, contemplation and writing to enrich his knowledge and understanding of his field, but there is never enough time. It isn't built into the structure of the job or his life with his young children. Time for that pleasure has to be stolen from other, more pressing demands.

At the same time, Arthur feels an inner demand to make enough money to support a comfortable style of life. In his profession, he can erase his penny-pinching student memories by working just a few more hours each day, and at the same time he can become a good provider like his father.

He wants more of everything, and it isn't possible. He wants more time with his children. They are fun and loving and make him feel good when he has time to play with them. Though when he does make the time to play, he often thinks he could have been reading in a leisurely fashion or working for more money.

Arthur's parents survived poverty, and money became the prime value to them. But he grew up affluent, with a wider range of value choices, and he developed more scholarly values. Now he is struggling to reconcile his parents' values with his own, but more and more he is leaning toward scholarly pleasure in private while showing his children a very secure middle-class material world.

By deliberate policy, Arthur's children are taught not to value money too highly. It is OK if they lose some or give some away as loans to friends who won't pay them back. It is even OK to get it without working for it, just because they need it or he wants them to have it.

Arthur teaches his children to handle money in exactly the opposite way from what he learned. He was taught to guard it, earn it, watch it, save it, not share it, never waste it and expect to be yelled at if he ever lost it. He grew up to be a good worker, a good provider and a good money manager. He learned to keep his eye on the dollar, and he has a hard time making charity donations or spending money on himself. But if he were the only influence on his children, they would grow up to be quite generous and sharing but might not become financially prudent or controlled.

By deliberately creating an experience with money opposite to his own, Arthur is repudiating what he was taught because he considers it to be irrational and excessive. From time to time, his parents' beliefs break through and he has to suppress his desire to lecture the children on their irresponsible money management. He is angry and self-righteous and wants to yell at them, "What do you mean you gave so-and-so a quarter and you didn't get it back?'"

To correct his parents' excesses, Arthur may have swung too far away from the valuable parts of their teaching. By throwing the baby out with the bathwater, he may have created an experience for his children from which they in turn will have to recover. They may be missing a lesson about necessity and limitations!

When Arthur wants to lecture his children about losing a quarter, he is unconsciously recalling his parents' unacceptable, excessive style. If he suppresses that desire to yell at his children the way he was yelled at or if he discounts his desire to yell as insignificant, he misses a vital message and will continue the excess. He must pay attention to this desire to yell and wonder about it. He must learn not to be afraid to have some feelings similar to his parents' feelings. Only then will he be able to reexamine his position on money.

Arthur learns from his wife, who corrects the excesses in his policy toward money. But had he ignored that shouting voice within him as a source of crucial information, Arthur could not have seen what his wife saw.

Now let's look at the other part of Arthur's conflict—the love of book learning. He wants very much to establish this love in his children while they are young because it was not encouraged in him by his parents. There were not many books in his house and very few, if any, children's books. It was not one of the things money was spent on. Arthur loves to read to his children but finds that he isn't doing as much as he should and that he doesn't receive nearly the kick out of it that his wife does. She enjoys every minute of it and becomes animated and as naturally excited as the children by a delightfully funny section. When Arthur reads, he pretends to be like her, but he is really annoyed at the money spent on children's books, even though it is minuscule in comparison with the money spent on his serious books. He also begrudges the money his wife spends on novels. Most of the time, Arthur doesn't criticize her because intellectually he agrees she is doing the right thing. But his feelings can't be denied. As his reading time with his children diminishes, his dream that he will be their intellectual teacher becomes less and less viable. More and more his wife becomes their intellectual instructor. He enjoys watching and facilitating the process but also feels a tinge of envy and disappointment.

Arthur's idea of himself as a true intellectual is modified after being damaged. He is one who admires intellectuals and he is smart in some areas, but he is not an intellectual himself. He just can't be what he really isn't. He is disappointed, but the experience with his children teaches him what he is as distinguished from what he wants to be. He is quite different from his parents, but he is not so totally different that he can make of himself a "true" intellectual.

At work, Arthur, now 30, wants more time to pursue the intrinsic pleasure of scholarship. His compromise between his parents' commercial values and his scholarly values worked during his twenties while he gained the satisfaction of making it in the world. But now he wants more of his kind of pleasure for himself. He likes himself better and feels more whole and satisfied when he is engaged in meaningful scholarly work. He does not get a kick out of making money. In fact, he has just been stubbornly trying to erase, through his children, the stinging hurt he felt from his mother's icy words and his father's thunderous shouts over issues of money. But Arthur is still surrounded in his head by revived parental images.

His wife sees only the stubbornness of his attitude and worries about the effect it is having on her children. The conflict within Arthur becomes a source of tension with his wife. The conspiracy they formed during their twenties unravels: she no longer can confirm it as adequate. Arthur doesn't like her knowing more about him than he knows. Why can't she just close her eyes to this?

On the issue of books, he envies her naturalness and the fact that she had books read to her as a child. He again feels inferior to her and resents her even more. She is hurt by his attitude. She accuses him of shirking his reading obligation with the children. She doesn't know that he is avoiding reading with them because each experience points to the painful truth that he isn't what he wants to be.

Soon Arthur loses sight of his internal dilemma and becomes enmeshed in a battle with his wife. She becomes the one who won't let him be what he wants to be. It is she who stands against his growing desire to do more scholarly work. She is the one telling him he is not a true intellectual or a superior parent. As the witness to Arthur's disillusionment with himself, his wife becomes, in Arthur's mind, its cause.

Like Arthur, we all know our rigid idiosyncrasies as parents. We know that our partners know them too. And we know theirs. We witness their living conflict with their parents, and they witness ours. We each are in touch with the other's most tender spot, and we can choose to treat it with care or use it for warfare.

We recognize our idiosyncratic rules by the way we stubbornly defend ourself against our spouse's better arguments. Our imperatives may be trivial and silly, such as rules about how old the baby-sitter has to be (over 50) or the schedule of piano practicing or walking around in bare feet or snacks and chores. Or they may be fundamentals that will influence our children profoundly. We may relate to an opposite-sex child with overwhelming seductiveness or overwhelming hostility if our own sexual identity is too compromised or rigidly encased. We may have a program for our child's life that doesn't include our child's wishes or capacities; we may ruin both the child who follows our program and the child who defies us and is frozen out of our affection.

The child who follows our program of imperatives spends his/her adult life trying to escape the hell of never being able to live out his/her own life without guilt; the child who is frozen out of our attention lives his/her life feeling unloved or misunderstood.

When we impose our imperatives on our children, we make them feel powerless. All of us perpetuate this crime, generation after generation. All we can do is minimize the damage done to our children by fighting through, as directly as possible, our own battles to become ourselves. The more we accept our fear of becoming an inevitable copy of our parents, the further we can go in distinguishing our own qualities from theirs. When we deny that fear, we have to fortify our denial through our children's lives and thereby perpetuate a great crime against them.

Wanting and demanding more *intrinsic* pleasure for himself, Arthur was in the *first step* of a career move. He was developing a more independent adult consciousness and breaking away from a compromise with his parents' values. Through the arguments and experiences with his wife and children, he had come to see that he was not what he wanted to be.

Each of us lives out the same formula. As we seek intrinsic pleasure, we become necessarily more self-concerned. Self-concern and accepting our need for intrinsic pleasure eventually force us to bring a previously undeveloped quality into our life.

It is the emergence of undeveloped and previously forbidden personal qualities that is the key to the first half of this formula. If our compromise with our parents' ways and values demanded toughness in our twenties, gentleness may be the quality we seek. If we needed to be obsequious and timid, speaking with more authority is what we will work on. In similar ways, it may be greater discipline, joyous fun-lovingness, or any number of other human qualities that we lack which will suddenly seem crucial.

We can't escape having been a child in our family, and we can't deny that we were exposed to certain idiosyncrasies in that life. At one time our parents' world was the only world we knew. However, it is now time to repackage ourself with a larger portion of those qualities we were previously *afraid* to include.

One 31-year-old science professor, the son of a famous historian, convinced himself during his twenties that he was not ambitious like his overly ambitious father. While struggling to overcome a writing block, he discovered an intense, murderous rivalry with his father that revealed his own undeniable ambitions. Once in touch with his intense ambition, his writing block disappeared, and he began to make some choices about how to direct, harness and modulate that aspect of himself.

A 33-year-old man felt stifled in his own family by the overly polite atmosphere. Upon reflection he recognized that his parents' slightly abrasive style with each other was also a part of him. He decided to let some of that emerge, since it rubbed away the artificial covering of family problems that needed attention. He began to encourage up-front abrasiveness in his family and purposely set out to change the tone of the family life until it felt more real and alive to him than it had for a long time. He had denied this useful quality during his twenties because he had agreed with his wife that abrasiveness was really "nastiness." His wife came to agree that her own family's ways were too distant and cold rather than "polite."

As we open up, we must face the nuts and bolts of change, the things about us that make us uncomfortable or unhappy. We must become aware of our similarities and identifications with our parents. We want to avoid blind repetition of their patterns on the one hand and not reject useful or pleasing patterns of theirs on the other. We must consciously choose the patterns we do want as part of our adult personality. This is the essential development process of the thirties.

3. Component Assumption 3

"I CAN SEE THE REALITY OF THOSE CLOSE TO ME QUITE CLEARLY."

The major false assumption of the thirties—"Life is simple and controllable. There are no significant coexisting contradictory forces within me"—has a third component assumption: "I can see the reality of those close to me quite clearly."

During our twenties, as we struggle to shape our own independent lives, we do not deal with the demonic images or the conspiracies we have formed in our relationships. In our thirties, as we open up to life's complexities, our irrational demons interfere more palpably with our lives, particularly with our relationships.

The three conspiracies which we could not confront in our twenties now are exposed in our thirties. They are:

1. Being married to someone who has a negative characteristic identical to that of one of our parents.

2. Re-creating our parents' marriage within our own by becoming like one of our parents.

3. Insisting on one-mindedness.

As we attempt to grow and become more intimate, we come face to face with our demonic childhood consciousness misinterpretations of our loved ones. Therefore, the component false assumption of this chapter is most challenged by a committed, intense living-together situation—usually this is a marriage.

Marriage and Demonic Images

In our early thirties, both partners are working to discover and satisfy their inner selves. But the boundaries of each partner's problems become confused. Neither of us is sure where our individual needs stop and our partner's needs begin. Children add yet another level of confusion. To straighten out our borders and make our growth work clearer and easier, we must improve our marital dialogue in our thirties. Our partner must know and appreciate our pressing concerns; for what they perceive as selfish or stubborn behavior, we may feel is our way of resolving a conflict essential to our future. To continue our psychological work, we must ignore the charge of selfishness and refuse to measure ourself or others by predetermined formulas of what a husband or wife "ought" to be.

STEVE AND MARY

Steve is 34. Mary is 33. He is working toward an MBA. When she asks him to study at the library on Sundays, he says she has no right to ask him to leave the house. She becomes furious. Later that day he says that she is right; the next day she apologizes for overreacting. They each resume the thoughtful goodwill stance toward each other that has characterized most of their relationship.

A few days later, after he is particularly nice to her, she asks curiously, "How come you are so nice to me lately?" He responds, "Because you have been so nice to me." She doesn't believe him; she's irritated but doesn't know why.

Underlying her initial "overreaction" and later irritation at him is the suspicion that he is being nice because it is expedient for him. Four years ago, during a successful career as a programmer, he decided to go to school for an MBA. Now it is two weeks before his final exams. Because she works full time and also cares for their extraordinarily difficult 9-year-old adopted son, the last six months have been hectic for both of them. The child has no friends and must be supervised constantly. He has a medical problem which requires that he be routinely driven to doctors, rescued from embarrassing social situations, and have day- and nighttime medication, which must be monitored. He makes amusing, bright, insightful wisecracks, but on a moment's notice, he may shout across a supermarket that Mary is a "fuck-ass."

Mary asks Steve to go to the library on Sundays because she doesn't want to tiptoe around the house or curb their son at every moment so that Steve can study. Since their son is her responsibility during this period, she feels that Steve can at least put himself out one day a week to make it easier for her.

He, of course, reacts from his point of view. Overworked and anxious about the exam, he wants to do what is easiest for him. Everyone should accommodate to his needs.

He recants after hearing both her anger and her point of view. "You're right. I didn't think of it that way before," he says. That helps her, but she suspects that he is saying she is right only to quiet her anger and decrease the tension in the house. She feels he is acting not out of consideration or enlightenment but out of selfish expediency—to shut her up.

At this point in the dialogue, Mary is left with two versions of her husband: one benign and one demonic. The benign version is that Steve is a man trying to work things out between the two of them. Upon confrontation, he is decent enough to own up to his error and make an attempt to repair it.

The demonic version is that Steve is a man who can turn the charm on and off, a man who controls and frustrates her, who has put her through hell for the last six months by choosing to be a selfish pig. Now he chooses to be nice to exploit her powerful desire to have a good relationship with him. He doesn't need a good relationship; he just wants to shut her up and keep her from complaining.

Because she understands the pressure he's under, she tries to be good and kind and help him through this period. On the other hand, every time she thinks he is playing her for a fool and manipulating her, she wants to yell and scream at him. She wants to deprive him of his victory over her.

These two versions of reality each feel right at times, yet they contradict each other. The version Mary accepts as real determines how she feels, responds and interacts with Steve. When he is benign in her eyes, things are good between them, and potential friction between them passes unnoticed or prompts a good chuckle. When he is sinister in her eyes, she responds accordingly—with defensiveness, irritation and a desire to strike back.

It is obviously crucial that Mary determine which version of her husband or what combination is correct. Certainly both kinds of men exist in this world, and people do change from one to the other over the years.

The question then becomes: how does one come to know what "really is" in this situation? The answer: by an ongoing dialogue between the two people in which the evidence is sifted and weighed.

Mary and Steve had their share of trouble in their twenties. From her point of view, he was not warm, loving and communicative enough. From his point of view, she was too demanding and insatiable. They talked about the issues, and each decided that although the other was wrong, they would continue to try to live with it and teach each other how to improve. They would compromise to please each other, but since both believed they were right, they each felt they were doing the other a favor that should be appreciated. It was a forced, fragile compromise in which each tried to will away his or her demonic image of the other. They tried not to see how demonic they each felt the other was, for if they were right, they would have to separate once the evidence proved their worst suspicions. During periods of stress, they tried to live within a simplified version of reality—"I'm really good and he/she is really bad."

Now in her thirties, Mary is willing to concede that her simplified, demonic vision of Steve *might* be manufactured in her head.

A month earlier, during the bad times, when Mary offered to take their son out of town for the weekend, Steve reacted with jealous suspicion and accused her of going off to have an affair. She felt hurt by his lack of trust, even though she was angry enough to flirt with the idea of an affair. She reacted with righteous indignation at his remark. Although he thought he was right, he regretted the emotional storm that ensued.

During the good times of the last week, she again offered to take their son out of town. This time, when Steve thought it was a good idea, Mary was hurt that he wasn't jealous. She thought he was not voicing his mistrust just to keep her from being angry again.

She had the "ah-ha" reaction familiar to all of us, when our favorite suspicions seem to be confirmed. The "ah-ha" reaction is especially strong when we are beginning to believe we might be wrong. It reinforces our confidence again in our ability to "know" in a subtle way our loved one's inner workings.

I pointed out to Mary her two contradictory views of her husband. If he had voiced mistrust of her second offer to take the child away for the weekend, she would have been hurt and angry, especially since she was feeling loving now and was not even guilty of mental infidelity. But when he didn't voice his mistrust, she was able to label him as unloving and insensitive to her. Either way, she had evidence that he was the demonic one. Instead of discovering the real Steve, she was declaring he must be demonic, then looking for the best evidence of it. In turn, when Steve spots this pattern of hers, he feels there is no way he can please her. By labeling her insatiable, he totally misses her problem and introduces his demonic image of her into the puzzle. This, in turn, feeds her demonic image of him—"He does not understand and love me; he only sees me as his demanding mother. He defends himself against me as if I were bad and makes me feel even more unloved." The cycle of this marital seesaw goes on and on.

Steve finally agreed that Mary could, with their son, go out of town for a weekend. She knew he had no reason to be jealous now. With this, Steve was once again loving in her eyes, and she felt cared for by him.

But something unsettling remains. She doesn't like the idea that he doesn't seem to worry about missing her. She understands that she has been in the same position herself and knows that she has wanted to "get rid of him" on Sundays. But it still hurts. It hurts because it is too close to her childhood, when she was constantly feeling unloved by her alcoholic, disturbed parents. They acted as if they would just as soon get rid of her if she gave them the slightest trouble. When the past and the present become too similar, Mary loses her orientation, and the past becomes the present. The hurt of the present is entirely tolerable as long as it is recognized as a *present* hurt. As long as the past remains the past, it does not click the demonic version of her husband into place.

Mary must get to the position where she can recognize the old rule from her childhood, which is: "I can only be a *victim* of insensitive, unloving others and impotently complain and hope someone takes pity on me." She must modify that to: "I am not impotent. I can bear the kind of demonic hurt I always feared, and with my adult consciousness I can see what it means and consider my response. I am not being unloved, abandoned or misused in this situation. I am a partner in a marriage, not a child to my husband."

This kind of dialogue and thinking can help us sort out what needs to be sorted out in married life. We must turn toward the complexity and confusion, thrash around a bit among the contradictions, and finally sift and sort evidence until fact and fiction settle out.

In the case of Mary and Steve, it might have been otherwise. Many of us do marry partners with exactly the qualities and tendencies that traumatized us in childhood. It might have turned out that Steve was planning to get rid of her and their difficult child after becoming an MBA. Like her alcoholic parents, he might have had an incapacity to be close and loving. If so, Mary needed to know it soon, because the rule organizing the experience of our thirties teaches that dreams in life will come true only if we directly surmount the obstacles in our path.

In our twenties, we formed conspiracies, tolerated demonic images of ourselves or others, and brushed aside a host of other irrationalities because we were so intent on setting up our lives. Now, as we open up in our thirties, those old conspiracies and demonic images are like yokes around our necks. We no longer have the same self-image or see the same direction to our lives.

We demand that everyone, particularly our partners, recognize our uniqueness and change their false, fixed images of us held over from our twenties.

Shifting Conspiratorial Compacts

Especially during their late twenties and early thirties, spouses tend to feel *too* dependent on each other. Each of us in this era of our life comes to recognize that, in some pervasive and inchoate way, we have given our loved one's opinion, glances or moods *too much power* to affect and determine us.

Steve and Mary each felt their basic happiness was *totally* controlled by the other. From Mary's point of view, Steve could withhold closeness, affection or communication at any time he wanted and thus destroy her. From his point of view, Mary could be angry or dissatisfied at any time she chose and thus destroy him.

As a couple, we play a power game with each other that may explode at any time. Behind the facade of everyday living and loving, tensions and petty disagreements is a fusillade of hate ready to burst out when the power game spins out of control and loses its balance.

During personal stress and change, the balance *always* shifts: the other becomes even more important to us, more powerful and more in control of our happiness. We forget that we have any power at all over the one we love. We feel totally vulnerable and impotent.

During these times, we hate and love most deeply. We hate when our partner misuses his or her power and is insensitive to our vulnerability. We feel racked with pain and deeply humiliated by our gaping wound. We swear we will never open up again, never trust, never submit ourself to this humiliation again.

We also love most passionately during these times of stress. We change when our partner *doesn't* use his or her power against us. We love our partner most when he or she could devastate us but doesn't. That's when we are most convinced they are *not* our secret enemy. We are always seeking that pure, clean, consuming love and closeness, that elusive transcendent quality, that makes us break our protective vow never to trust again.

If we are devastated too many times, we harden and begin to hate. Our relationship becomes a battleground. We maim and try to destroy each other. We withhold the medicine of love. We attack where our enemy is weakest—at his or her self-image. We cut off our mate's supplies in bed. We outflank our husband or wife with the children. We mow down our partner in front of company. We cut him or her off from friends and family. Marriage becomes hell.

We can slip into it so easily that in the midst of the worst battles, we don't even know what the war is all about. Not only do we not know how to stop it, we don't even know how it began!

In my view, there are three essential ingredients to the witch's brew that conjures up this hell on earth:

1. We have real differences to negotiate.
2. We overestimate the other's power.
3. We underestimate our own power over the other.

SALLY AND BURT

Sally, at 27, is a strikingly beautiful model with a razor-sharp mind, a glaring lack of confidence, and a surprising homegrown quality, considering the hardness one expects in women who have made a career of their looks.

Burt was a bachelor until he married Sally two years ago at age 32. He races cars and dirt bikes, has an easy, flirtatious way with women and a comfortable, reassuring way with men.

Sally and Burt have been at war for the last year, and Sally has moved out. Burt painfully records his love for her in tearful declarations and urges her to keep talking to him so that he will come to understand. Sally says she loves him still, but she also hates him too much to ever trust him again. She doesn't want to talk about it; she just wants to stay apart. Sally feels she has suffered deep humiliation. She feels she has been a fool and a coward to have stayed as long as she did. She can't conceive of ever going back.

Burt can't understand how it all happened. He waited until he was 32 and married the first woman he ever loved. They had nothing but fun during their courtship; they laughed a lot and shared the same scenes. She seemed to get a real kick out of his racing-crowd friends. He saw that although she was bright and independent, she seemed shy and lacked self-confidence, but he was sure he could pull her out of that with his good humor. He was sure he loved her. He admired her brain and was proud of her beauty. But he didn't understand her lack of confidence. After their marriage, he took her for granted.

Sally had had her share of lovers and good times, but with Burt she found something special. He was special enough to marry over the protests of her parents and the warnings of a few of her friends. She had a fixed image of a marriage; in that context she felt totally devoted to him. She didn't take him for granted at all. She tried to please him, to dress more as he liked, to fit into his way. She liked being part of an official couple.

The differences began to show during parties. Assuming Sally was really just like him, Burt would drift into conversation with whoever was next to him. He never gave a thought to where Sally was; he knew she could take care of and enjoy herself. He wouldn't hesitate to embrace a friend's wife; he felt free to comment to Sally on the way home about some other woman's breasts or shapely legs. After all, wasn't she, Sally, the most beautiful of all women? How could she ever feel jealous or unloved? He knew he loved her; how come she didn't?

At parties, Sally felt shunned, avoided and unattended. She didn't like his implied comparisons of her with other women during their conversations on the way home. She was eager to be with him, yet he didn't seem eager to be with her. Just once during the evening couldn't he come over and touch her and reaffirm their bond? When she joined him in a conversation, he never seemed to make room for her or go out of his way, in consideration of her shyness, to make her feel part of the group. She felt like a puppy dog trailing behind him. Her sense of pride and independence suffered.

Incidents accumulated, and feeling more unloved, Sally's affection tarnished and turned to possessiveness and jealousy. She felt smaller and smaller, even "dirty" because of her mixed feelings. They argued about spending money and what kind of clothes she should wear.

She couldn't understand how he could continue to hurt her at parties after she told him how she felt. Why was he not helping her gain confidence in herself? Why was he cutting her down where she was most vulnerable? "Everyone thinks he's so great and loving, but privately he's a monster. What is he taking out on me?"

Burt was getting bigger and bigger in her eyes, while she was becoming more powerless. Each slight became exaggerated. She was now afraid of him.

Ironically, she was becoming bigger and bigger in his eyes, although instead of showing the hurt, he became defiant and stubbornly proud. If she was hurt by what he did, why didn't she speak up as it was happening? Why did she wait a week to tell him what he had or hadn't done at a party the week before? Before their marriage, she loved him for his ways; he wasn't acting any different now. Why was she trying to change him, why was she making him feel so guilty when he hadn't done anything wrong? Burt felt a little boy's defiance; he was sure that the woman he had loved and trusted enough to marry was now using her extraordinary power over his happiness to criticize him and make him feel like a small, guilty boy.

One night in the midst of an argument in which she felt painfully vulnerable and he felt painfully criticized, he said, "OK, if you can't stand me, why don't you leave?" She went upstairs with her tail between her legs. She was not ready to leave, but from that moment on, she hid her anger. She brooded and collected grievances; months later she devastated him by moving out.

In visits with me, Sally came to understand that while she felt powerless, in fact she held tremendous power over Burt's life. She asked Burt about the revealing blouse he had bought her. Hadn't he tried to remake her sexual image to please himself, regardless of what she wanted to be? Wasn't he callously denigrating her and making her feel like a cheap whore?

To her surprise, he admitted trying to change her image, not to hurt her but to diminish her power over him. He thought if he could encourage her to walk around the house naked sometimes or to go nude bathing or to wear a more revealing blouse, their sex life would improve and he would get rid of the feeling of being dirty. He wanted her to be more like him to neutralize her power over his sexuality. He needed to remake her, not because he enjoyed controlling her but because she was too powerful an influence over his mind.

Now, let's look at Burt and Sally in terms of the three essential ingredients of marital hate.

Burt and Sally had real differences to negotiate. They had different levels of social confidence; they had different views of what it meant to be a loving couple; they were in different places about bodily exposure and dress; and they had different backgrounds regarding money and how it should be handled and spent. But none of these differences was unusual or irremediable. Every couple has a comparable list of differences.

Burt and Sally overestimated each other's power. For Sally, Burt had become the sole determiner of her self-worth. He held all the power: his every action or remark was an evaluation of her—was her barometer of self-worth up or down today?

Because she was the only woman he trusted enough to marry, Burt felt she had total control over his happiness. He took her for granted to minimize her power over him because he felt she had begun to misuse that power.

They underestimated their real power over each other. Because Sally felt powerless, she had no way of understanding her real power over Burt. She had no way of knowing how devastated he would be when she left. She thought he would just pick up his old ways—a new girl would be on his arm and in his bed before the smell of her perfume was off the sheets. She had no way of knowing that he feared her power to control his life. He felt she was looking down on him. While he was trying to get her to be more like him sexually so that he wouldn't feel morally inferior to her, he had no way of understanding his power over her. He didn't believe her when she told him he made her feel so bad. It couldn't be that way.

So Sally and Burt slid right by each other in their marriage until each became convinced that the other was purposely and callously out to ruin his or her pleasures and growth in life.

Burt and Sally's *overestimation* of each other's power, which is part and parcel of every intimate relationship, is a particular hazard during the late twenties and the early thirties. In this period of rapid change, power fluctuations in our relationships become quite volatile. That is why we must come to grips with the inherent complexity we all share as human beings. We must know our values and others' *fully enough* to let our partners know and appreciate the full dimension and complexity of our terrible vulnerability.

As we open up in the thirties, the conspiracies which supported our relationships in our twenties also open, releasing our dreaded childhood demonic images. To rebuild our relationships successfully, we must overcome these demons and accept the self within each of us that demands to come out. We must then see each other authentically, through adult eyes, as the people we really are.

4. Component Assumption 4

"THREATS TO MY SECURITY AREN'T REAL."

The major false assumption of the thirties—"Life is simple and controllable. There are no significant coexisting contradictory forces within me"—has a fourth component false assumption: "Threats to my security aren't real."

While we are opening up to our inner world and the hope it offers, we are also squeezed by the network of relationships and the tangle of routines we have accumulated over the years. They all make demands on our time and energy. A simple hobby, such as tennis, has become a ritual which demands regular attention every week. We don't have enough time to be with ourselves.

We feel an urge to push away the strictures on our lives in order to plumb more deeply new aspects of ourselves that need our time and attention. But because our new directions threaten the lives we've already established, our first approach is to say, "This isn't real; I can forget that I ever saw it so clearly; it was just a flash." But this won't work, for the insistence of new thoughts and urges characterizes the early thirties. Ideas won't be denied just because they're troublesome; they spring back at us and refuse to be ignored. Time is not pressing yet (as it will in the forties), but our dissatisfactions won't go away. We can't rationalize them out of existence.

CAREERS: This age period is a natural time for career commitments to deepen; either we extend ourselves anew in the career we've chosen or we enthusiastically move into a new one. The commitment—"This is really going to be my life's work"—creates both a sense of security (because at last we've chosen) and a sense of insecurity (because we've lost the experimental attitude toward work that characterized our twenties). Earlier, we were ready to change jobs and to leave what we were doing at a moment's notice. Now, with our new commitment, our horizons have shrunk. We have sacrificed adventure for security.

INTIMACY VERSUS SPACE: Couples find themselves wanting more of each other but more "space" too; circumstances determine which need is more urgent. Men who leave their families, complaining of being cramped, burdened and bored, say they "have to get away." Yet often they find themselves back in the same situation. This is a painful time for women too: some seek more intimacy, while others want to run away because they feel smothered by too much closeness.

RETURNING TO SCHOOL: This is a period in which both men and women return to school—whether to enhance a career, to begin a new one or, for those who have been raising a family, to begin a career for the first time.

MORE FUN AND MORE BODILY PLEASURE: It's also a time when we recognize that we've been working too hard and taking life too seriously. New bodily desires and emotional sensitivities command our attention and arouse our curiosity now.

SETTLING DOWN: Many men and women who've been single find a surprisingly strong and unexpected urge to settle down, to stop running around.

HAVING A BABY: Many women who haven't yet had a baby find themselves with a strong urge to have a child. Women who already have children find a desire to have another child during their early thirties—usually the last one.

STOP BEING A BABY: There's a sense at this time that we must stop the babyish indulgences we've carried over from our childhood. It's time to grow up and finally stop being a perpetual student, a chronic rebel or the family's black sheep.

STOP FIGHTING PARENTS: We view our parents through different eyes at this age. They've changed and we've changed. As Jane, a 30-year-old woman, remarked after a visit home, "My parents don't want to control me any more. I was all prepared for a fight. I was like that Japanese soldier they found in the Philippines last year—ready to fight a war that's been over for years."

Tom, 29 years old, had to acknowledge, while reading a letter from his father that would have burned him up six months before, that his father was right when he said that Tom had better get moving if he was to get anyplace in life.

Divorce: Breaking Up a Family

If we have children, our involvement with institutions and routines is multiplied by their friends, the car pools, the other parents, the neighbors, the relatives who want to visit, and arranging lessons, shopping and recreational outings. If we have any time left over, there is a husband or a wife ready to make demands on it. Even doing what we want, we end up feeling surrounded. Family living isn't easy, and real compromises have to be made. Not having enough space for ourself is built into the family institution!

Once we start thinking about divorce, we ask ourself a series of soul-searching, soul-wrenching questions. "Am I running away because I am too thin-skinned to hear the truth about myself from my partner? Am I running away because I don't have the guts to bear the responsibility I brought into this world? Will I suffocate here? Am I trying to be a teenager again? Am I just seeking sexual variety in all this? Will I be more satisfied with my new life? Am I copying someone? Am I rebelling against my parents? Can I make it?"

"Can I make it?" is a real question for more women than men, particularly if the woman has not been working in recent years. If she has lost confidence in her ability to support herself, she is in a different position than her husband, who at least feels confident economically.

On the other hand, if a woman has maintained a career or is adequately prepared to return to work, she is much less afraid to think about divorce. In fact, many women want to work as a hedge against financial vulnerability; then they feel they can pursue the trouble spots in the marriage without backing down because "he might leave me stranded."

Indeed, our whole emotional system seems organized by separation fears from our earliest years. As young children we want to be loved to ensure that we will not be left. We are comforted when we can win a smile, a laugh, or a hug from our powerful parents. The more we feel their empathy and attention, the more influence we feel we have over our world and the more secure we feel we are from separation. Those of us who were treated without much empathy as children felt powerless, vulnerable to being left in a helpless state, and resentful that we had to perform to be "kept."

Each of us feels some of this in our intimate relationships, but some of us are cursed with a much larger dose of insecurity. In a couple, when one partner clearly has more power, the other partner automatically starts to feel like a "thing" again. One solution to the often unendurable pain this creates in the "weaker" partner is to rebalance the power, as Sally did by separating from Burt. Another solution for many women is to return to work. A third solution, which both sexes sometimes try, is to have an affair. And a fourth and much healthier solution is to find some way of breaking up or modifying the outdated childhood illusion that we are powerless.

LUCY

Lucy, at 34, did the latter. For eleven years she felt Bill "had her by the balls" because he often threatened he would leave, cutting off the money he earned and she spent. Although she had been very ambitious and professionally capable in her early twenties, she was tired of working and was secretly quite pleased to quit when she got pregnant. They now had two children, who were not yet old enough for her to go back to work full time comfortably. However, she now had some leisure during the day, and she felt she deserved some reward for all those years of serving others—particularly since she had been more thoughtful and giving as a wife to Bill than he had been to her as a husband.

After some treatment, Lucy sees that in collusion with Bill, she has unnecessarily placed herself in a powerless position. Although she doesn't trust the way he handles money and although she has the time and he doesn't, she has still refused to write out their monthly checks. One morning a little while after she made this discovery, he hands her their income tax returns before dashing off to work; he wants her to sign them without looking at them, just as her father used to do to her mother. She refuses and says she won't sign them until he shows her all the year's financial information. He storms and fumes. She persists. While looking through the records, she discovers that the month of her birthday, when he said he didn't have any money to buy her a decent present, he had spent an exorbitant amount on his hobby. She then storms and fumes.

At the end of that same week, he needs her to attend an important business function of his company. "No, not until I get that watch you promised me for my birthday. Tomorrow!"

Tears. Sleepless nights. Great anxiety. When it's all over she says to him, "I've been a bitch to be so demanding, but now you see what it's like to be on the receiving end. For a few days I had all the power, and I used it on you like you do on me."

Lucy broke her twenties conspiratorial contract with Bill: "I will be totally devoted to you, then you will stop using your money to control me." She turned things around temporarily when she invented a direct way of teaching him what it felt like to be humiliatingly powerless. "Buy that watch tomorrow!" was the sign of her power and his humiliation.

Lucy's heady feeling of power that week was so strong that she won't ever think of herself as powerless again. She hopes that because she no longer feels small and helpless, she won't have to continue these extreme maneuvers to get power.

Men are just as likely to have been treated as "things" in childhood as women; the only difference is that it is not usually money that makes men feel powerless in a relationship. Other factors create the same feeling for men. A man may fear that his wife can leave him easily, especially if she is very pretty or sexy, if she is particularly independent, if she has a strong tie to her parents, or if she gives the impression that she looks down on her helpless husband and doesn't particularly need or appreciate him. When men feel on the short end of the balance of power, they set out to eliminate their unendurable vulnerability. They may do it with an affair, a separation, or whatever other action will display the power they have over their wives, including economic power if that will work.

Although the hurt-revenge-hurt cycle of these imbalances can easily escalate into divorce, most of them can be worked out within the marriage if there is a commitment to face the very powerful, primitive emotions that are at the root of the trouble.

Who's the Enemy? The Critical Question for Divorce

Is our partner the enemy of our growth? Does he/she really want to quash our needs, or are we just accusing him/her to camouflage our own internal prohibitions, which we are afraid to face? Most of the time it is some combination of the two.

On the one extreme, our partners usually see our changes as threats to their safety, so they often do everything in their power to stop us. If this is the case, then by various techniques of reward and punishment, they will try to convince us that we are morally obligated not be any different from the way we were or the way they need us to be. They invoke their way of looking at the world as if it had been revealed as the only way by God himself—in order to maintain their sense of safety. They may tell us we are horrible people for not seeing it their way. We may hear that we are not devoted enough or committed enough. Husbands and wives who talk like this are trying to convince us we are theirs! They are trying to take us back to our original starting point and substitute themselves for our parents.

We are at war! Husbands and wives who are excessively possessive, who try to control us either directly or by pitiful, guilt-provoking supplication, are enemies of our future. By their actions and questions, they let us know in no uncertain terms that they expect us to have no life except what they permit us. "You can like this friend but not that friend. You can talk to her but not to him. Interest A is respectable; interest B is not."

CHERYL

Cheryl, at 28, is married to a man who, because he is in a family business, has to live in a very conservative small town. She is extremely bright and quick witted and has penetrating insights into people and situations.

When she was 9 years old, her mother was called to school and told that her daughter was an extremely gifted writer. Her mother replied in front of her, "I taught her that." Cheryl never wrote another imaginative story.

At 27 she finally acts on an urge to write that by now has become unbearably strong. She recognizes that even though she hasn't really written since she was 9, she always felt she would someday become a writer. As she pours herself into her work, the battle begins, because her husband believes that the sexually explicit romantic novel she has begun to write will ruin him in the community. Since he can't stop her from writing altogether, he demands that she write something else.

In addition to fighting the massive odds against writing a successful first novel, Cheryl must also battle her husband. Every argument with him also is an interruption of her work, so every argument becomes further evidence that he is willfully sabotaging her efforts. More and more, he is becoming her enemy.

Cheryl finishes her book, sells it to a publisher for a ten-thousand-dollar advance, then divorces her husband and takes off for a new life with her two children. She has now become a successful enough author to live off what her writing will earn her. She couldn't live with an enemy of her talent, for an enemy of her talent is an enemy of her essential self.

She was willing and able to fight the prohibiting enemy inside herself, but she could not forgive the man who was supposed to be her ally for kicking her when she was down.

On the other hand, many of us convince ourselves that our husband or wife is our enemy because we need an external enemy. We can't afford to admit that it is our own internal prohibition we are trying to break down.

If Cheryl never "found the time" to write or if she decided without testing it that her husband didn't want her to write because he couldn't tolerate the change and upheaval in their life, she would have been creating an enemy before an enemy existed. Anticipating future responses and making them an excuse for inaction is camouflage for the anxiety aroused by contemplating a battle with an internal prohibition. Only *after* defeating her own internal enemy was Cheryl in a position to judge whether her husband was a real enemy or not. Often, in similar situations, we find that after defeating the inner enemy, the outer enemy disappears, either because our spouse/lover/boss/business partner responds positively to the new self we have become or because he/she was never the enemy in the first place. (No one could really have argued if Cheryl's husband had said that she couldn't be taken seriously as a writer because she hadn't written since she was 9 years old—until she produced a four-hundred-page manuscript and then went to the trouble of trying to sell it. She didn't just put it in a closet after she wrote it; she went the whole way and *demonstrated how serious she was*. An essential ingredient.)

When we're spooked by some unspeakable inner fear of our own growth, we usually unfairly demand an absolute assurance that our partner is in no way opposed to our growth and change. In the absence of that selfless, absolute assurance, we conclude that he or she is solely responsible for holding us back. Once we have that idea, we pursue the evidence relentlessly to secure proof. We harass, insinuate, misread or provoke our partner until we can seize on some palpable bit of behavior that we can use to convince ourself that we are right. With all our maneuverings, we may have indeed *created* an enemy, who, once aroused, counterattacks.

Too frequently, divorce is the outcome of this process. In the midst of all the angry recriminations, one or both of us build up so much anger that we become afraid to talk about it. Like a moat around our castle, our silence protects us from the danger of our fury. We turn off. We icily decide the relationship is over. We walk or run away. We won't discuss it openly any more.

Often it's not over at all; it's just the pattern caused by our internal prohibition that's temporarily stopped dead, to be continued in some other relationship under some other roof. The relationship is ended not because the issues are unresolvable, but because one of the partners is too afraid of the inner fury that might be set loose if it continues.

It can be a very costly error not to master the seven-step inner dialogue in our twenties and thirties. If we have not learned to confront our inner prohibitions, by the time we approach our forties we are likely to mistake our partner's incomplete support for total opposition to our growth. The forties are when many of us end up with ugly, unnecessary divorces.

So, once again, to decide whether to proceed with a divorce, we must determine whether our partner is the real enemy to our growth. Just because our partner *feels* like the enemy doesn't mean he or she is. Both the real enemy and the person we are falsely accusing of personifying our prohibition *feel* the same. We must sift all the facts and contradictions and catch ourself if we are distorting a benign event into a demonic one. Only when we see our partner clearly will we know what we need to do.

Aftermath of Divorce

Whether we acknowledge our feelings or not, some bitterness or depression is inevitable after a divorce. We can view a divorce from two viewpoints: adult consciousness and childhood consciousness.

Adult consciousness: My spouse and I are both free, independent agents. We have split up by choice, because of different rates of growth, because the conspiracy upon which our relationship was built became untenable, or because the shifts in the direction of our lives were incompatible.

If we split up because of valid, adult consciousness reasons, we feel sadness, a sense of loss and disappointment, but we know we can love again.

Childhood consciousness: I am ashamed of our failure and frantic at the loss of a family way of life. I should have been able to stop this divorce. Something must be wrong with me. I am terrified of having to create new patterns all over again.

If we view our split with the eyes of childhood consciousness, we are likely to see ourselves as failures, measuring ourselves by the impossible expectation that children have: that adults can always control their future.

In reality, most people view their divorce with some degree of both adult and childhood consciousness. To resolve our confusion effectively, we must allow both consciousness perspectives their full reality. We cannot suppress either view. Using the seven-step inner dialogue outlined in Section I, we must let the contradictory feelings emerge before we can resolve them.

In the aftermath of divorce, we often find out how much we have been living with the values and hang-ups of someone else's head; in addition, we frequently discover that we have been projecting our needs onto them so that they might do our work for us. Once we are alone, we begin to find what our own inner needs and values really are; we have to rely on our own impulses and intuitions, unfiltered by any other person.

Often, recently divorced people turn to self-indulgent behavior, especially drinking or promiscuity, to rediscover themselves. By defining anew the boundaries of our self and our values, eventually we prove that we own ourselves; then this kind of testing, frantic need to discover who we are ends.

After a divorce, we must also deal with our ex-partner's negative opinion of us. In recriminations and bitter accusations, he or she exaggerates our problems and faults as a way of rationalizing and supporting the decision to split. After years of love, we are left with "She/he hates me, so I must be awful," or "She/he is awful, and not a word of what she/he says is true."

The truth is that generally our ex-partner's complaints about us are accurate to some degree but not as much as he or she claims. Therefore, since the complaints do usually reflect real problems in us, we must consider whether these problems are real; and if so, we must face and resolve them. Once we have faced our internal prohibitions and inadequacies, our ex-partner's view of us will no longer hold any exaggerated demonic power. We will know viscerally when our partner's power over us is spent. As one man put it, "I no longer hear her words through my gut."

Some people make their ex-partners members of an extended family—the way grandparents or aunts and uncles used to be. They allow their ex-partners to take the kids on weekends, out for dinner, or away on vacations. Some ex-spouses even become friends. Once we resolve the guilt and blame and work through the anger, ex-spouses can make valuable friends. After all, who knows us better?

Section V
35–45
Mid-Life Decade

Major False Assumption to Be Challenged:

"THERE IS NO EVIL OR DEATH IN THE WORLD.
THE SINISTER HAS BEEN DESTROYED."

At the end of our twenties, with our place in the world somewhat secure, we could afford to rediscover vital talents and instincts we had been suppressing; we could consider amending
our life course to include them. During our early thirties, we
acted tentatively to make some changes and fussed and fretted
about the rest, uncertain whether allowing them to surface
would uncover treasure or trouble. We didn't know whether the
dissatisfaction and restlessness we still felt reflected greed, immaturity, and an inability to enjoy life or whether it was the sign
of a superior vision within us.

Now we see more clearly, and consequently we are more
frightened. For we know that we *must* act on our new vision of
ourselves and the world. The desire for stability and continuity
which characterized our thirties is being replaced by a relentless
inner demand for action. The sense of timelessness in our early
thirties is giving way to an awareness of the pressure of time in
our forties. *Whatever we must do must be done now.*

Time, the messenger of finality, is the ultimate limitation in life. It strips away our last remaining illusion of safety and makes existentialists of us all. We stand naked and exposed, toe to toe with life. Our naiveté is lost forever. The illusion of our immortality is dying; in a crunch, no all-powerful hand is going to save us.

As we challenge the last major false assumption, "There is no evil or death in the world. The sinister has been destroyed," we are vulnerable, and that gives us access to the deepest strata of our minds that we have ever examined. It's our final natural opportunity to deal with that deeply buried sense of our "demonic badness" or "worthlessness" that has curtailed us from living as legitimate, authentic creatures with a full set of rights and a fully independent adult consciousness.

To achieve an adult sense of freedom, we must pass through periods of passivity, rage, depression and despair as we experience the repugnance of death, the hoax of life and the evil within and around us. To enjoy full access to our innermost self, we can no longer deny the ugly, demonic side of life, which our immature mind tried to protect against by enslaving itself to false illusions that absolute safety was possible.

We must let go of our childish desire for absolute safety or we lose the opportunity for fundamental repair. We can falsely reassert our innocence and continue to rely on the protective devices to shield us from our demonic view of life, but then we will have to relate to others as cardboard figures rather than as passionate, hurting and loving human beings.

Most of us oscillate in small swings between the denial and the acceptance of our vulnerability. Eventually we work our way deeper into our core, to form a new understanding of the meaning of our life uncontaminated by the need for magical solutions or protective devices. Gradually we come to heal our deepest splits—never completely, but as best we can.

Five Component Assumptions

The component assumptions of the mid-life decade are:
1. The illusion of safety can last forever.
2. Death can't happen to me or my loved ones.
3. It is impossible to live without a protector (women).
4. There is no life beyond this family.
5. I am an innocent.

1. Component Assumption 1

"THE ILLUSION OF SAFETY CAN LAST FOREVER."

The facts of life continually assault our illusory sense of safety. Friends, relatives and parents get crippling diseases or suffer near-fatal accidents. Stiffness, aches, pains, weight gain, receding hairline, skin changes and countless other small signs of aging are a cumulative message about our human frailty. Separations, divorces and infidelities are epidemic; they are all around us if not in our own lives. At work, our juniors see us as "one of the older ones." There's an age bias in industry against people over forty, so our options narrow; we lose the sense of safety that comes from a belief in our easy career mobility. But these potent facts of life are weak, easily forgotten messages compared with the fundamental shift in our sense of safety that comes from the time-ordered metamorphosis of our intact family.

The Loss of the Intact Family

In one way or another, we are losing the last vestiges of our parents' protection. Even if both parents are alive, vigorous and independent, a role reversal takes place, and gradually we are standing in their place.

We are in the thicket of life, working away at our inner world and working with our children, our spouse and our career, while our parents have pruned away their involvements and live a more simplified life. Their parents (our grandparents) are usually not alive, and the intensity of their involvement with us has also diminished as they have progressively lost the authority we once invested in them.

As adults in the 35-to-45-year-old range, we can still remarry, have children, or start a new career. Our parents generally don't have these options.

Some of us are now in a commanding position at work and feel powerful in the world. While our parents may have been there, they've lost power through retirement or reduced responsibilities. Some may still have wealth or political and business clout, but they don't have the feeling of power that goes with day-to-day operations—with being in the middle of things.

In sundry other, subtler ways, the world now belongs to us and our generation, not to them and their generation. It is the reversal of roles: when we were growing up, whether we liked it or not, we had to acknowledge that they had the authority in the world then; whether they like it or not, they must acknowledge that now we have the authority. (It is important not to confuse authority with infallibility. They may have been wrong in the exercise of their authority, and so may we.)

So whether our parents are healthy, independent and vigorous, declining or deceased, this is our time in life; we are the full-fledged adult, not they. As we go from 35 to 45, it becomes clear, sometimes painfully clear, that we are the only, the final authority over the conduct of our own lives.

As our parents measured their age by our growth, so our growing children tell us that we are getting old. Only yesterday the children were chubby babies in diapers; now they are time clocks ticking away the years of our life. They go through the same rites of passage we went through in our adolescence. They have to learn how to handle their new sexuality, their bodily changes and the growing awareness that it's time to leave the sanctuary we have provided for them. Our awareness grows with their awareness.

Before we know it, our sons and daughters are driving cars; soon they want to take those cars farther and farther away for longer periods of time. They push for more room, more signs that we agree that they're competent and able to care for their own safety. The limitations of our control over their safety become apparent. As their emotional and sexual involvements in-

tensify, they must work out their hurts without our help or interference. We see them making mistakes and not listening to our
advice, and often we have to suppress a terrible feeling that
they're just testing us.

All our hopes and dreams for them, our ideas of what and who
we brought them up to be, have to be modified and reconciled
with reality. If our child was to be a sensitive artist, then his
limited talent or lack of enthusiasm may become more and more
evident as his teenage years go on.

We come to feel very strongly that something is slipping away
from us. Our parents are becoming more and more peripheral to
our lives, and our children are also becoming less involved in
our joint family life. It is only a matter of time before "it" will
all end.

Parents: Power Play in Three Generations

As our family changes over our mid-life years, power shifts ac-
celerate. Our parents hang on to whatever power they have over
us to fortify their sense of safety; we hang on to power over our
children for the same reason. Our children are still young
enough to be somewhat reluctant to fight hard for power because of that old dilemma: when they take power for themselves, they lose a piece of their illusion of safety. For the same
reason, we allow our parents a small, but often irritating, degree
of power over us.

By our mid-forties some of us have worked out the power
shift with our father or mother in a significant and meaningful
way because we have had to take care of a dependent parent
who, like a child, could not care for him- or herself. If the parent
accepted his or her dependency with dignity, our relationship
was that of mutual adults.

If a parent can't accept our help with dignity and becomes a
demanding and insatiable child, our opportunity to parent is a
mixed experience. It lacks the comfortable mutuality of two recognized adults who both acknowledge that their respective positions are dictated by the impersonal and inexorable flow of time,

not by some intrinsic superiority of one over the other. When an elderly parent regresses and is demanding or insatiable, his or her behavior makes us feel like a child who still can't satisfy father or mother. If our adultness is not accepted, we have to control our rage and salvage a difficult situation. But we feel guilty because while we're being dutiful, we don't feel dutiful. Instead, we feel very angry.

Children

Much of what is going on between us and our children is muffled. Sometimes we are sure that the way they react to us is only hurting their chance for success in the world, but we can't put our finger on what it is. Occasionally, we try to figure it out and confront them with it, but to no avail. They disagree or think we're crazy; anyway, they don't feel they need our help. We fall into lectures that turn into clichés concerning responsibility, sensitivity, fortitude, ambition, laziness or hanging around with the wrong crowd. We know the right issues aren't being addressed, but we can't find the right issues.

One moment we act toward our growing adolescent children as our parents acted toward us; the next moment we retreat and make a conscious effort to act the opposite way. Much of the time we aren't sure what the right way is. Sometimes we feel we are doing what we can. But when our way seems to be failing, we lose confidence and wonder whether we're failures as parents. Maybe we should have stuck with our own parents' methods—after all, we've not done that badly.

These concerns increase in importance when our children are between 18 and 22 and seriously challenge the false assumption "I'll always belong to them." At that point, we have no more direct control and authority. Oh, we may still have influence or be available to give advice or help in a crisis, but our children's character and personality by then are being shaped in the inner workings of their minds. And they have a vested interest in keeping us out of their heads.

If in this period we're facing up to our own inner demands, we can accommodate our children's inner demands, give them the necessary room for expression with a minimum of conflict. In fact, if we embrace our own growth, we can directly challenge their fear that neither we nor they can survive their independence. On the other hand, if we "stonewall" against changing and insist that our main role *is* to be their parents, we can force their changes into less healthy but nevertheless necessary expression. Like the flow of a powerful river, the need to grow can only be diverted, never totally dammed.

Sometimes we're finely tuned to our children's weaknesses; perhaps they don't have enough of a certain personality characteristic or attitude that we want them to have. They know it's true and feel our knowledge as an untenable pressure that makes it harder for them to acknowledge and claim the problem as theirs to work on.

But sometimes we have an exaggerated response to a certain characteristic because it is one that we have and don't want them to suffer with as we do. We thought we had taught them otherwise. Often it is a characteristic we've overcome, and it feels as if we have passed it on to them.

We must sort out these different possible interpretations. If our child is ignoring a weakness, then that must become clear to us both if it is to be worked on; both must see it as a weakness and not an arbitrary fiction of our parental imagination. On the other hand, if we exaggerate or misunderstand a child's "problem" because we need to live through the child, we must see that clearly enough to work on it; it is then our problem, and we need to face it for our own growth.

But the true dialogue necessary for this essential sorting out requires an equality between parents and children almost impossible to achieve at this time. In our typical power relationship with our children, we feel we have greater insight into "truth" and tend to undervalue or veto our children's positions.

It is hard for us to keep in mind that our young ones still overvalue our statements and opinions concerning the way they conduct their lives. They seem to be so independent, so defiant

at times. When they slap us in the face, verbally or symbolically, we find it difficult to understand that they're often trying
to cut us down as an authority just because they need to become
their own authority for their lives. They feel us watching them
even when we're not with them.

Also, it's hard for us to remember that we still want to hold on
to our power over them. Even if we can point to a hundred ways
in which we've relaxed the parental reins, our children can point
to at least ten important ways in which we haven't.

It's not malice that moves us to hold on to power over our
late-teenage children, and it's often not love; it's an attempt to
keep our own feeling of safety intact. If we can't keep them
confined under our roof by routine or regular hours, if we have
to let them wander the country or be off at school, we can at
least symbolically keep them a member of our family by exercising some power over their minds. *Keeping them in the family is
the key*. As long as we can maintain the family despite the terrible pressure or emotional shambles, we can retain much of the
feeling of safety that is slipping away from us.

Our children can't appreciate that this is our last family; they
will go on to form a new family. We can't appreciate that after
our children grow up and out, there's another life for us to lead.
The nuclear family is the only form of family life many of us
know. But it's not the only form of family life possible, and living without the illusion of safety is still life.

2. Component Assumption 2

"DEATH CAN'T HAPPEN TO ME OR MY LOVED ONES."

This second component false assumption, the illusion of immortality, is challenged from two directions: the illness or death of a parent and a complex set of signals about mortality as part of the life cycle.

The Illness or Death of a Parent

When a parent is threateningly ill, there is a horrible sense of gloom that "it" is inevitably going to happen. At the same time, we repeat, "It can't happen, it can't." All our life we've feared losing our parents. As a young child we anticipated our catastrophic reaction to that event and more than likely had nightmares about the loss. Our early bedtime rituals included conjuring up magical ways to keep "it" from happening. We went into our parents' bedroom in the middle of the night to reassure ourself they were still there and to touch them to make sure they were alive. After a nightmare, our fear overwhelmed our grasp on reality, and it took restless snuggling and burrowing into their surrounding warmth and smells before we were assured they were alive and on duty.

For a short period of time, the dream reality of their death and the snuggling reality of their aliveness overlapped and created a pocket of consciousness where there was neither life nor death. Through this mechanism, we learned to push away the terror of their death without destroying totally our fear of it. Therefore, when a parent's death finally does threaten or occur, we have a long background of rehearsal. In a sense, the event is a reexperience: it has already happened countless numbers of nights. It has always been reversed by waking up; but this death can't be reversed. The safe feeling that "it is only a dream" is lost forever. Life's limited time slams us in the face like a steel door, and the limitation of our powers is never so pitifully clear as when time temporarily becomes the *only* reality.

During the period of mourning, which, in its various phases, lasts at least a year, sequences of denial alternate with periods of grief. When we deny death, we try to turn the uncontrollable reality back into a terrible dream that will be reversed when we wake. We try to return ourself to the magically protected belief that "these things don't happen to me."

If we are too successful in returning ourself to that protected pocket of consciousness, we may eradicate the death at the cost of our sense of vitality and life. While we may free ourself from grief by the denial, we will take on the characteristics of the parent we lost. This usually occurs in subtle ways, but it can occur in quite obvious and exaggerated ways, as it did with Jim.

After a very short period of grief, Jim, a 38-year-old businessman, took over his dead father's business position. Within months, his colleagues began to report an almost uncanny resemblance to his father that had not been present before.

He changed from an easygoing person to someone more rigid and conservative, like his father. He started to walk with a slight limp. He changed tailors and lost his previous flair for color. Even his diction and little mannerisms changed. Only people who knew both him and his father appreciated the uncanny sameness.

After two years, Jim complained of feeling older and "tighter," as if he had less private space in which to move. His grief finally broke only after some psychotherapeutic help. After acknowledging it, he felt great relief, looked years younger, and recognized in retrospect that for most of the two years following his father's death, he was not himself.

If we live through the mourning period with a minimum of denial, we experience the grief as memories that bring tears when we think they can never recur—lost poignant moments together, the voice that will never be heard, the skin that will never be touched, and the look, the gesture that will never be seen again. Each memory we cherished hammers home the painful message of finality. And it has to be hammered home time and time again to be believed.

It is absolutely essential to bear the pain of the mourning period if we are to stay in touch with ourself. Any pocket of hope that our parent's death is only a dream falsifies reality and closes off a section of our mind. The *pain* of remembering and longing and realizing what can no longer be destroys any hope of cheating death—and it thereby keeps us open and alive.

No matter what form the mourning takes, after the death of a parent the world is a different place. For a period of time it is emptier or lonelier or less meaningful. Some of us see it as cruel, harsh, ugly and a stupid place to be. The hypocrisy, the petty values of everyday life become glaringly apparent in contrast. Touching other human beings deeply becomes life's meaning for many mourners, while others return to some sort of religious involvement. Still others forswear religion as useless, as if in some way they believe that a true believer doesn't suffer losses.

When our parents die, the fear of our own death becomes exaggerated. Sometimes an intense fear of dying triggers an obsessional preoccupation with health. Most of us feel more vulnerable, as if our parents were a shield standing between us and death; now that they are gone, we are next—and it can happen at any time. If one parent is still alive, we can maintain the illusion that death is an orderly event which we are protected against by someone else. This is another invisible childhood protective device, which we retain well into adulthood, to preserve our illusion of safety.

On the anniversary of the death of a parent, we usually experience a brief reactivation of grief. As the death becomes more distant with each succeeding year, the anniversary reaction has less power. Eventually, if we work through the guilt, it may appear to be no more than a long-lasting, unexplained mood change.

For some of us who feel independent of our parents, the death of a parent leaves us with a few tender words unsaid and a great longing for just a few more minutes of aliveness. Others of us feel cheated that our dead parent can't witness what we are becoming, as if final peace with ourselves depended on their satisfaction with us.

Other Messages About Death

The shock of our own mortality may not be brought home by the illness or death of a parent. It can be delivered just as surely by a combination of external events and our own work on our inner self.

These external happenings may be the reversal of roles with our parents, the attrition of feelings of power and safety because of our changing roles with our children, our place at work, the accidental deaths of our friends, and the physical signs recording the passage of years. All these factors add up in a unique way in each of our lives to deliver an unmistakable set of signals.

If the weight of external happenings doesn't break through our illusion of immortality, our own vigorous growth efforts may cause the cave-in, as articulated by one patient, a successful 37-year-old executive: "Up to this point, life was all uphill, with no thought of an end; now it is as if I am at the crown of the hill and can see the downslope for the first time. Death is a long way off, but it definitely is there."

In its most malignant form, the dawning awareness of our own mortality can manifest itself in a sudden outburst of exaggerated symptoms: acute anxiety or self-destructive, dangerous behavior. One prominent writer wrote about a wild year in which a newfound obsession with cemeteries was paralleled by drunkenness, overuse of drugs, gambling, high-speed drunken driving and provocation of dangerous criminals. All of this began in his thirty-sixth year and has since disappeared; with a kind of frantic craziness, he was trying to overcome some existential terror.

The Male Response to Death

Men seem to be more surprised at the fact of mortality than women. They often react to the news of a death as if someone has played a dirty trick on them. In mid-life they can become preoccupied with the topic of death for long periods of time, during which the deaths of friends or relatives around their age scare the hell out of them. They lose confidence in themselves and confuse their awareness of death with their situation at work.

Many men see work success as the route to immunity from death. I am not talking about the products of their work or their children living after them as the symbolic route to survival after death. Rather, those of us who are most shocked by the awareness of our own mortality had a pact with the world: if we continued to be good boys and worked hard, if we sacrificed and succeeded, the fear that we would be annihilated, which terrorized us as little boys, was never to return again. One of the appeals of a business career is that the business world has banned human frailty; it has sanitized the natural processes of biology and replaced it with the dictate that success can cover up any flaw. It's a tempting vision, because it connects with the way many of us want to see the world. If one success doesn't do it, then the next level of success certainly will. We never know when to stop, for success and total peace might be just beyond the next bend in the road.

Underlying the terror of death is often not the fear of death per se, but the childhood consciousness version of what being dead is like: we are convinced that in death, we are buried alive and remain conscious and helpless for eternity; we are convinced that death is intense aloneness and the *experience* of being eaten away endlessly by worms and vermin.

We can break our protective pact with the business world in any number of ways. Often, by becoming more successful, we learn what more success can't do. Each rung up the ladder brings different (often more) responsibilities and worries along with our coveted prerogatives and privileges. Nothing essential has changed. We never find ourself completely without a boss or pressure to perform. We never find surcease from the problems of family—whether with our parents, children, wife or ourself as son, father, husband. This disillusionment with work as a magical protection against death reaches a critical awareness level in the mid-life decade. When it ceases to function, when we feel the cold breath of death on our own neck, we experience the demonic dread that it protected against; in this way, work and the fear of death are intimately related.

Faced with this intense anxiety, some of us redouble our efforts at work and reinvest in its illusions with a passion. The relentless pressure to make a quantum leap into the world of fantastic success, to end death with one magic stroke of achievement, increases. We move faster and faster, work harder and longer, and take on more and more projects. We take chances that are out of character for us.

Often we have to lose some of our biggest gambles before we can bring ourself down. Depression after a big failure is one exit off the track. If we keep on succeeding, the pace itself will eventually wear us out. Strokes, bleeding ulcers, or sudden crushing pains in the chest—if we survive them—can also be another way off the track. Heavy drinking and/or heavy womanizing and/or desperate "good times" are all part of the same syndrome— while we are running away from the demonic childhood fear behind us, our life is being dominated by it. It's a no-win situation, built on denial.

The other way the immunity pact with work is broken is our disappointment with what we have achieved; some social scientists call this the achievement–aspiration gap. For the blue-collar worker it may be a bitter feeling—"I've worked all these years, used up all my energy, and what have I got?" For the middle-class man who set out to reach some rank or achievement, it can be a deep sense of personal failure and worthlessness. Bitterness follows as he comes to realize that he mortgaged twenty valuable years of his life, gave up freedom, fulfillment and flexibility to pursue a dream he never realized.

After our immunity pact with work is broken, we are open to the deeper recesses of our being, and we search our souls for unexpressed areas we were afraid to touch before. We know

now that being a certain kind of man no longer grants us magical protection or immunity from death. No matter what or how much we achieve, we die.

RALPH

Ralph, a 41-year-old executive in a large supermarket chain, is told to prepare himself to take over a top executive post in the company, one step away from the presidency. He's worked his way up from stock boy and is a loyal, hardworking, dedicated, efficient and productive employee. He appears to be a good eagle scout—grooms and dresses himself like a stereotyped clean-cut, short-haired executive and family man. With the increasing responsibilities for the overall day-to-day operation of the food stores, he finds himself spending less time with his family. He feels guilty and estranged from his sons. He especially feels bad about missing their Saturday morning Little League baseball games (he and his father had spent time together only on the baseball field). Lately, since he's been obsessed with the promotion, he can't help seeing that his wife is right when she points out he's not listening to her.

He is in the middle of two pulls—the fantasy of the job and its rewards and the reality of time not spent with his children and wife. Because he married late and his children still are pre-teenagers, the pull of his family is strong.

One day while sitting at his desk, he gets terribly angry at his immediate boss over an imaginary conversation about his sons' Little League game coming up the next Saturday. Ralph decides that he will go, no matter how much his boss frowns or raises his eyebrows or in some other way calls his loyalty or motivation into question. In the next breath, Ralph convinces himself that he's going to have to learn to play golf, which he'll have to play on Saturdays, just to keep his new job. He'll *still* be giving up his family time, even when he's no longer in charge of day-to-day operations! He may be willing to learn how to make better speeches and eat rubber chicken at civic banquets, but he's *not* willing to play golf on Saturdays, by God! Or so he tells himself. The money, status, recognition and power are awfully tempting. He's torn, frightened and angry.

When he actually does announce to his boss that he's taking off Saturday, a very rewarding conversation replaces the imagined stormy one. His boss not only makes no new demands for more loyalty and sacrifice, but turns out to be a real human being. He asks the same questions Ralph does, has already been through the same mill, and doesn't mind at all whether Ralph plays golf or goes to a Little League game.

Ralph's decision to acknowledge that his family was more important, despite his fear of losing his job, cracked his fantasy vision of the work world as the place to finally satisfy unsatisfiable fathers. He feels markedly relieved. His adult view now is that the office is a place to go to earn a living and work out a certain kind of life satisfaction.

Ralph had learned to please all the various fathers of his life (his boss, etc.) to smother his great fear of them. He learned how to be like them as well as to please them, and he felt safe only as long as he was acting in character as a pure company man. And, indeed, his demonic childhood fear of the dangerous father, which had moved him to be a good eagle scout for the company, *was* responsible for much of his success. But he did not need to be a perfect eagle scout to keep succeeding.

If we don't challenge our loyalty to work or question our ambition, we will never learn exactly how frightened we are that our life will be smashed and ruined by a dangerous, angry father.

Ralph was shaking in his boots when he talked to the boss about the Saturday arrangement. He was clearly reacting to the fantasy father, and after it was all over he understood the difference between the boss as another man and the boss as he had fantasized him.

By overcoming his fear of his own weakness (by allowing himself to experience it) and by realizing that it was not his destiny to be controlled by dangerous fathers and he was not therefore still a weak boy, Ralph was able to admit to his "weaknesses"— that is, human emotions not subscribed to by he-men and fantasy bosses. As a result, he became softer, more flexible and easier to be with. Ralph became less competitive but not less effective. He was more in touch with his memories of the soft, tender father who had picked him up and carried him around when he was a toddler.

GERALD AND MARIE

All his life, Gerald, now 42, has been a hardworking man living on the edge of difficult decisions. He had taken the risks necessary to develop a successful commercial literary career from his nonliterary beginnings as a 25-year-old shipyard worker. He sees what needs to be done and he does it. He pays a price for bluffing, being unprepared, being uncertain, being wrong, being forced out and failing; the product he ultimately forges out his talents is at least half determination.

Marie, his estranged wife, 34, has her own charms and strengths. Although she has a distinctive flair for living, she feels indecisive and absolutely dependent on Gerald. She is considering resuming their marriage after an eight-month separation, during which she has been living with a sweet but "too weak" man. The experience has taught her a good deal about herself: she feels she has paid Gerald back for several affairs he had during their marriage; she feels he deserves it. So does he, and he waits agonizingly for her return while he takes care of the children.

As Marie is considering returning, her indecisiveness becomes painful for all concerned. She almost begs Gerald to tell her, "Return, now!" He knows if he takes charge again, it will work for a while; but in a few months, she'll complain that he forced her to come back before she was ready and that he is controlling her life again.

Though it causes him great pain, Gerald tells Marie to make up her own mind. His obvious pain makes her feel guilty, and because he won't tell her what to do directly, she feels that the guilt must be a devious part of his plan to control her.

Gerald finally understands that he *has* helped foster her dependence over the years. He sees that Marie may not let him stop acting the role of parent, even though she resents him for it. He wants to express his pain directly without being cast as a controlling parent, but he's forced to act self-sacrificing and bear his hurt in silence because it simplifies reality for her. At the moment, Marie can't face a very complex world.

Gerald feels his pain, knows he adores her and misses her presence, and is pained by her suffering. He will do anything for her except act as her decision maker and life ruler. He wants desperately to be with her, but he can't stand relating to her in her victim role.

Despite their pain, they remain finely tuned to the nuances of each other's concerns. They talk with intense feeling for hours and days, trying to come to a resolution so that they can return to each other. They both want the same thing—a relationship based on equality—but she can't be convinced he won't control her, and he's not convinced she'll allow him to be her husband rather than a father.

In retrospect, Gerald recognizes that their "ideal" love relationship—at least, all their friends said it was ideal—was warped by the pattern of her dependence, to which they both subscribed. When his wife was most dependent, he had his affairs—and always with independent, strong-willed women.

Later, Gerald's several years of psychological work brought dividends. He saw with great clarity that his masculine, paternal, strong-man role had robbed him of his self-contact, his sensitivity, his pain and his totality. Even if it meant losing the person he loved most dearly, he realized he had to stop playing that part. To live with Marie from behind the barrier of his supermale role was to lose her anyway and to sacrifice himself as well.

In the mid-life decade, men remodel their definition of maleness with the sense of urgency that characterizes this whole period. As the end of the decade gets closer, the sense of urgency increases.

Ralph—who, by being such a good eagle scout all his life, gained power and financial rewards far beyond his initial ambitions—had to destroy his self-image as the obsessively devoted and loyal son of the fantasy fathers he somehow thought ran his company and controlled his success. By doing this, he could become the father/man he wanted to be to his own sons. But he made that decision only when he felt he couldn't put it off any longer.

Gerald had to have "relief from masculinity," from the super-successful male image which helped him rise from oblivion to fame beginning in his twenties. Now he wants to be understood and accepted by the woman he loves as the nurturing male he has become. But to do that, he must give up control and become the kind of male who does not force the world to bend to him. Then he can know the world beyond the limited mold he has repeatedly fashioned with himself at the center.

Work as a Protective Device

A man's work, then, is supposed to bury all his childhood demons, all the injuries that have made him feel humiliated or small. The work mythology of this society blends right in with every little boy's early childhood cures of his "smallness" by fantasy.

As small boys we had no hesitation about telling our parents that when we grew up we were going to be Superman or a cowboy or a fireman or a doctor or a certain movie hero. When asked why we wanted to become a doctor, we might have said, "So I can give kids shots"; perhaps we wanted to be Superman to save our mother from danger; we might have wanted to be rich so that we could have our daddy at home with us or so that we could get rid of our envy of other, more prosperous families or our shame of being the poorest in the neighborhood; or we might have wanted to be a cowboy because city traffic frightened us. We only have to ask the next small boy what he wants to be to find a fresh example.

But those fleeting and easily accessible statements are only the tip of the iceberg. Little boys work on curative fantasies all the time in their play; through play they develop their understanding of the world. They build an unassailable self-image, become mentally invincible, protected against the hurts and slights of everyday life—particularly the disappointments they experience at the hands of parents. As they get older they spend long hours daydreaming about their role models—invincible men who never feel slighted or small like a child.

Jungle adventurers and detectives never feel helpless and confused like little boys. Corporate presidents don't vomit in their clean offices. Men with money never get less candy than their brother. A powerful man always commands his woman's attention. She waits for him to get through with his important business before he, the important man, has time for her. Quite a reversal from the "Don't bother me now—can't you see I am busy?" line that every boy hears from his mother.

Our desire for absolute invulnerability and other compensation for all hurt gradually is layered over by more realistic-*appearing* goals. Our future plans are influenced by the adult men with whom we have close contact, especially those who make us feel big by taking an interest in us. The more interested they are in us, the more we value their qualities or life style or occupation. Obviously an interested and involved father has the greatest influence on us, but teachers, uncles, coaches, distant cousins, older boys or neighbors can have great impact. By the time we're in our twenties, we're forced to choose an occupation out of all these influences, combined with our sense of our own natural talents.

The job decisions we make during our careers really represent our attempts to hand-tailor a work situation that has room for all those disparate parts of ourselves that we were made aware of by the influence of others. Most of us who reflect back on career choices we made during our early years can see an emotional pattern unfolding through all the happenstance and "practical" decisions. In retrospect, it seems mysteriously inevitable.

We pursue careers with enthusiasm because we accept the mythology of the work world that a man can become invincible with power, money and status. The system preys on our narcissistic weakness—the so-called ego massage, or "stroking." No one can pass up a promotion. The rewards of rank proclaim that the higher the rank, the bigger we are and presumably the less vulnerable we are. The implication is that we can become so big that when we "get there," we'll be totally invulnerable.

Yet no man in his forties can kid himself that work success will make him invulnerable to sickness, to personal problems, to death, alcoholism or neurosis. There is too much evidence to the contrary all around him. In essence, men sell their souls for a feeling of triumph with so little lasting power that they constantly have to sell more of themselves to buy more of it. When the craziness is finally exposed, they feel cheated.

There are two polar reactions to this insight: (1) We can accept it and begin to dismantle the myth that work success will protect us from hurt and thus find whatever intrinsic meaning our work has for us as persons. (2) We can deny the insight and forfeit the relief it brings.

When we deny the insight, we become progressively duller and more one dimensional as work-centered people. Since we have to stay away from all those "weak" feelings that sometimes define our humanity, we have to stay away from deep knowledge of ourselves. To drown our deep feelings, we inundate them with drinking, work, outbursts of anger or whatever other avoidance technique will accomplish the same purpose.

When dangerous thoughts threaten to break through, we feel pressured and ascribe that pressure to work. We manufacture a work worry to cover it if none is present. We become frightened by the first whiff of depression.

Some of us may begin to challenge the conviction that depression is intolerable. We may let a minor depression run its natural course and learn that depression not only is tolerable, but is actually better than the sensation that we have no feelings. We may even let ourselves experience some significant disillusionment and the relief that follows.

But the moment we he-men hit a raw nerve, we run back to the magic balm of work. We resign ourselves to a life with occasional but *controllable* pain but no passion—a life with no surprises; unfolding without growth.

ACCEPTANCE: NO MORE OVERTIME BLUES

RICHARD

When Richard's immunity pact with work was broken, he decided not to be a law professor any longer. He followed a strong urge to go into private practice. The next year, he was financially very successful but not happy. At 43, Richard found his interest in the law flagging for the first time in his professional career, and he also found himself with strange symptoms that made him suspect he had a rare wasting disease of the muscles. He experienced abdominal pain and became depressed even though a GI series proved that the pain in his belly was not cancer. He stopped playing tennis because of the intermittent weakness in his hands and his newly clumsy body movements, which only he seemed to notice. Despite assurances from his law partner, he was convinced that he had lost his mental sharpness. Fortunately his wife was patient and caring throughout all this. For Richard, life had taken quite an unexpected turn.

In five weekly sessions we uncovered the following. His father had been a medical-school professor. His two uncles were successful practicing doctors who looked down on his father, believing he was too frightened to go out on his own as a doctor. Both his parents, in turn, saw the uncles as greedy and taught Richard not to be like them.

Until he was 11, Richard was a "bad boy" who deserved the beatings his father inflicted upon him. He wouldn't follow rules, he was vengeful, he teased and hit his sister almost mercilessly, he broke things too often, he was too competitive with his friends, and he became too angry when he didn't get his own way. By the time he reached college, he was a prince of a fellow with no traces of the angry child. During law school he intended to go into practice until the last semester, when he so admired a certain professor that he decided to become a professor himself.

During the next fifteen years he developed a reputation as an excellent, sympathetic teacher with extraordinary patience, understanding and forbearance. To others his research and his administrative efforts were moderately successful, but privately he felt himself to be a complete failure in those areas of his life. Even though he worked hard, often six and a half days a week, he knew there was something wrong in the way he conducted himself. When it came time to make an administrative decision, he was too indecisive: it took too long and it took too much out of him. He was terrified of being wrong. Whatever he decided had to prove right in the future even though he knew the future couldn't be predicted 100 percent. He felt he might be hurting someone if he was wrong.

In his research work he couldn't muster the right amount of aggression at the right time to push his work and seize the recognition he felt he deserved. Again he was afraid of being too aggressive.

At 40 he began to rethink his commitment: though he loved teaching, he really didn't like the research and administrative work. Since he could continue to teach part-time and begin a private practice, it made sense to switch. He saw then how his life as a professor had been a massive protective device against his greedy "badness." While discussing the move with his wife, he felt good about it; but when he discussed it with his mother only a half hour later, she made him feel like a greedy bad boy in less than five minutes. To be a professor and forgo the higher income of a private practitioner was a statement to the world that he was not greedy; that he was, in fact, like his father; and that he wasn't at all like the uncles that he had secretly admired.

He decided to leave the university for private practice anyway. At the height of a financially successful first year, his muscle symptoms and depression appeared. Six months later he came to see me.

Richard left academia feeling that he was weak and a failure, so he was somewhat unsure of himself and depressed when he entered private practice. Once he started to be successful, it was time to renegotiate money agreements with his new partner. He began to feel weak and indecisive again, but this time he also felt a countersurge of aggression and anger at what he thought was unfair. Often he'd retreat from a direct confrontation, but he never forgot his feelings of anger.

The whole subject of aggression and what amount of it was OK under what circumstances began to dominate his conscious thinking. He experimented with the idea that he could be strong without being guilty or that he could be firm without being a "bad boy." As this became clear to him, he began to open up issues at home with his children that he had failed to open before because he was afraid of his anger.

Finally, at a restaurant with another couple, he had an experience in which his old "bad boy" fury came surging up for a moment; he contained it, then transformed it, taking a moderately aggressive action that was exactly right for the circumstances. The maitre d' at the restaurant had kept them waiting for more than half an hour with a number of phony excuses. After an instant of fury, Richard went up to him and said, "You've been keeping us waiting much too long—I'd like a table now." Within five minutes they were seated. For days afterward he glowed with pleasure. He had become quite a different, freer person.

Transformation of the Meaning of Work for Men

We've seen how work can be used as an illusory protective device against whatever we fear most. For Richard it was fear of his own aggression and greed; for Gerald it was fear of admitting he could not control everything that ever came up; and for Ralph it was fear of displeasing angry fathers. Each of them had to strike a new balance to allow unexpressed elements of their characters to emerge.

In the same way, those who fear that people will take advantage of them have to learn a less fearful view of others. Those who have always rebelled have to learn to live with authority. We must all balance our lives to develop the suppressed aspects of our personalities.

Achieving a happier balance may precipitate a career or a life-style change if a man has options, although many people, especially blue-collar workers, do not have great options.

Richard explored and dealt with two of the five basic motivations that give work meaning. When Richard broke his immunity pact with death and gave up the "cure" of *"getting bigger,"* which is the first motivation for work, he was free to redefine his career within readily available options and quit doing university administration and research in order to do what he enjoyed more—private practice and teaching. He "quit" working just to get bigger.

That exposed his idiosyncratic *psychodynamic* reason for working. He worked at the university to prove he was not greedy like a child or like his uncles. His work in private practice exposed both a positive and a feared part of himself: he liked the autonomy and direct responsibility of private practice, and he liked money—he was more like his uncles. He was also like his father inasmuch as he loved to teach. He had to fight through the symptoms in order to license himself to live out his own psychodynamic form of career, but the inner necessity to follow through on that motivation for work finally prevailed.

The psychodynamic meaning of work is closely allied to but not the same as working *to express and exercise a full range of talents and capacities,* which is the third basic motivation for work. In every job, new challenges appear that require the use of latent capacities. By the trial and error of this process, we come to recognize competencies hitherto unknown and constantly expand our self-definition. It is important to utilize these capacities, as did Richard in teaching and private practice, *whether or not they are connected with parents or past conflicts.* Being able to do what we do well makes us feel vital and makes work a labor of love.

The fourth motivation that gives work meaning is *necessity* and the fifth is *being part of an organization or field that has its own extrinsic meaning,* either because it is growing fast or because it serves an important public function, such as medicine or government.

The transformation of meaning in work in mid-life can be thought of as a reproportioning of these five basic motivations that give meaning to work. When we are young men, we work primarily out of necessity, to get bigger, and to be part of something that is in itself meaningful. After working for twenty years, we can't work for those reasons predominantly and still stay mentally alive. We must do work that confirms our talents and expresses a psychodynamic theme close to the core of us. Time is too valuable to be spent at a distance from our authentic selves, though we still can't ignore necessity, we're still tempted by rank, and we can temporarily be swept along by a fast-growing organization.

Although there are stockbrokers who decide to take up cabinet making and carpentry, the changes aren't always so drastic. One minister may become an activist, while an activist minister may become more of a scholar. One family doctor may go into teaching, while another may set up a clinic for the poor. One mathematician who's always been a loner may change to an institutional setting, while another who has worked for IBM all his life may move out so that he can finally do what he wants. One executive may develop a greater concern for money, while another may lose interest in pursuing it so hard.

Achieving the right balance may happen slowly, over a period of years, and we may take many missteps before we hit upon the best transformation for us. For a year or two, work may seem to be utterly boring and devoid of meaning. We strike the right balance after we embrace our "weakness"—which allows us to feel like true men.

This switch of meaning structures that requires us to embrace our weakness can cause apparently inexplicable and irrational-appearing behavior during the mid-life period and is an underlying dynamic in mid-career changes, mid-life transitions and mid-life crises. Some of us have relied too much on the "cure" of love and work and have not evolved. We're addicted to rank or status long after it has served its initial purposes, because we need it as defense against the personal inadequacies that we've not attended to and that now seem, in their warded-off state, insurmountable. For us the mid-life period is a crisis of choice because we feel deadened inside and know on some level that if we don't connect work with our core selves through our real talents and our own psychodynamic reason for working, then that deadened lack of interest, that push-ourselves-through-the-day consciousness, will prevail for the rest of our working lives. On the other hand, "getting there" seems like an impossible Evel Knievel daredevil leap across a deep canyon. Potential disasters lie ahead if, impelled by an untested deep intuition that may be wrong, we leave our safe, familiar, socially sanctioned niche of business-as-usual.

Given this impossible decision-making position, we're usually paralyzed until our unconscious attempts a rescue by forcing us to do something. This usually occurs by the breakthrough of some negative and potentially disastrous behavior or symptom, such as hypochondriasis (fear of cancer, heart attack, muscle-wasting disease), drinking too much, absenteeism, self-destructive affairs, poor job performance, poor judgment on crucial matters so as to engineer a failure, or deliberate and provocative destruction of a marriage. These behaviors and symptoms are all part of the dialogue with ourselves and with our employers in an attempt to reach psychological constructs that can give meaning to the rest of our lives and rescue us from the deadened life we're leading, in which our work is not a labor of love and our love seems to be all work.

If we don't understand these symptoms and behaviors as part of an attempt to grow and if our employers read these behaviors narrowly as just poor performance or poor motivation, we try to hide what's going on (but we can't) and our employer begins to label us in a way that limits our future in that company. If the employer cares, he tries to motivate us by the ordinary, but now ineffective, carrot-stick considerations of rank and prestige. When those fail, the labeling process is complete, and our future is sealed. If we remain there and our attitude does not change, we are the future deadwood of the organization. If we successfully master the mid-life challenge and revitalize ourselves, we may move out of the company and they'll lose our valuable experience.

In short, when work loses its illusory magical protective powers and when we are more in tune with our instincts and impulses, we become *authentic* adults, true to our innermost selves. We generate our own interests, motivation and values. Because we have decided which things really have meaning for us, we see clearly just how we want to spend our time. We no longer fear bosses or idealize and imitate mentors. We stop being false protectors to women and require instead a relationship of two independent adults.

As we demand higher levels of authenticity around us, we automatically become generative: we provide a model of a real person rather than a collection of roles. Our children and our juniors learn more about life from us.

Men's moves toward authenticity in the mid-life period are initiated by the dawning and sometimes cataclysmic awareness of mortality. Next we'll look at the same process in women.

3. Component Assumption 3

"IT IS IMPOSSIBLE TO LIVE WITHOUT A PROTECTOR"
(WOMEN).

As I have just explained, in the mid-life decade, when the fact of their own mortality first seems inescapable, men are shocked and often traumatized for long periods of time. Their life-cycle changes follow on the heels of that disturbing news.

Upon the realization of their own mortality, however, women feel an increased mandate to act on their own behalf. Whatever fears have interfered with a woman's achieving a full life up to now must be confronted and mastered. The greatest inhibiting fear for a woman is caused by the false assumption "It is impossible to live without a protector in life." This is a component false assumption of the major false assumption "There is no evil or death in the world." The component assumption derives from the archaic version of femininity that has been socially reinforced for almost all women now in their mid-life decade. This outdated version of femininity says: a woman can exercise power only indirectly, through a man. Feminism obviously has challenged this confining definition of a woman's options, and today women engaged in acute mid-life struggle enjoy enormous support as they strive to implement a modern definition of femininity: "I can engage my personal powers directly."

JANIS
Janis, an intelligent, competent 37-year-old woman, tells me that if she had a flat tire on the freeway, she'd call her husband rather than the auto club. She must know there's something fundamentally wrong, since that sort of decision implies she needs him in order to live through life's hazards. She must pay dearly for that kind of protection.

Janis has been a professional singer for ten years; she makes more money than her husband and travels extensively in her work. Yet she is still afraid she can't survive without her husband's protection.

When I press her to explain in detail what necessary powers and abilities he has that she doesn't have, she can't give me any. Despite Janis's intellectual conclusion that she doesn't need her husband's protection in any specific practical way, she still feels that in some ineffable way it would be too *dangerous* to be without him.

By contrast, when a man contemplates separation from a woman, he thinks about the loss of comfort and being cared for; he fears being lonely, being depressed; he may be afraid he won't ever find another woman. But he isn't afraid he won't be safe or won't be able to survive the hazards of life, even though he may be afraid he won't be able to survive the pain of the loss.

This, then, is the issue women must address and battle before they can tap their personal center of power.

Taking Back the Power

Women can take back the power they have lost to control their own lives only by proving through definitive action that the assumption just stated is indeed false. Janis has to learn to call the auto club instead of her husband. Some women have to go on trips alone or go to work or take over the family finances or prove through extramarital affairs that they can risk losing their protector. Whatever it is, each time some idiosyncratic fear is overcome by effort and self-discipline, a woman feels more whole and complete and realized. Developing dormant skills and talents can make a woman feel an exhilarating sense of drive and power, especially if in doing so she knows she is overcoming her myth-based fears.

Taking back power over her own life is extraordinarily difficult because it forces a woman to confront the core trauma of life—that we are all irrevocably separate and mortal.

Kate, a bright, pretty woman with an air of brisk efficiency, has always claimed she consciously chose her life as a suburban wife completely intent on helping her lawyer/politician husband. However, at 42, she admitted why she had never wanted to go further toward independence: "As a child I felt I was forced to be precocious. When I married I suddenly found myself clinging for the first time in life, and at this point I'm not sure that I want to change. It's awfully lonely out there. When you can take care of yourself, you're no longer a child—you can die."

Jane, a 36-year-old woman in the midst of the same struggle, said, "I've been tormenting myself with so many questions in the past month that I actually put myself in a horrible depression. I have, however, found a great deal of strength within myself that has somehow kept me going and made it worth it. My poor family feels responsible for my 'problem,' though I've made it clear they have nothing to do with it. They hope it will pass and I'll be the same old me. But I know I'll never be the same person I was a year ago—if I ever get through with all of this. The nightmares every night are the worst."

As a woman battles to recoup her power, she has to figure out the proper area in which to do battle. Is it with her husband? At work, with an uncooperative, oppressive boss? Or is there a deep inner struggle with her childhood fears of death, which are reemerging as demons in her adult life?

Alice freed herself from the myth that she needed to be protected when she confronted and overcame her sense of inferiority.

ALICE

"I resented him. He loved his work, and we were living out his life style of money and possessions. I had no life of my own, and he wasn't giving me one. I thought if I divorced him, then I'd have to have a life of my own. I had fantasies of turning back the clock, running around with a lot of men and being free and doing something with my life. But I couldn't think of what to do for work. I encountered this deep sense of inferiority and lack of focus that I always knew was present. I'm strong, but I wouldn't take on this fear of my inferiority unless I had to. It's too scary.

"That summer of my fortieth birthday, I spent the whole time visiting with friends, bluntly asking them about their marriages. It was my own personal research topic. Finally I decided that *I* was my problem. Terry had never stopped me. I had stopped myself. From that moment on, I stopped resenting Terry and decided to carve out a life for myself within the marriage.

"I'm going to take whatever it is he can't provide for me. He doesn't like it that I'm not there to take care of him all the time, but he's really pretty good about it. It's like it is final-exam time—I *have* to do something for myself. I no longer have to wait for fate to make me do something, like Terry suddenly dying or us getting a divorce."

Most women in this society are not able to break through the protector myth without in some measure blaming their husbands. They believe their husbands have taken away their power and are refusing to let them regain it.

Women who are now in their mid-life decade were taught as children that the only way to get power was to marry it and that to marry power it was necessary to have the power of physical attractiveness. They were also taught that men were attracted to helplessness in a woman as well as to her looks. Therefore, as long as a woman appeared helpless, she could control the power of men and make them safe to be around. The most glaring example of this is the "Southern Belle," but she has Northern, Western and Eastern sisters. The other side of this myth is that a woman who demonstrates power and skill will have no claim on a man's power, or if she does entice one, in time she will lose him.

Of course, there is very real power to be gained by apparent helplessness: an attractive young woman who appeals to a rich, powerful older man can become a millionaire overnight without having to go through the twenty years of grueling effort and slow uphill climb he did. A man can't do that except in very rare circumstances.

But as women get older and lose some of their physical attractiveness, as they grow to resent their demeaning situation, as they become more confident about their abilities and see how incompetently the world is really run, they feel that they are wasting their resources and intelligence. They are ready to challenge the myth that men don't love women who have their own power. They refuse to be anybody's little girl any more.

When women begin to take back their power, they watch the men in their lives very closely. "Does he love me more or less now that I'm changing?" Well, husbands love less when change costs them something; they love more when change benefits them.

But a man's ability to give love is easily confused with his being able to grant permission to his wife to take charge of her life. Without realizing it, she thinks, "I need his permission to change." Is he then granting it or withholding it? A husband can't *let* a woman have *her own* power. It's not his to give.

When a woman tries to win her husband's approval or his consent to her change, all is lost. It is the slave asking the master. Even if he agrees, the fact that she had to ask means he still owns her power; therefore she is not one whit freer of his protection. She may do different things with her time, but she has not reclaimed her self. A woman who constantly studies every nuance of her man's behavior to determine his *real* feelings on any given matter is still living with the childhood consciousness belief that her husband/protector owns her power. Such a woman feels bolder and more confident if "he" seems positive; if "he" is negative, she feels defeated and disappointed.

In time she sees him as the enemy of her growth and freedom; she develops the feelings of violence and hatred one imagines a prison inmate feels toward a sadistic, teasing jailer. He is a mean, commanding, selfish little boy. She is a frightened, victimized woman who has been reduced to the status of a child while doing all the work of a mother.

By this time, the woman has completely forgotten that originally she only pretended to be helpless. She gave away her power and is perfectly capable of taking it back—except in her mind. She now believes in her own helplessness. She has to fight "him" to the death for it. She can regain power over herself only by gaining power over him.

To complicate matters, a woman's fantasy may be a legitimate insight into her husband's psyche: he may really want to control her and keep her powerless.

Another possibility is that by subtle provocation a woman can turn her husband into a real enemy to match her fantasy.

Sorting out these possibilities is crucial to the outcome of a woman's struggle. The dialogue becomes: "Is the struggle purely between me and the false assumption that I need a protector in life? Am I wrong in accusing my husband? Is he refusing to let me go?"

If a woman's struggle is primarily internal, after she regains her personal power she usually can renegotiate her relationship with her husband on new terms.

Now let's examine one of the other possibilities: how and why a woman would cause her husband to become jealous and controlling.

JANIS REVISITED

I had seen Janis, the singer, only five or six times two years earlier. Then she had come for treatment because she felt so panicked she couldn't sleep or eat or work. She was constantly on the edge of crying; her husband had left her in a fit of rage four days before. All she could think about was how to get him back, even though she wasn't sure she wanted to live with him any more. He had left because of her chronic and vociferous dissatisfaction with his way of life. She freely admitted that she had forced him to leave.

Robert was 42 then. He made a good living, but because of the nature of his business, he didn't work many hours. Ruggedly handsome, he loved outdoor sports and spent much of his leisure time boating, playing volleyball and working around the house. He loved to spend time with their teenage children. Although Janis enjoyed these activities and the family's good times together, she also felt he wasn't intellectual or ambitious enough for her. She couldn't get him to change. When she saw him turn on the TV or go off for some more fun, she felt a gnawing dislike for him that she could not hide, even though she had complete freedom to enjoy the more intellectual, musical, aesthetic part of life with her own friends.

Basically, Janis interpreted Robert's way of life as a strong indication that he didn't love her. She felt that she was never first in his eyes—even the children got more of his attention. When they were alone together, they did have a good time and a good love life, but she felt ashamed of him in company.

Treatment with Janis ended then because Robert had come back and they had begun to talk. All she wanted at that time was to resume the marriage; she was afraid to explore any further.

In the two years that intervened before I saw her again, Robert had changed more to Janis's liking. He had changed fields and was making a better living; moreover, his new business required him to read law and professional books eight to ten hours a day. But when he watched television at night or didn't want to go to concerts with her or preferred movies she thought inferior, she felt the same way about him as she had before.

In the first hour this time, Janis says she just doesn't love Robert any more, but she can't bring herself to tell him. She feels she's suffocating with him, especially after returning from a month-long singing tour that included luxurious living in France. In his presence, she feels mentally turned off, and she feels he turns the kids off. For the last few weeks, she's been angrily withdrawing from him. She knows she'll force him to leave in a rage again because he won't be able to take it much longer. She's *forcing* him to leave her because she's afraid to *tell* him to leave. She's scared that she'll panic the minute he leaves and beg him to come back. She can't bear the idea of being alone.

Robert has surprised her so far by his uncharacteristic response. When he sees her irritated, he has actually become more attentive rather than angry. The other day he sent her flowers!

All of this is told in a fragile, tentative, soft voice that does not fit her at all. She says she feels she's in a cocoon and must break out; she must have her freedom. She doesn't want to hurt him or the children. Although she loves and wants to be with the children permanently, right now she just wants to get away from them all. She's afraid that if she speaks out too strongly to Robert, intense pain and hatred will burst forth. Yet she's even more afraid of the long-term hatred felt by couples who stay together only because they are too afraid to be alone.

She's acutely aware of her contradictions. She earns more money than he does, but she doesn't want to have to make a living; it's too scary and lonely to *have* to do it. She feels intellectually superior to him but still needs him to take care of her. She wants to be free, yet she has freedom to do whatever she wants. She thinks he doesn't want her to be around the music business, but she recognizes that he puts up no obstacles to her going on trips, to meetings or to concerts. In fact, her only indication that he doesn't want her to be around the music business is that he doesn't like to go to concerts with her.

She catches herself in midsentence when she says, "He allows me to handle my own business. He 'allows' me—I sound like a kid getting permission from a parent." In fact, her husband never involves himself in her financial affairs at all.

When Janis describes her mother, the deeper reason we are looking for becomes quite apparent. She does not respect her mother. She ruined all her children's lives because she lived with an alcoholic man for forty years, hating him when he was drunk and mean and forgiving him when he was sober and mild-mannered. Her mother sat there year after year, silently loathing her husband but saying nothing directly.

The parallel with her mother's life was shockingly clear. In fact, in place of her usual tentative and fragile speech, there was a confirming high-pitched squeal of anguish: "But I don't want to be like my mother! All my life I've tried to be different. I'm not like her. I work, I am more intelligent, I do things differently."

But there was an undeniable correspondence: Janis pictures

herself imprisoned by an intellectually inferior husband the way her mother was by an alcoholic husband. She is frightened to live without a man because her mother was afraid to live alone. She is incapable of being direct because her mother kept silent. She watches her kids be turned off by her unintellectual husband, just as her mother let her kids be turned off by Janis's unpredictable father. And she can't risk hurting anybody because her mother would never hurt anyone.

Her current family life has become so thoroughly blended with her memories of her original family that she feels she has become her mother all over, that her whole life is now charted, that she has no more options as long as she stays with her family.

In fact, Robert does not constrict her freedom or independence at all. *What he does not do is endorse her way of life or values as the right way by becoming like her.* Her career ambition and aesthetic sense and creativity are aspects of herself that are different from him—but they are also different from her mother. She wants Robert, by his actions, to demonstrate to her that those parts of herself are all right for her to have and to use. She wants permission *from him* to be different from her mother. But she has not completely given herself permission: the image of her mother's life remains the only right way for her to be.

At work, she is direct, forceful, aesthetically motivated and ambitious. But she is scared, tentative, tongue-tied and helpless at home. It's easy to project an internal prohibition—"I feel overpowered when I'm with him"—onto someone else—"He overpowers and controls me." He's not the jailer, and her mother is no longer the jailer. She's shackled by her unacknowledged belief that she doesn't dare be different.

Like Janis, women can make their husbands into masters to cover and explain their feeling of being locked into the boundaries of their mothers' lives. It is all too common. I've seen a woman throw away her literary talent because she was convinced she dare not be more than a housecleaning wife like her mother. I've seen a woman disavow her executive talents because her mother was seemingly ignorant. I've seen a woman walk away from her financial talents because her mother couldn't handle money.

In each of the above lives, these women felt controlled by something they couldn't understand. Despite contradictory information, they each came to believe it was their husbands who kept them down. The woman who gave up her literary talents was married to a well-to-do man who begged her to get hired help. The fact that he was not as compulsively neat as she was gave ample evidence to her that he was secretly demanding that she spend all her time cleaning up after him. And so on.

A little girl's first protector and first model is her mother. The goal of a girl's life when she is two feet tall and mother towers over her is to be like mother. To be like mother is to be safe.

In the mid-life decade, when all of us pursue our authentic self with the urgency born of the pressure of time, women must face the most primitive destructive anxiety of their earliest years. They must break through the constraints of "mother's" solution to life and face the terror of being quite naked and alone in the world without a rigid program for the future. They must learn to experience and contain that helpless state long enough to know their most demonic infantile fantasies—being the victim of an angry, ever-controlling, jealous mother who won't let her daughter grow up. Only after the demonic has been experienced at its full power—a basic technique suggested in this book—only then can real current threats be distinguished from ancient childhood fears.

MIRIAM

Miriam, at 41, has proved her competence in a profession she started in her early thirties. She's constantly renegotiated the terms of her relationship with her husband over the last five years, and any outside observer would say that she's a strong, independent woman, by no means in the shadow of her husband. She has separate friends, separate interests, she travels alone. And she loves her husband. However, the marriage is on thin ice.

She's declared unequivocally that she must have absolute sexual control over her own body. Torn up by episodic sexual jealousy, her husband no longer feels he can trust her. He feels she's pushing him out, and he can't find a way to stay in contact with her. She's destroyed their way of life, and he can barely control his rage at her. But despite all this, he still loves her deeply. His goodwill and patience are exhausted; he's tired of being the enemy.

Two years ago, during a vacation together, after a week of long, sensitive interchanges, she saw that he was not her enemy, that he did love her and wanted to be with her. He just didn't like the idea of her needing other men.

Then she had a dream in which her household was invaded by her mother and her aunts. She was adult, strong and firm, but she wasn't strong enough to make them leave the house—and the young boy in the dream was not strong enough to help her against these harpies. (Miriam actually had spent the first four years of her life with her mother, aunts and grandmother while her father worked six and a half days a week.)

The next night she had a primitive dream in which women were having intercourse with other women and she was having a baby by another woman.

The third night she dreamed her mother was dying of cancer but would not confide in her. Her mother was still protecting her against the cruelties of life and denying her full confirmation as an adult capable of sharing the pain of mortality.

Since those first insights, Miriam has declared her husband the enemy again. This protects her against the real adult issue of separation and against her childhood fantasies about mysterious, unfamiliar penises and mothers as sadistic harpies who will always haunt her and never let her grow up. She can't free her internal demons, so she's better off, she thinks, dealing with an external oppressor/protector in the form of her husband.

Once grown women have contained these deep irrational fantasies about the first women they ever knew, they are better able to engage their female friends as people without fear of hurting them or of being hurt. When women no longer have to defend against a fantasy attack from a primitive mother or no longer have to act helpless while facing mother-substitutes disguised as men, then they can reclaim their power to be adults.

A final outdated childhood fear that women must conquer is a deep anxiety that an angry maleness is buried deep inside them which is ready to spring out if a woman shows her anger or aggression.

In their late thirties or early forties, women begin to get disillusioned with their husbands' caretaking ability. Reality forces them to give up the idea that a magical protector will always take good care of them and make them unfailingly happy. But this myth does not die easily, and many women experience a demonic fury that they refuse to face. This repressed anger at men for not taking care of them ends up being turned inward, against themselves, and in this way such women deny themselves the opportunity for release and growth.

A woman who has not been working may have a problem finding something to commit her energies and talents to because of real obstacles, overwhelming fear of the consequences, and her concept of work at this stage of her life.

Because a man *must* work, he tries to believe that his work is something special. Endowing work with a forthcoming magical reward helps a man overcome his hatred of the idea of working just to survive. Because from childhood many women are told that they do not have to work, they do not invest work with any magical payoff. They don't overestimate what work can do for them.

In fact, women can utilize their full strength in the career world only after they're convinced that no magical payoff awaits them at home for being a good girl. When that dream of a magical payoff is shattered, many women feel, for a time, that they've been fools to have spent so much time in the way they have. They can't help feeling taken advantage of or misused and bitter. Was it their husbands or the world at large that led them astray?

Feeling betrayed and alone dredges up powerful earlier feelings of betrayal that were part of childhood when parents made promises but didn't deliver.

So women beginning work at mid-life start looking for a job or a career with a large dose of skepticism. Unlike their husbands, not believing that work will produce any magic for them, they judge a job by its intrinsic value and its fit with their talents and needs.

The real obstacles are the limited availability of jobs, the difficulties of balancing the needs of a home and a job, and the fact that having been out of the job market for so long can lead to painful comparisons with the husband's status in life. These real obstacles force women entering the job force at mid-life to start at an all-too-real disadvantage.

Fantasies expand on the real obstacles and combine with feelings of betrayal to make actually taking a job a dangerous activity.

Virginia, described in the first section, said, "I imagine myself working ten days a week, becoming president of General Motors, and having no time for them [her husband and children]. I will be completely cut off in my new world, and he will be destroyed by my success."

She's going to get all the power he refused to provide for her; he'll be sorry! As if the power she's seeking is his to give!

Nancy hated men who stole the limelight—as her brother had at home. She was afraid to use her talents because she was sure a lifetime of fantasies of revenge against her brother would be put into action. She had many talents and always quit when she began to be successful. Now 40, it really was time for her to reenter the career world; but she was afraid she would lose control. To Nancy, seizing career opportunity was not merely taking a job; it was opening a sluice gate on uncontrolled hate.

Some women are caught up in a particularly common and intricate fantasy pattern. Because they gave their husbands all their power, they have reestablished their sense of equality by considering themselves to be quite superior. Given a chance, they could do whatever their husbands do better. They could make more money or achieve higher status. They can easily see the men's mistakes, and they wouldn't make them.

If these women go out into the real world, they risk losing the secret superiority that covers up their feelings of powerlessness. If they go out in the world and don't manage to be extremely successful, they have, because of their fantasy, proved themselves to be more dependent than they have ever allowed themselves to admit. A modest competence would seem an absolute failure.

Entering the job market taps women's primitive competitive urge and the hunger for power, revenge and status that they had to deny as good little girls. Once they see how much they lust for it and need it and fear it, once they no longer deny it as a part of their nature, they are free to entertain their own fully adult powers.

Because women had to suppress their awareness of their power for so long, it is possible that its reemergence frightens them. Men have practiced their aggression and competition and status seeking and have been encouraged to do so. They have learned some rules of conduct, sportsmanship and fair play that at least regulate the brute forces at work. Until recently, women have not had the opportunity to openly express aggression and anger, so they're sure that uncontrollable monsters are going to pop out when they open the door.

When women really tune in to their inner power, the wild fear disappears, and they develop a quiet, extraordinarily gratifying sense of authority. In meetings of twenty or of only two, they know and trust their own minds and so are not intimidated; they learn to speak out as they see the issues. They continue to go through anxiety, but now they don't feel continually shaken or threatened. As they face their fears, they can sense their own growth.

To take back her power, a woman does not need to go to work. She can use her self-determined freedom as she will. For women who've lived in a traditional marriage until their mid-life decade, going back to work or starting a career is only one way to support and affirm their new sense of who they are. Some women pursue interests in politics or in social, cultural or artistic endeavors; it matters only that women use their powers without reservation. They must make a commitment to pursue something. Commitment is what discriminates mid-life activity from the activities of the preceding years. Earlier, a woman might simply be intent on getting out of the house and away from the car-pooling full-time-mother routine. Now, with the press of time, the meaning of extracurricular activity changes: a woman pursues projects with power and commitment and a sense that she is acting to develop herself.

For some women this new sense of personal power allows them to let down their guard with their husbands and become better friends, sometimes even partners in work or in other shared activities. Rivalry and competition between husband and wife disappear once they both acknowledge that he is no longer responsible for making her life work out. They can enjoy their friendship as two independent, vulnerable human beings.

ANN: FROM CAREER TOWARD FAMILY

Ann, at 35, had an abortion and experienced a depression that has now lasted two weeks. She's earned twenty-five to thirty thousand dollars a year for the last four years as an actress, and she has hustled for it. She works hard and is serious about her career. The one thing she's never been able to do well as an actress is cry on cue: it doesn't fit her image as a resilient, self-reliant, tough, capable person. For the first time, she has begun to cry spontaneously. The other day, while at an interview, she found she had no enthusiasm and couldn't put on the happy smile she needed to get the job. While walking out of the interview, she began to cry. Daily, she alternates between feeling good because her future as an actress looks good and then feeling that her life is dismal and a failure because she has no one to share it with intimately and no child to take care of and to whom she can show her deep capacity to be a loving mother.

Ten years ago she had a depression which was more debilitating. At 25, she was trying to make up her mind whether she should continue her acting career or go to law school. Suddenly she landed in a depression; she went home to her family, where she could do little else but reread Sherlock Holmes novels, play some gin rummy with her brother and occasionally take a bite of food. At the end of six weeks, she decided to commit herself to acting and to move to LA to pursue her career. Since then her career has gone well, although she has not become a star.

She has had one serious relationship with a man, which lasted seven years, and has had other intermittent but intense relationships. But all these relationships have left her feeling hurt and lonely. She has many supportive friends, but she recognizes that she has always been afraid of a commitment. When people get too close for too long, she feels absolutely smothered and can hardly breathe. When a man thinks she is terribly beautiful and she finds him looking at her adoringly, she just wants to run away. On the other hand, in the seven-year relationship with Bill, she felt she lost her own center and her drive; she became his satellite and idealized and adored him the way most men treat her. She has never been able to maintain a sense of both freedom and closeness.

During the last ten years, she has been more like her father than her mother. Her father is strong, tough, self-reliant and is quite a doer in life, while her mother is more loving and open but dependent. Ann considers her mother weaker than her father. She has elements of both her mother and her father but has never been able to integrate the two. She's tired of being tough and self-reliant; she wants someone to take care of her and wants someone to take care of—this means both a husband and a child. All her married female friends seem to be going in the other direction—they all want careers because they feel their families have robbed them of their personhood. She feels exactly the opposite. She feels angry, as if part of her life has been taken away, because she has not been "allowed" to have a family. She is desperate to do that now because it is getting too late.

Her career transition and her desire to be a mother and a wife are intimately connected. Her career has peaked because there is a limited market for actresses with her characteristics and of her age, so work seems to be harder to get. But the work has never completely satisfied her; she is very bright, and acting has not exercised her intellect completely. She never did go to law school, but several years ago she got involved in a public law case and helped raise money for it. She learned about the issues and temporarily became a reporter for a local radio station and reported on the case and its ramifications. This was her most exciting work experience. A somewhat analogous job, developing ideas for television and movie production, is open now, and she and the people who know her feel it would be exactly the right job for her, although it's difficult to get. Her eyes sparkle and her face comes alive when she talks about this new possibility.

The lull in her career has allowed her to see that work was a protective device against intimacy. She often turned toward her career just at the point when she might have developed a real intimacy with first one man and then another. Her loss of interest in pursuing her career aggressively is her way of suspending her protective device in order to allow a strong urge to marry to come to the surface. The abortion and the depression that followed have made her appreciate the power of her need to have a family. Part of her fear is based on her old childhood idea that she will have to give up her life to any man who loves her. She still believes that you owe someone who cares for you anything they want and that you can never say no to pursue what you might want. Now Ann has shed her defensive structure. Though she's confused and can't decide whether she's ruining her life or making her future, at least now she is acting on her instincts and taking charge of her own happiness.

Several studies contend that by their late thirties, women who have never married become very interested in marriage or some deep, abiding relationship. They are as surprised by this powerful, unrelenting urge as their married counterparts are at the urges they feel impelled to act on at this time. But married and unmarried women at this age are all working to conquer the same false assumption: that they need a protector in life.

Career Development for Women Executives

An enlightening doctoral thesis by Margaret Hennig, *Career Development for Women Executives*, written at the Harvard School of Management in 1970, profiles twenty-five women presidents of industrial companies. The backgrounds and career development of all these women are remarkably similar. They illustrate one way of facing the mid-life transition.

All the women were born in 1915 or 1916, and each was an eldest or only child. As children, they all went to work with their fathers often. Each played sports vigorously, extending exercise to the point of strain and really focusing on *winning*.

All the women had educated parents, and each claimed that her mother and father alike pushed autonomy, ambition and daring for her. The fathers wanted no role discrimination by sex, and the mothers' only concern was that their girls retain feminine manners.

As adolescents, the twenty-five women were high achievers. They preferred boys to girls as friends, and they dated but without much sexual contact.

Within three years of graduating from college, each had become an administrative assistant in the company she would later head. Each became attached to a boss who was supportive, like her father. The women played down sex and acted like men; they trained themselves to be rational, unemotional and to tell an occasional dirty joke. They were never seductive with men and never had sex with men in their company or line of work.

Although none of the women expected to become president of her company, all expected to hold an important position eventually. At around 26, each woman decided to concentrate on her career and to hold off on marriage till the age of 35 or so. They wasted little time on personal matters and moved up the ranks with their bosses.

While establishing their competency in the world of men, they bent over backward to be the kind of women they thought corporate men would respect—logical, unemotional, tailored work machines. By the time they reached upper-middle management in their mid-thirties, they found they didn't need to try so hard to fit in. With that security, they could relax the tight hold on themselves. Until then, the motto shared by all was "Think like a man, work like a dog, act like a lady." Each put her sex drive "in storage," acted very controlled and unseductive with men, and had no close relationships, either with other women or with family. But by their mid-thirties, all twenty-five women experienced a similar depression.

The personal confidence resulting from having "made it" combined with a temporary middle-management career plateau to make their jobs less consuming and less exciting. This exposed the emptiness of their lives outside of work. The life costs they had agreed to pay at 26 "until they established themselves" were now being reevaluated as the prospect of being unmarried childless middle-aged women became unavoidably imminent.

Their depression was not, in my opinion, just the sudden realization of their life situation, which was not inherently depressing, but was a depression common at the beginning of a profound transformation. In order to pursue a life outside of work, a life that was virtually nonexistent, they each had to recapture a part of themselves: the once valued "emotional woman"—an image they had rejected in the service of being respected corporate women.

For these women, the protector myth was a deeply buried issue. Since they feared that in an "emotional" relationship, they would have to surrender to a man, they had opted exclusively for careers. They chose to become their own protectors. But by 35 the dissatisfactions of a rigidly closed life became apparent, and the women opened up to these other parts of themselves.

The question of whether to marry became the crucial life-course decision, encompassing not only the question of whether marriage would enrich or injure their personal lives, but also the question of whether the time requirements of marriage would damage their chances of eventually making top management or, more devastatingly, whether a husband would force a decision between career and marriage. But these gnarly questions were academic and premature, since none of the women had an emotional involvement with a likely husband.

First, it was important for them to have time to experiment and to exploit the opportunity to relax their tight hold on their feminine selves. They each made a deliberate decision to give themselves that time by letting their career plateau for a year or so, by delegating responsibilities to subordinates, or by uncharacteristically refusing added responsibilities. They changed hairdos, dressed with a new flair and color, and became conversationally open. Some became social butterflies. All braved the initial stares, double takes, kidding and whistling of people who knew them and, with time, learned to like and respond to being looked at in a way they hadn't since their early twenties. They became interested in themselves—in what they had become and in what they were becoming.

Although many of the change devices were temporary (the social-butterfly period or the radical new hairdo) and some of the exhilaration of bold, dramatic change wore off after a while, these women knew they had "changed forever. I learned to understand and accept and, yes, like and enjoy another very real part of me. . . . I was a new and stronger person for it."

Hennig found that at this point in their lives, all twenty-five women, who later went on to become corporate presidents, had taken a moratorium from career ascent to concentrate instead on developing private lives. Half of them married (to professional men either widowed or divorced but with kids). All of them expressed tremendous relief at no longer having to "plan every word and deed before acting." Rather, they allowed their feelings and instincts to emerge. They developed friendships with other women, became more open to social exchanges at work, and were more likable and more capable of enjoyment. All the women who risked a career moratorium discovered that *their new openness was precisely the trait which advanced them from middle to top management.*

Another group in Hennig's study, with exactly the same family background and career development, felt the same depression at this age, but because they were afraid they would be swallowed up by their personal lives (or the men in them), they pushed ahead without a break. These women never advanced beyond middle management because they were just too rigid, too closed for top management.

The women who chose a moratorium were able to conquer the protector myth because they felt secure in their careers (no man could take it away) and because their instincts and impulses were too strong to deny.

Once women shed their protector myths, they are free to experience a broader range of social contacts and to expand their own personalities. They can appreciate work for what it is and feel a new confidence in their own ideas. They are free to take on traditionally male concerns because they know it will not devour them or make them men. Like the women executives, they can allow their womenness to surface. Once the protector myth is conquered, women are free to become whole and *authentic.*

4. Component Assumption 4

"THERE IS NO LIFE BEYOND THIS FAMILY."

This component false assumption of the major false assumption "There is no evil or death in the world" can paralyze a couple in mid-life and prevent them from working through the problems in their marriage. Because dialogue or conflict would endanger the stability of the old marriage conspiracies, the growth struggles and anxieties inside each partner have no forum. If the conspiracies are not worked through, two harmful outcomes are possible.

On the one hand, the marriage may stabilize along the old lines, forcing each partner to relinquish the possibility of new personal growth (a loss of passion). There may be surface peace, but the building internal tension will finally burst forth from the partner who feels more alienated, lonelier or more deprived of the opportunity to deal with his/her inner needs.

On the other hand, renegotiating the conspiracies is truly a dangerous business. Although each partner may benefit eventually, renegotiation threatens the very survival of the relationship. The internal changes we demand of ourselves at mid-life are so powerful that most of us forget our fifteen-to-twenty-five-year investment in the relationship; we push our renegotiation to the point of thinking about separation. Facing the terror of being alone finally makes us question very seriously whether there *is* any life beyond our family. This usually causes us to slow down, but preferably we still continue the essential demand for change.

Renegotiation of Sex in Marriage

Sex is perhaps the most explosive issue to renegotiate in this period. Four forces bring it to a head: our sense of time urgency, the end to parental inhibition, our children's sexuality, and recent cultural changes. We feel this is our last chance to explore new sexual or romantic territory. Soon we'll be fifty or sixty and our youth will be over—our bodies will be less attractive, and somehow it won't be right any more. Someone we know has enjoyed these new sexual or romantic experiences without disaster, why not us? Now that we have final authority over our lives and understand the depths of life, sexual pleasure seems more innocent. Maybe it's as good as its reputation. Since we no longer feel guilty about sex, we see it as our right to pursue new pleasures.

Over the years we have become very parental. By that I mean that we usually feel and act differently around our friends or colleagues than we do around our children. We may have fun with our children, but we also feel older or duller or prohibited from being or saying totally who we are out of deference to them—as if they're only allowed to see certain parental aspects of us. As they grow older, we show them more, and each of us remembers finding out bit by bit about our parents' secret personalities.

This phenomenon is especially potent in matters of sex. Weekends or vacations away from the children are sexual adventures. At home, with presumed sexual innocents around, a wet blanket is thrown over sexuality, even in the absolute privacy of our bedroom.

But as our teenagers and young adults become more blatantly sexual, family jokes or conversations about sex begin to include them. As the children experience sex, we feel a new surge of interest ourselves.

If we can abandon our inhibiting parental roles, our sex life suddenly improves. Our parental inhibitions come from a childhood consciousness belief that parents are essentially asexual. It's a powerful wish, and we often say or hear our friends say, "I know my parents had a sex life, but really I just can't imagine the two of them enjoying it. I certainly can't imagine them doing what I do or feeling the way I do."

As we drift into our parental roles, we take on that image of our parents and, through no fault or intention of our own, become dull sexually compared with the way we were in our pre-parental days—and compared with what we'll become again if we can change as our children grow.

During the years of the wet-blanket pattern, we struggle to keep our sex life alive and interesting. Some of us resign ourselves to this inhibition as if it were inevitable and everlasting. Others consciously try to create romance or engage in creative sexual experimentation. As our teenagers become sexual, we recognize how hard we worked at sex in the past!

When the children leave home altogether, we experience a greater release from inhibition. We're private citizens again; we feel younger rather than older. The great burden is lifted, and we have time for ourselves and our partners. Eventually we find our children's visits both a joy and an interruption of our privacy. When that begins, we feel a bit guilty about the resentment and try to keep it buried.

Not only are we released from parental inhibition by our children's chronological march, we're also spurred on by envy and jealousy of their youthfulness, their shapeliness, their sexuality and their opportunities in life, some of which are closed to us. But some, of course, are still quite open.

As mothers, we are attracted to our sons and their friends. After reading a magazine article about older women with younger men, we may wonder what it would be like. We find that our husbands are slightly aware of what's going on and are reacting competitively with the boys. One of the young girls comes into the room in tight shirt and without a bra, and we feel a flash of hatred and envy of her firm breasts as the young boys turn to her.

As fathers, we do what we can to avoid staring at our daughters' curves or their friends who make a game out of seducing us; we do what we can to keep our wives from knowing. Our sons' girls are awfully appealing, and sometimes we daydream about being in their place during this sexual revolution. It was never like this in our day. From time to time we wonder whether our anger at our sons is really jealousy.

The obvious change in the recent values about sexual freedom hardly needs mention. Those of us now in the mid-life decade were taught that sex was restricted to a monogamous marriage that was supposed to last a lifetime, for better or for worse. Dedication to the other's welfare was paramount and self-sacrifice was noble then. Nowadays "self-actualization" is what the culture touts, and while concern for others is fine, it is never supposed to go to the point where one has to sacrifice one's life or goals. Although romance and love and broken hearts are still the dominant topics of popular songs, the heartbreaks are because people have to "move on," to do their "own thing." In our frame of reference, that was a betrayal of a lifelong contract. All these elements—the change of values promoting self-actualization, the prevalence of sexual stimuli in the culture, the free-sex ethic, the decrease in our parental inhibitions, the emergence of our children's sexuality, and our sudden sense of urgency ("The time to do it is *now*!")—all these combine to form a very powerful push into extramarital sexuality.

Although many of us now in our mid-life decade may have had more than one marriage or several extramarital affairs, the great majority of us have lived in monogamous, faithful marriages—until now. Statistics tell us that a virtual epidemic of infidelities, separations and divorces takes place in the mid-life decade. Statistics also tell us that the double standard is dead.

There are many motivations for having an extramarital affair, including pure sexual desire, a search for love, the impetus for the breakup of a barren marriage, anger, an urge for revenge, the acting out of an old family drama, the need to find an unlived portion of oneself or to risk the loss of a protector, and the very real wish to break through to one's innermost core of dangerous passions.

The arrangements vary from "Don't talk about it and don't do it" to "Don't tell me if you do" to "Once but not twice with the same person" to "Out of town is OK or strangers are OK, but not friends." And finally, there is the completely "open" marriage, in which all details are shared and anything from a *ménage à trois* to bisexuality to swinging with other couples is not uncommon.

But whatever the motivation or the arrangements, all extramarital sexual relationships must be seen against the background of two psychological dynamics: (1) Monogamy is a solution to the oedipal conflict but not a resolution. (2) All the rules of life that were learned in childhood are now being questioned.

Monogamy Is a Solution to the Oedipal Conflict

The family as an institution has a long history and serves many purposes both for society and for its individual members. One purpose for the individual is to form a union with another person that helps end our loneliness and our feeling of being "left out"—which in our bitter childhood consciousness memory means being left out of our parents' intimacy. Our "left out" hurt was soothed when we became part of a couple.

It is bad enough when the arrival of a baby intrudes on our relationship and brings back the feelings and the demonic images that are the childhood consciousness emotions of a "left out" child. At least we love the baby. But an adult rival intruding upon a marriage is a different matter. We cannot love the rival as we love our child, so by definition one of the partners will feel that horrible, left out, betrayed feeling again. Then fury and anguish really begin to pour out.

NEIL AND SHEILA IN MID-LIFE

Neil and Sheila experienced the swamp of human passion and pain over sex and infidelity and the interwoven issues of collusion, aggression, drives toward freedom and archaic demonic feelings and fears as only a couple in mid-life can.

Neil is 43, Sheila 39. They're each successful in unrelated careers, with no sense that they have to be more successful. They're both agreeably busy in their lives and manage to conduct their household affairs cooperatively with the aid of hired help. They have a 6-year-old daughter, whom Neil was more eager to have than Sheila initially. Now they both adore her. They've been married for ten years, each for the first time.

Both have migrated into exactly the professional position they feel best suits them. Neither is reluctant to use authority; however, they are not considered hostile or commanding or unfair by their business associates. They are civilized and chatty when they meet for dinner during the week; they spend Sundays together with their daughter. They are each quite likable and enjoy both shared and separate friendships. To all the world, they are a successful couple. But though they won't talk about it, Neil and Sheila both know that beneath all this proud harmony, there are strains and tensions. The source is in the bedroom.

The surface calm is shattered when Neil discovers Sheila has a lover. The underlying tension erupts with frightening violence. Neil becomes enraged and threatens to kill the lover. For the first time in their marriage, he hits her. She's petrified and convinced she's unleashed a madman, and to my eyes he is quite convincing as a dangerous, angry heavy. Fear and tension accompany him like his own private cloud.

For several nights, Neil takes long drives, and in a fit of despondency, he prepares to drive off a cliff. He drives past the same spot several times, each time feeling an almost irresistible urge to get it over with. He feels crushed, despondent, that his world has been destroyed forever. He has a thirst for revenge against the lover, whom he knows, and a consuming hatred for his wife. She did this to him just when he's been feeling most loving toward her—in fact, when he's been treating her just the way she asked him to! While he's knocking himself out trying to please her, she's carrying on behind his back!

They come to treatment as an emergency, both afraid of his violence. She's literally quivering. In the second session, years of unhappy love experiences and misunderstandings come tumbling out. It's a vivid testimony to how much can be suppressed by two civilized people.

By not dealing with the issues, Neil and Sheila have constantly misinterpreted each other's actions. Empty charges and countercharges ricochet back and forth like bullets fired without reason or cause. Each feels wronged, misunderstood—each believes the other ought to be grateful because "I'm so kind, I carried him/her all these years."

Throughout their marriage, they had proclaimed images of each other as warm, loving, dependable partners. Now Sheila and Neil each began to reveal their secret, demonic images of their *real* mate.

SHEILA: "I've been a fool. He's cold and calculating. All those years he made me feel like a woman, he was just trying to get control of me."

NEIL: "She is cold and unloving. First she teases me, then when I respond, she throws my affection back in my face. I'm not gonna take that punishment. What for?"

Under the pummeling of his insistent "Why did you do this to me?" she responds with anger and exquisite pain: "You didn't want to touch me any more. In my mind, I begged you and begged you to hold me, just touch me. I'm dying. You make me feel so ugly."

Later she adds, "It was too late when you tried to be affectionate. I had already given up and didn't trust you."

Confusion reigns. Neil and Sheila maintain contradictory images of each other. At times their conflict is total, yet in other moments, mutual love and caring are equally palpable.

He feels righteously indignant over her infidelity and at the same time responsible for the anguish she experienced over the years because she loved him and wanted him so much. She feels hurt beyond repair by him and therefore deserving of her experience with the other man. At the same time, she feels responsible for the wreck of the man she sees before her: torn and twisted because she spurned him. It's a vicious cycle. Neither will forgive; neither will repent, so their anger builds. When Neil initiates lovemaking, Sheila must ask herself, "Is this the good Neil, who loves me and makes me feel worthy of love? Or is it the manipulative Neil, who is trying to control me with his affection?" The contradiction is paralyzing. She doesn't know how to respond.

To compound the problem, Sheila must also decide which of her selves Neil is approaching: the loving, "good" Sheila or the heartless, "demonic" Sheila. Neil is caught in the same dilemma. Instead of two confident, autonomous adults living in the present, Neil and Sheila are like four people, two each, caught between childhood and adult consciousness.

Although they hear each other talking, neither understands the other. But they do see hot-blooded passion, and it shocks them, for they had come to see each other as cold, calculating and distant.

So far their lesson in facing problems is extraordinarily painful, but at least their demonic images of each other can no longer be accepted without question. They're alive in a new sense and mean more to each other in their bitterness than in their calm. But it could have been a violent disaster.

Neil never anticipated his violence and fury. No man ever does. The ex-wife of a psychiatrist friend of mine had to get a judge's restraining order to keep her husband away from her house. He beat the door down twice. In Neil's position, we all experience self-righteous indignation, together with a confusing sense that somehow we deserved this hurt.

Before infidelity, our spouse took our parents' place and so satisfied every woman's original oedipal drive to possess her father's love and every man's oedipal drive to possess his mother's love. Now we know that our sense of ownership of our spouse's love was an illusion which quieted our intense oedipal desire. This traumatic lesson forces us to recognize these possessive drives. It should also teach us that if we can truly master our childish drive to possess, our adult consciousness and sense of our own inner freedom will make a qualitative leap forward.

Infidelity can start us on a long and painful journey, at the end of which we can see our partner as a separate, independent being over whom we have no possession. But most people don't get all the way, and some don't get beyond the first step—they just feel betrayed and destroyed for the rest of their lives.

Questioning the Rules About Infidelity

Monogamy was probably an unquestioned commitment when we entered our marriage, but now as we find ourselves halfway—at mid-life, literally—all the other rules we've always believed about life are being questioned, and the validity of monogamy also usually comes up for review. We may know some couples who have violated the rule of fidelity without any apparent loss or others who have experienced great trauma because of it. Certain novels and movies and some celebrities proclaim loudly that fidelity can and should be junked for each of us to reach our full measure of humanity.

So if we no longer consider the rule to be divinely inspired, our decision about breaking it usually comes down to "I would like to try it, but it would hurt him/her too much." Is our partner's pain to become the new guideline to action? Or must this decision be a purely personal matter? For those who perceive an extramarital affair as a personal issue, the other person's pain seems to be a form of bondage much like our parents' worrying was during adolescence.

Those who refrain from infidelity because of their partner's pain feel they are making a more or less calculated decision to trade off the possible gains and perhaps a piece of their individuality for a more peaceful union with their partner, concluding, "That's just the way it has to be if two people are going to have a chance to live happily together. It may be a sacrifice, but it's a necessity."

But whether extramarital sexual relationships come up, are talked about and faced or not, sex is an issue that will be reopened in mid-life.

Through our children, sex passes through our living room almost daily, waking us up and reminding us, through competition, envy and jealousy, that it's still quite alive inside us.

Our teenager or young adult also brings up for debate all the philosophical issues that we brought to our parents twenty to twenty-five years ago, but wrapped in the attitude of this current generation. He or she forces us to take sides on issues of life style, sexual morality, duty to authority, hair length and dress, politics and government, work and leisure and the nature of relationships between the sexes. Even the issue of whether a family is necessary is raised and seriously questioned.

Listening to our teenagers makes us aware that for years we've given hardly a moment's reflection to the assumptions underlying our life style. Their questions often cause our attitudes to change. Their generation's values about the right way to live modify our generation's values—as we internalized them.

Just by growing up and trying to figure out how to live, our teenagers exercise the powerful need they have to find our inconsistencies and hypocrisies. Although we may defend our values to the death, the way of life we set up based on the plan we shaped in our twenties is under attack. Our certainty that it is the right life for us diminishes. That certainty may have been necessary to see us through the difficult work and sacrifice required to establish and maintain a life that included both family and job. But now at mid-life we don't need it. We need *uncertainty*.

One 39-year-old man summarized this questioning consciousness for me: "I find myself making decisions in a new way. I ask myself what would I do if I only had two more years left to live? How would I use my time and resources?"

When we ask that question, a life centered on the self becomes a priority. The form, rewards, costs and obligations of a marital relationship are among the first things to be questioned. Noel Coward wrote a famous song identifying the issue, "I Travel Alone":

The world is wide and when my day is done,
I shall at least have traveled free. . . .
When the dream is ended and passion has flown,
I travel alone.
Free from love's illusion, my heart is my own,
I travel alone.

As our illusions of safety crack, as children go their own way, as years of complicated living generate hurts, this sentiment becomes very tempting. As women return to work and take back the power they delegated to their protectors, they want to find out what kind of life they would have had if they hadn't accommodated their particular spouse/protector. As men come in touch with their greater need for closeness and sensuality and want a life outside work, they have the same question. What have I missed by being married to her? What love or closeness or adventure have I been deprived of?

The question becomes: how much of a separate life do I need to express my emerging individuality and my differences with my spouse? When the children leave home, the whole marital arrangement has to be restructured.

Engaging the Change Process

There are two patterns for marriages that have remained intact until the mid-life period, depending on whether the man or the woman has been doing the most growth work. The classic pattern is for the man to begin struggling to leave the form of his life that is suffocating him; he points his finger at his wife, who represents all the values they held jointly before. Usually the woman defends the old values, confirming to the man that she really doesn't understand him and probably never did. By that time it is irrelevant to him whether the woman was forced to entrench herself in domesticity in response to subtle derogations until she became a caricature. He just wants out.

The other pattern is the mirror opposite: the woman complains that her husband hasn't grown apace with her, that he is impossibly insensitive, that he is deadened and unavailable.

In between these two extreme patterns are most of us who are alternately tugging and following, but always struggling. During one period we're sure the other is impossibly behind us and will never make another move, while during the next period we're threatened.

Both of us are driven to rework our concept of the male and female aspects of ourselves. Underneath the old conspiracies, at mid-life we are negotiating to find room for our newly forming selves.

To oversimplify it, as men we're striving for release from our stereotyped masculinity and opening ourselves up to need, uncertainty, anxiety and ambiguity. As women we're striving for release from our stereotyped femininity and taking on new strengths, autonomy, freedom, novelty and self-confidence. Both sexes will do this with an ever-increasing pace as the midlife decade goes on.

Gail, at 37, is trying to break out of her pattern of constant car pooling and busywork, and she manages a summer afternoon at the beach, a treat she hasn't given herself in more than ten years. She's sure her husband doesn't want her to spend her time that way, because he has remarked, in the midst of complaining about his work, "While you were sitting on your ass at the beach . . ." She feels his remark is a message of control. I suggest it might be envy. She's surprised but then says, "Of course!"

A woman who sees her husband becoming more vulnerable, more desirous of companionship and fun, something she'd always thought was best for both of them, sometimes wonders whether it is too late for them as a couple, whether he has waited too long. Sometimes a woman is scared to see her husband soften, as if some mythical protector is gone from both their lives. Sometimes she resents his becoming more lovable just when she was ready to write him off as hopeless and set out on her own.

In a strong, flexible marriage in which all issues are negotiated through dialogue, both partners can continue their necessary growth and change—but they must expect turmoil, confusion, arguments, blame and plenty of anxiety.

As we redefine ourself and our old relationship, we dream of being alone, and we ask, "What would I be like if I hadn't married her or him?" This leads to a series of experiments, such as taking courses, meeting new friends, reestablishing old rusty relationships, and doing what we've always been hesitant to do because he or she would disapprove or think it silly. Often our adventures are sexual, since they are usually the most forbidden.

These experiments are a crucial part of separating out who we are as we define ourself more by our own experience and less by our marital partner. If along the way we find a new lease on life that gives us a new center of vitality, we may be bitter because we think that our partner prevented us from developing this aspect of our life, this essential part of ourself. We'll remain bitter until we recognize that no one took anything from us. We sacrificed these undeveloped parts of our personality as much as our partner did—to a conspiracy that we are now strong enough to break. We're about to see whether we can form a new relationship based on empathy and respect rather than illusion.

Conspiracies Must Be Broken

Most of the major conspiracies remain intact during our early thirties, undergoing only slight surface modifications. Some of the major conspiracies are:

1. I'll be the parent—you be the child.
2. I'll be the smart one—you be the dumb one.
3. I'll be the worker—you be the player.
4. I'll be responsible—you can be irresponsible.
5. I'll be the healthy one—you be the sick one.
6. I'll be the leader—you be the follower.
7. I'll be the tyrant—you be the victim.

8. I'll be decisive—you be wishy-washy.
9. I'll be the taker—you be the giver.
10. I'll be right—you always be wrong.
11. I'll be the educated one—you can be ignorant.
12. I'll be highbrow—you be lowbrow.
13. I'll be friendly—you be distant.
14. I'll be the protector—you be the protected.
15. I'll be hard—you be soft.
16. I'll be sensitive—you be rough.

Any couple can draw at least two or three from this list. Either husband or wife can take on any of the roles; sometimes we alternate. But no matter what the choice, whenever we accept a limiting role, we violate our self. It is always unhealthy to sacrifice our identity for the stability of the relationship. Even the smart/good/sensitive/caring/strong role is a violation, because it does not allow the "badness" in us to surface. Thus we are prevented from facing our demons and returning to our passionate inner self.

CONFRONTING THE CONSPIRACIES: YOU DON'T GET SOMETHING FOR NOTHING

Richard and Sarah

Richard is 38, Sarah 36. They've been living out the following conspiracy for the last ten years of their thirteen-year marriage. Richard is a perfectionist, a smart, strong, complex, talented, tyrannical teacher. He sees Sarah as stubborn, resistant, dependent, simple, and always angry at him though she covers it up with affection.

Sarah sees herself as the victim. In her view, she's really very strong, maternal and responsible to put up with the little-boy tyrant, because despite his talents and success, he's really so insecure.

To the public they're both handsome and vivacious and smart in different ways. He's smart in book learning, subtleties and social graces. She is direct, earthy and very funny. He circles around a topic, zigzags around the periphery before he reaches the center. She barrels into the center. Over the years, they have maintained the public facade of a good marriage while the emptiness grew between them. She complains he's too bossy, unloving and not tender as he was in their early years together. He complains she refuses to make use of her talents out of spite because she's too stubborn to accept his help.

At a party, Sarah claims Richard pushed her to make friends with a famous artist, whom she already knew and did not want to know better. She became angry and did exactly the opposite of his bidding: she walked away from the artist. At the end of the evening, the artist came up to her to make a lunch date. Later, at home, she said to Richard, "You see, my way works better than yours. I don't like your playing up to famous artists as if they're so important. You should consider yourself as important as they are; you're a famous musician and a handsome and intelligent man. You shouldn't manipulate me to be friends with him." He responded by saying that while he used to be impressed by famous people, he has outgrown that. His motive was quite different from what she interpreted. He was indeed somewhat imperious about asking her to act friendly, but only because he has seen her avoid contact so many times with people that he knows she wants to be in touch with. He's seen her act in a haughty and superior way out of fear of rejection rather than disinterest in the person. For years he's wanted her to overcome this problem. He's tired of shouldering the burden of their social life because she won't follow through on telephone calls.

Richard feels Sarah has not carried out her responsibility as a partner in the marriage—either at home or in their social life. She admits that she does not call people because she doesn't want to bother them and that it must reflect some sort of hidden inferiority on her part. Since her earliest years in a rather forbidding Catholic school, she has been holding her head high waiting for people to come to her; she never makes a move toward someone else, and now she recognizes that she's afraid of appearing small and rejected.

Sarah is a great beauty, and because of this she's been able to protect herself and get away with her aloof attitude. She wanted Richard to be as kingly (the famous, handsome musician who's impressed by no one) as she is queenly, so that together they could carry the same attitude and her defense would be fortified rather than questioned. She was annoyed when he saw her protective device in action, and she fought it off by accusing him of being a tyrannical little boy. Now she sees that although at times he really is tyrannical, in this case he was a friend and an annoyed partner who helped her expose an internal prohibition.

Because Richard refused to let an evening end with her labeling him tyrant, Sarah had to face her internal prohibitions. As she opened up and shared the history of the origins of her attitude in grade school, Richard saw that she stopped being, for a moment at least, the superior perfectionist who ridiculed him like the father he could never please. Her style of seeing things simply and directly, in black and white, was a style that always made him feel judged. It often inspired his perfectionist counterattacks on her.

This cycle of misinterpretation, confrontation and reinterpretation is what happens when conspiracies unravel.

FRANK AND WINNIE

Frank, at 42, was feeling generally weak and unmanly. He was having a hard time deciding about a career change and frequently dreamed about death. In a university extension course about career change, during small informal group sessions, he began to talk about his wife, who constantly brought up old hurts and blamed them all on him for not being the kind of man who liked to talk about things. Since his wife was right that he didn't open up all his feelings, he felt that she was also correct in assigning him the blame for all the past hurts. He tried to make it up to her by listening, talking, arguing as long as she wanted him to now; but he felt it was an endless punishment.

One man in the group suggested that the problems in any marriage were produced jointly, and though Frank might owe his wife a degree of openness, he did not owe her interminable angry discussion sessions.

The next week, Frank returned and reported that he had told his wife that she was unfair to blame him for their early marital difficulties—as if she had nothing at all to do with them, as if he had all the power. In addition, after arguing for several hours, he said, "Look, I just can't take it any more. This is me. I will return to argue with you later on; now I need a rest." She was miffed at first, but they managed to resolve it as the day went on.

Several days later, he found her crying—for reasons that didn't appear to relate to him. The day after that, she seemed quite relieved and told him she had just parted from her lifelong Catholicism. She had lost her belief in God, which, even if it was a great loss, at least meant that she was responsible for herself. Now bad experiences or bad feelings were not someone else's responsibility. She no longer felt angry at her husband, nor did she feel that he was responsible for everything. She had a new sense of freedom.

Frank had helped her by establishing boundaries in a direct and honest way: "I am different from you, and I can argue only so long." But his manner confirmed the importance of their relationship to him: "I will return to the argument at some future time, because it's true we need to resolve these things." Although Winnie didn't like what he said, she apparently began a process in which she ended up crying to mourn the loss of a belief system that she had treasured. She came to a new understanding of herself: "I believe in my independence and separateness and feel a certain amount of freedom with it, and therefore I no longer blame you."

For the first time in many months, Frank felt the energy necessary to pursue the difficult task of determining his future. He feels he can do it now because his relationship with Winnie has opened up and made him aware of other possibilities in his life. Work and love, we see, interlock.

Frank also told a story about his father, who around age 40 became an ever more beaten man while his wife became stronger and more imperious. His father aged rapidly, then died a few years later. He had battled Frank's mother until he was 40, but in Frank's view, then he just gave in and died. Frank was worried that he would replay his father's life. But the knowledge that he could work out problems with his wife without being destroyed by her gave him a new power source.

Underneath each repressed fragment of the self lies a repressed fragment of a feared memory. It requires a substantial expenditure of energy to keep it so repressed. Once it is released, accepted and integrated into our coherent, whole self, it becomes a new source of power, releasing energy for the process of active living.

DEVELOPMENTAL ENVY: NEIL AND SHEILA

The marriage conspiracies of Richard and Sarah and of Frank and Winnie are of the kind that can be corrected relatively easily. But others reach into the core of each partner and form the bedrock of the relationship.

When they first married, Sheila made Neil feel like a man and he made her feel like a woman. "I turned him on. I could tell. And it made me feel attractive sexually for the first time. I mean, I didn't suddenly have slender legs or a great shape just because he kissed me, but he wanted me, and that was as much as I could ask for."

Neil and Sheila gave each other all the warmth, all the civilized talk, all the love they seemed to need—until the baby. With Cheryl's arrival the proud harmony of their life together had become mysteriously out of tune. Can a baby so devastate a marriage?

Before Cheryl, Sheila and Neil had been living out a silent conspiracy, a secret agreement unknown even to them. Over time, this pact had become the unchallenged law of their relationship. The implicit accord went something like this:

"Neil, I depend on you to make me a whole, loving person.

Through your affection and love, I attain my own womanness, so if you'll continue to do this for me, I'll always love you.''

"Sheila, you allow me to be tender, soft and loving. Without your trust, I would have to be hard, aggressive, the kind of man I hate to be, at least at home. Continue to do this for me—I can't do it for myself—and I'll do whatever you need.''

Fair enough. Scratch my psyche and I'll scratch yours. If my sense of self is a gift from you, what does it matter? We'll always be together. . . .

Before their child was born, Neil and Sheila spent all day Sunday in bed, making love, eating, chatting and reading the paper. After Cheryl's birth, Sheila felt Neil put the child between them. In fact, she felt he was hiding behind Cheryl to reject her sexually. She began to resent Neil and the child for the loss of love she felt.

Neil interprets the facts differently:

"I wanted a child. She didn't want a child. I know that. . . . Her work was important, just as important as mine, but she had the baby anyway. I liked that.

"I get up early, so I figured on weekends I'd do her a favor, let her sleep late, and I'd get to spend a little time with my daughter. You know.

"When she'd wake up, I'd bring the kid in bed, and we'd lie there, all three together, with her in between us. I thought when the baby naps, and they nap all day at that age, we could make love.

"Sheila got irritated. I couldn't understand it. I was trying to be tender, a good father, to care for my daughter and have a loving family. I'm not a macho aggressive type, not at home anyway. But she didn't want the kid in bed. . . . Made me think she wasn't much of a mother. I couldn't let Cheryl feel that. She'd be scarred for life you know. I covered for Sheila. I loved the kid enough for both of us. 'Course I never let Sheila know I worried about her as a mother.''

The cycle of misinterpretation started then. Because he thought she was an inadequately loving woman, both to him and to his daughter, he began to cover up his feelings. In addition, he felt punished by her anger when he thought he should have been rewarded. She sensed he was covering up and was secretly critical of her. She became irritated and aggrieved as her suspicion was confirmed—the baby that she gave him out of love at the sacrifice of her career time was taking his love from her. She had been a fool.

Sheila feels that all the years he made her feel womanly were designed to get control of her. Now he's withdrawn the affection she needs, and she's forced to try harder to please him, which makes her still more dependent on him.

Their sexual relationship is unsatisfactory to both of them. By the time he recuperates from a long bout with hepatitis, their sex life is finished. Their demonic views of each other are confirmed. As he's recovering his strength, she feels it's time to resume their sexual relations. But Neil is avoiding any recognition of her affectionate nursing care and therefore is depriving her of any affirmation of her being a loving woman. She begins to see him as the selfish little boy her mother told her all men were. Once more she's gone out of her way to win his affection, and once more he's withholding it coldly to keep her working at it. She "knows" he's unendingly critical of her, even though he hasn't verbally criticized her. She's hurt by it.

Neil sees her outward behavior but has no knowledge of what she's really experiencing. He sees her intense ministrations and implicit demands for affection as a request for a sexual performance he doesn't feel vigorous enough to accomplish. He's just returning to work and drags himself through the day and just barely gets by. When she's easily hurt, he's sure it's because she's feeling sexually frustrated and dissatisfied with him for not being manly enough. He feels she's terribly unfair and insatiable. He begins to withdraw any affectionate touching from her so as not to stimulate her or aggravate the situation more. He has an intense need to please her, which frustrates him; he feels weak and inferior and guilty because he can't please her, but he's also angry at her for putting him in this position. In his mind, she is in absolute command of his sense of manliness—in exactly the way she feels he's in absolute command of her sense of womanliness.

At this point, their conspiracy has broken down, for Neil no longer feels like a man or Sheila like a woman. Their childhood demonic views of the opposite sex have come alive again. Years of chronic dissatisfaction have whittled away at their love cure. Rather than face the fact that their conspiracy isn't working any more, Neil and Sheila are blaming each other for willfully and maliciously withholding the magical "cure" the other possesses.

After the hepatitis, when they do resume lovemaking, it's difficult for him. He feels it's because he's trying too hard to please her; she feels it's evidence he's withholding again, and she's irritated. Sheila's irritation and impatience convince him that she'll never let him please her and that he'll never do it right in her eyes. If he manages to do it right, she'll be irritated again a few hours later anyway. When he blames her, she feels guilty because she knows she's feeling angry and unloving; he's right that she hasn't been warm. Sheila wonders whether there's something wrong with her sexual attitude toward him. More and more she feels defective, as if she has to try harder to please him. She ultimately feels controlled by his penis, as if his loss of interest is a measure of her sexual defect. She becomes self-conscious and loses her spontaneity. Intercourse becomes such a horrible, confusing battleground that she'd gladly settle for just touching and holding.

Neil doesn't believe she will settle for touching and holding; he thinks it's patronizing and an indirect form of saying he's only man enough to do that. He withdraws from touching and holding as well as intercourse. He also feels there's something wrong with him, for he knows he's angry and isn't making love with the right emotion. It's not love, it's battle.

They avoid discussing it and settle into a life without physical intimacy. Every few months they try again but can't do it. He reads her very carefully to see whether she wants to. She's wary. He interprets her wariness as reluctance. He approaches her tentatively and indirectly. She interprets his tentativeness as a lack of real interest and feels teased and disappointed.

Over the years, the failures cause them to clamp the lid on the topic even tighter. Sheila becomes convinced that Neil is content with the situation as it is, while she's dying from lack of love. She believes that because of his anger toward women, he's keeping her from having a sex life. He's become, by this time, completely identified with her own primitive childhood consciousness. She *has* to break out of the deadlock she feels he has her in: she deserves a love life, and he deserves to lose her if he won't love her.

So she begins an affair, out of desperation. She feels that it's absolutely right for her to do this even though it flouts the ethical boundaries of her marriage commitment. The affair for Sheila is the beginning of change. Through it, she withdraws from the conspiracy and says, "I am a woman whether you make me feel like one or not."

As she begins to feel loved outside the marriage, she stops being so dissatisfied with Neil. In the bedroom she can be friendlier, even affectionate, because he no longer has the power to deny her her womanness. Sheila has overcome her internal prohibitions, albeit temporarily, by using another love cure—her affair—to mask her need for a man to make her feel like a woman.

Neil feels *developmental envy* toward Sheila. She has grown and is free now to help herself, but he still believes he can't help himself. "I need her to help me and she won't do it." (If the conspiracy were still working, she *would* be able to cure him.) Neil feels that he's earned the right to have her cure him because he lived with her and suffered because of her. "She's flying now and I'm lying here on the ground alone." This is a fine definition of developmental envy, by the way.

In this state, Neil is incapable of sexual pleasure with his wife or with any other woman. At this point, the future of their relationship depends on which reality he chooses. He has two options:

288

1. Childhood consciousness: In this view, Neil continues to feel that Sheila took something from him—his sense of maleness—and he must stop her. He becomes her enemy and tries to deny her the benefits of her affair in any way he can. This view forces him into seeing Sheila as his internal prohibitor. She will have no choice but to leave him.

2. Adult consciousness: In this view, Neil acknowledges that he has an internal prohibition which prevents him from defining his maleness by and for himself—it has simply been exposed by the end of his conspiracy with Sheila. Though he may fear that his problem is deep and perhaps irreconcilable, he must try, through the seven-step inner-dialogue process, to resolve his archaic demonic images of women. In this view, Neil overcomes his envy of Sheila's development: "I must support her well-being because her growth is good for both of us; it does not take anything away from me."

For Neil to end his pathological dependency and break through the conspiracy, he must be able either to have an affair with pleasure or to make love with Sheila successfully. If he can't, his feeling of emasculation will dominate his consciousness and he will be stuck with his internal prohibition.

The case of Neil and Sheila is a paradigm of developmental envy and resolution of conspiracies in mid-life. It is complicated by a real threat to the relationship—that is, Sheila's affair and Neil's lack of interest in sex. However, the conspiracy had not worked for years before Sheila initiated change.

But even when sex is not a threat and the conspiracy is still functioning, the same dynamics occur. For example, if a woman accepts her own intellect at the same time that she knows her man has no special claim to mental powers, she may expose his fear that she does not love him deeply enough, if he is harboring such a fear. As we noted earlier, people often marry as part of an effort to achieve wholeness. Our aim in these instances is to marry someone for qualities he or she possesses that we lack— as though the other person would become a piece of us. We fool ourself into thinking we won't have to develop the desirable quality; we need only marry it. For instance, women often hook up with men for their seeming intellectual power. When a woman recognizes her own powers of intellect, she overcomes an internal prohibition in herself and exposes the conspiracy with her partner, if there is one, for he may feel that he must maintain superior intellectual power at all times or he will not be a man and not be worthy of love. If so, he then envies her development because he feels stuck with a defect that he fears is permanent.

Once again, the options for him are to attack her newfound intellectual confidence or to correct his own mistaken view that he is really unworthy of love and thus overcome his own internal prohibition. She has initiated the action, but now he has the opportunity to respond.

If we could freeze the action here and if both the initiator and the responder had perfect insight, absolute emotional control and objective distance and if both were penetratingly articulate, they would have the following ideal dialogue:

Initiator: I'm embarking upon a new step in life that challenges my old ways of seeing myself and the world and leads to an unknown outcome that may threaten you and me. But the true enemy to my growth is that part of me that has forbidden this step. As suspicious as I may be that you, in your threatened state, are the true enemy of my growth and as much as I may try to see it that way for my own temporary comfort, please understand that I mean you no harm and love you no less.

Responder: I hear clearly what you are saying and see the wisdom of your insights and respect the integrity of your need to take such a step. But you must understand that I can't help feeling that my safe world is being put in jeopardy by your need, not mine. Your growth is causing me real pain. I will try to keep in mind what is happening, but I won't always be able to deny that part of me that responds automatically to someone I love causing me pain. For if my loved one causes me pain, it's easy to believe that he/she, whom I have trusted, has betrayed me— that is, wants to cause me pain.

This ideal dialogue may never actually take place, but it is the only psychological climate in which individual growth steps can occur without sacrificing the marital relationship. It is a very delicate balancing act which requires both people to be aware of two views of the other simultaneously—the goodwill view *and* the demonic view. Each must recognize that his or her demonic view of the other exists and that it has an archaic origin in childhood consciousness.

Neil and Sheila have helped us see the interior of a marriage and the years of accumulated grievances, misinterpretations of motives, feelings of victimization, and abuses of power that shift back and forth between the partners over the years.

For some there's a great reward in store for reworking a marriage in mid-life. The old power battles over maleness and femaleness are reduced to almost nothing. The old conspiracies are abandoned. In their place is a relationship based on empathic acceptance of our authentic partner, who is not a myth, not a god, not a mother, not a father, not a protector, not a censor. Instead there is just another human with a full range of passions, rational ability, strengths and weaknesses, trying to figure out how to conduct a meaningful life with real friendship and companionship. From this new dynamic, many different forms of marriage may follow: two very separate lives, in which husband and wife come together only periodically, as their rhythm of relating dictates; total sharing of one life in work and leisure; or variations between these two extremes. In any case, it is a relationship of equals, without rank, position or self-abrogation.

Divorce as a Casualty of the Process

Given the volatile emotions of marriage, couples often divorce before they've had a chance to work through their problems to come to one of the optimistic endings described above. At divorce, both partners usually are left with love for each other and a feeling of bitter hurt. If only they had held out a little longer, they might have fought through the problems. Yet every time they see each other, the anger resumes. Each hears the past misinterpreted by the ex-partner, and each feels that his/her current actions are still being misunderstood. Even a satisfactory new life can't eliminate the pain, because the old unfinished business still lingers—especially the desire to correct our ex-partner's demonic version of us. If only we could get inside our former mate's head and tinker with the machinery, we could release his/her hold over us. When our ex-mate's opinion continues being too important to us, we can be sure that we're still defending ourself against him or her because we haven't been able to admit that his or her view is partially correct and rework it. As we'll see in the next chapter, we must come to a new relationship with our "badness" before we can be freed from other people's definition of us.

Divorce can also be the result of having worked through the conspiracies to the recognition that there is little basis for a relationship. In that instance, both partners may be able to see the necessity for the divorce without bitterness; they've grown apart and have become so different that they share only the past. They have no basis for developing a future. Then both partners usually consider the divorce a marvelous release. Even if they never remarry, they are free to pursue a new life more suited to the selves they are at mid-life.

Living with the Conspiracies Unchanged

Those couples at mid-life who dare not risk challenging the conspiracies they formed in their twenties remain on the same old track, with two possible outcomes. Some couples will rerun the same old arguments in a stable, studied, repetitive way and live with a constant low level of bitterness. Such marriages become cold wars in which the partners recognize on some level that they've sacrificed a piece of their growth for the stability of their marriage. Each resents the other for it, failing to accept responsibility for his or her own decision. The other possible pattern is that of couples who seem to accept their sacrifice for the stability; they live without bitterness in some distant, peaceful coexistence, but they live without passion too.

As we have seen, mid-life is the time for resolution; we abandon old conspiracies, overcome remaining internal prohibitions and correct whatever distortions, misperceptions and misunderstandings that have prevented us from becoming authentic, whole people.

5. Component Assumption 5

"I AM AN INNOCENT."

"I am an innocent" is the final component false assumption to the major false assumption of mid-life, which is "There is no evil or death in the world. The sinister has been destroyed."

As the illusion of safety crumbles, as our mortality and separateness in life become more real, and as we challenge the belief that there's no life outside the family we've known, much of what we've repressed during our adult life comes back to haunt us. The gargoyles of human nature are exposed in the form of greed, envy, competition, vengeance, blame, hatred and despotic control. We see it in ourselves, but we see it in others first—something fundamental is happening to us: we have lost our innocence.

Our Darker, Mysterious Center

Our demand for an exclusive monopoly of our mother's love is at the root of each one of our deep loves and important rivalries in adult life; from that infantile source flows all love and all evil.

Our passionate attachment to our mother is never extinguished; it is only covered over during the years so that only carefully modulated, "civilized" amounts seep through into our loves and hates. There is only a faint, lingering whiff to remind us of our consuming childhood passion for total love, but it is strong enough to scare us—because it leads directly to the loss of our mother's love. The stipulation becomes "If I can control my natural aggressive desire to possess and own my mother exclusively, I will not lose her altogether." Thus do we become civilized!

But when we lose our lesser protective illusions during mid-life, we symbolically also lose the crucial illusion that we still have the magical protection of our mother's love. If we have lost that, we no longer have reason to keep our deepest passions at bay. We become demonic, rapacious, carnivorous, childlike, greedy. We demand more fun, more pleasure, more play, more novelty, more power, more respect, more resources, more stimulation, more intensity, more passionate dimension (grief and joy), more control, more equality, more dialogue, more truth, more subtlety, more nuance, more complexity, more understanding, more empathy, more freedom, more release from arbitrary constrictions, more personal expression.

More! More! More! The demand "Now or never!" threatens to erupt in gushes of ugly black bile. If I am the final authority in my life, why *can't* I have what I want? The selfish, greedy, impatient child threatens, in one impulsive decision, to destroy the whole fabric of our life and all that is safe and familiar.

The selfish, greedy child is indeed a dangerous element in us. It is also the source of our future vitality. The message comes from within our deepest desires and guides our future in a direction we've unconsciously decided we must go.

As children, before we had the mental capacity to control ourselves in any other way, we controlled our desires by refusing to know what they were. Our desires were seen as the cause of problems with our parents. During that era of our lives, we learned to turn away from our passions at the first whiff because we couldn't control ourselves in any other way.

Now we are thirty to forty years older and more capable. We can afford to know what we feel because, and only because, we now have the mental strength to control our desires. We can *contain* a passion without acting on it.

Many of us are not convinced of that. We fear that if we know what's in there, we'll spin out of control instantaneously. We are convinced that to *know* is to *act*. We are convinced that we wouldn't be able to deny ourselves gratification. Those of us who remain so convinced are condemned to alienation from our passionate inner core. We may appear mild, cold, conventional, rigid, unfeeling or angry to the outside world—but we feel colossally frustrated, cut off, cheated and potentially hot-blooded inside.

Michelle, who lives next door, is cheerful, peppy, funny, observant and good-natured. She loves her husband, adores her cats, is fun to chat with, teaches school, has no enemies and seems to enjoy life. All through high school and college she was a popular, fun-loving cheerleader. She recognizes no dark side of life.

But when she was 4 years old, she was hauled off to a child psychiatrist because she couldn't stop trying to slam her baby brother's stroller into the wall. She tried repeatedly to push his carriage into the street, and she pinched and socked him when he was asleep. When he was held, she would react with jealous rages followed by pitiful sobbing during which she pulled out fistfuls of her own hair.

So Michelle can't sustain her life by being peppy, fun, cheerful, observant, good-natured, fun to chat with and popular. She can't continue to be a cheerleader all her life. It doesn't work!

It doesn't work because on days when her own mother seems to pay more attention to her husband than to her, she sees her husband as a rival. On some days his work or some other woman's charms make her jealous. Her daughter or her son seems to stand between her and some ideal form of closeness with her husband. Someday her daughter is going to be prettier and sexier and funnier than she is, and her son is going to turn away from her toward a stranger. Someday her husband may no longer want a middle-aged cheerleader for a companion in life. Whatever it is, Michelle will continue to distort events, words and situations involving her loved ones and call up all the hurt, vengeance and retaliation in the pit of her memory. The tension will reign for days or weeks or months or years, because she's sure that all those who get close to her in life will discover that she is a 4-year-old brother-killer again.

If she learns to journey through her fear of the demons, she'll find that a flash of anger clears tension from the air faster than a stiff smile, that brooding jealousy can be dispelled by talking openly and warmly to her husband and children, and that living to satisfy her own desires lets her love more and releases her from performing according to others' standards and from the resentment that automatically brings.

We hide unacceptable, infantile goals behind acceptable adult goals, being on the surface smiling, aging cheerleaders. Behind acceptable ambition, one can often find immature greed—"I must have everything I want or I will hate the world I live in." Frustrate a driven, ambitious man and the greedy child pops out in temper tantrums.

Hiding behind the quest for expertise is often the demand to be above *all* criticism. The world's leading expert on a certain issue privately admits that though he knows his field better than anyone else, he can't stand being criticized. It tears him apart.

Hiding behind an unswerving commitment to marriage and monogamy are urges toward possessiveness, control, jealousy and competition. As the perfectly loved child, we had an incontrovertible right to an ideal state of oneness. By that impossible standard, we're all living in a state of deprivation and violation of our rights.

If it is greed that fires our ambition, we had better wrestle with it directly, for we will eat ourselves up trying to satisfy it in the world. If it is immunity from criticism and total, ubiquitous adoration we are looking for, we had better face the impossibility of the quest.

We can extract an adult measure of passion for life *only* after we wrestle with the childish, passionate demand for the *original* form of satisfaction. In the process, we have some pretty hard growing up to do. Riding these primitive passions is like trying to break a wild horse. We want to deliver a spirited and disciplined mount with both passion and civility, so we have to ride our horse with enough force to maintain discipline, but not so much that we ruthlessly crush the spirit we are trying to capture. We're bound to get thrown a few times before horse and rider finally become a powerful new unity.

If we turn away from those original passions, we resign our-selves to being half alive and try to convince ourselves that's the way life must be. We fortify ourselves with conventional wis-dom and mutter, "This is all there is to life, and there's no use upsetting the applecart or challenging fate. I've been like this all along; it's too late to change." We become more "typical" adults, repeating boring complaints about life, about our family, about duty, about hard work, about children "these" days and how bad the system is.

We become "middle-aged" well before our time: it may show with a spread of fat or with rigid thinking that is so predictable that our kids or friends can recite our speeches as if by rote, or it may show as an overfull and overorganized schedule. Which-ever form we choose, the result is that we push ourselves into less and less creative activities, as if dullness, repetition and plodding perseverance were desirable standards.

We justify most of our actions as a response to duty, which has called us in the shape of people or events. We do this be-cause we have to assert louder and louder that there is no mol-ten core of passion within giving us directions that tempt us to experiment beyond our self-imposed boundaries.

At least we feel quite virtuous and very maturely adult—and as far away as we can possibly be from our demonic, rapacious, carnivorous, childlike, greedy self. We are very safe!

All the evil of our childlike self will have been destroyed, along with its playfulness, curiosity, whimsy and novelty. But we can't stay "alive" without growing into our childlike self. If we're too "safe," we can't grow.

If we take a ride on the wild horse within us and contact our passion for *more,* our life becomes more highly charged and more dangerous. If our passionate desire for respect is not satis-fied at work, we have to admit our hatred for those who deny it and risk coming within an inch of quitting and losing our retire-ment, our income and our security. We must feel in our gut our passion for respect with such intensity that we could never again rationalize it away as unreal or neurotic or temporary.

We must risk doing something foolish for a change; we must occasionally do or say the unexpected; we must try stepping out of character just for the hell of it, just to see the surprise on everyone's face. For only then can we accept the idea that in childhood (or as adults in the grip of childhood consciousness), we were so afraid of demonic fathers that we endured whatever treatment came our way and didn't explore our options in life. We have been acting cowardly because we have convinced ourselves that others don't respect us as coequal adults, when it has been truly our lack of self-respect. But if our passion for self-respect is never allowed to surface in its full intensity because of our fear of the consequences, nothing can change.

If we want more money or more career success, we must come in contact with our powerful greed fantasy: wanting to have everything before we can sort out what we are really looking for in the way of satisfaction from work and money. A man who has been afraid to be too successful must experience the full intensity of his greed before he'll be able to let himself be successful in the real world; for only then will he know that in his ambition, he isn't being an omnivorous, criminal child. A woman entering a career for the first time must come in contact with her competitiveness, anger, power drives and vengeance fantasies or she will always expect to be punished for her ambition.

Once we have tracked, captured and successfully contained or modified our original, insatiable passions, the mysteries and complexities of the human mind and human interaction become awe-inspiringly open to us. The so-called irrational processes of human interaction are now acknowledged as real, and we now see that the time and energy devoted to them is not wasted or unnecessary but is life itself.

There are now so many sides to a story, so many views on a problem, so many solutions with so many different costs—reality is so rich in nuances and subtleties that we find ourselves in a far richer world than we ever imagined possible. We become as richly complicated, with as many new sides, as the world we live in. We are textured and grained just like the world we see. We become less predictable. We entertain ideas and concepts about ourselves and the world that were once too close to the demonic. We may get so in touch with demonic greed that we no longer value it. Many of us in our forties give up a high-paying job for a new life style or turn down a promotion that would eat up too much of our leisure time or develop an interest in a non-commercial aspect of our job or in training young people.

But to recap these rewards and release ourselves from the grip of childhood demonic images, we must trace the origins of our voracious childhood passions and fears and then contain their influence on our life.

THE SWITCH BETWEEN CHILDHOOD CONSCIOUSNESS AND ADULT CONSCIOUSNESS: NEIL AND SHEILA (CONTINUED)

Neil and Sheila are shocked to hear each other's demonic interpretations of behavior that each thinks is loving, patient and caring. Sheila still sees Neil as an untrustworthy, overly aggressive man who hides his anger behind quietness. He really doesn't love her; he just wants an opportunity to hurt her. Sheila feels like an innocent victim. She doesn't see her own anger, so she projects it onto Neil and assumes that he will act out his anger against her. Neil sees her as a woman he needs desperately but whom he can never get to love and accept him. He too feels innocent and projects his anger onto Sheila.

She's constantly asking, "Does he hate me?" He's constantly asking, "Does she love me?" She's ready in a flash to hate him for hating her. He's ready in a flash to hate her for not loving him. Both can handle *overt* anger and differences of opinion and criticism, but neither of them can tolerate what each is sure the other is *hiding*—the withholding of love and trust. The slightest indication that it *is* love that is being withheld triggers a vicious circle of confirmation and escalation.

Despite the fact that they are bright, sensitive and articulate people of goodwill and affection and commitment to each other, they had never been able to understand this cycle. They considered it just part of the mystery of marriage or of the man-woman relationship—to be suppressed while they concentrated on the vast area of their life together that worked well for both of them. They accepted the gulf between them that made them lonely and hoped the hurt would take care of itself.

But it didn't take care of itself. They can't live with such loneliness. It has to be faced. And part of the reason that it's no longer tolerable is inherent in their age. In mid-life they feel the need to achieve a deeper human contact, and they will eliminate at all costs anything which interferes with that end. Convenience, safety, old patterns and public opinion become weak in comparison. Being half alive is no longer acceptable.

Instead of avoiding the problem, they must face it and immerse themselves in all its horrible detail. Only a true dialogue that starts from the depths of where they are, regardless of how they got there, can get them out of it. During that dialogue, they'll have to risk learning something new. As Sheila said later in our work, "I've come to see that what I was so sure was real is not real. It's very disquieting and humbling. It was easier when it was all his fault."

As they continue to talk, a pattern crystallizes for Neil and Sheila; they begin to understand how the situation came about and, more important, what is still interfering with their love.

During the course of our conversations, Sheila intermittently appears frightened of him and maintains a sharp vigilance toward him even when he doesn't appear angry or threatening or even intense. In fact, the fury that possessed him in the first few weeks of treatment had long since abated, and he has a business-as-usual attitude, although obviously the topics and the sessions *are* emotional. Finally, Sheila is persuaded that Neil isn't a bundle of anger ready to jump on her. She becomes intensely curious about her fear. She monitors it carefully, while remaining quite convinced she must be right.

He's able to confirm that while she's often right about his anger, it does not exist to the degree she imagines. Her sensitivity to his hidden anger actually helps him discover and put into words what he's been afraid to state aloud. He quickly becomes quite expert in carrying out an honest dialogue and putting issues and emotions on the table. They both benefit immediately from her questioning of her fear reaction.

So by questioning, Sheila now recognizes that her fear does not mean Neil's anger is a definite reality—"I am afraid, therefore he is dangerously angry" was an illusion. Neil also realizes that a private menacing thought is just simple anger when expressed. He's not filled with dangerous thoughts, as they both had imagined. His words or thoughts don't destroy her. In fact, she even accepts some of his thoughts about her as accurate, while she debates others.

As the fear reaction disappears in the office, it appears in their bed. After a series of initial sexual successes, she begins to fear he's going to hurt her physically during lovemaking; and at the next office session, she states her fear as a conviction. He is deeply hurt. He's never hurt her and has always tried to please her. They both agree that early in the marriage their intercourse was rough and rugged, but she freely admits she wanted it that way and it made her feel desired. But now she's afraid of him. She agrees that he has never hurt her but still can't shake her conviction.

Sheila says she wants that topic off limits until they return to my office the next week. She's waited for eight years; she can wait one more week. It's too sensitive and confusing a subject for her. He accepts the condition.

During the week, in the midst of intercourse, she says, "Be gentle." Before she said "Be gentle," he felt very loving and gentle; after she said that, he felt very guarded, inhibited and hurt. To her it was just a warning; to him it was a statement that he was an aggressive brute.

In the following treatment session, she very accurately says that after she asked him to be gentle, he seemed hostile to her in bed. Neil easily tells her exactly what he had felt: he hadn't felt hostile or angry, but careful and inhibited. She was right that he became inhibited and somewhat withdrawn, but it was out of self-consciousness; he felt she was watching and disapproving of him.

In a flash of insight, she sees what has been happening. Whenever she feels him withdraw, she feels pain. Every time she feels pain, she feels he has hurt her. And every time she feels hurt by him, she feels he intended to hurt her. In her mind, he withdraws when he's suppressing his hostile intent. In this latest instance, she anticipated that he was going to be hostile, so she urged him to "be gentle," and thus brought about the "reality" she anticipated.

With tears streaming down her face, she manages to get out, "All of those years I thought he was so mean and wanted to hurt me! I guess pain is pain, and I built up this image of him as an angry man because I felt so hurt by his withdrawal."

Sheila begins to see how her childhood consciousness has intruded on her adult life. She understands that her false view of Neil was constructed as follows: "I have an inalienable right to be loved in my own way, and if he doesn't do that, if he withdraws from me, then he is sadistic and malicious, and *I hate him!*"

Now Sheila knows that she had still been operating on her childhood belief that men were mean and unloving. In fact, Neil is not that way except when she forces him to withdraw from her. The pattern is now plain for her to see. She has blamed her pain on someone else: "It can't be my fault that this is happening, so he must be doing it to me."

When Sheila recognizes that she has had childhood demonic images of men and a belief that her demons are caused by someone else, she has located the switching point to move from childhood consciousness to adult consciousness. She is ready to strip her archaic demons of their power and to move to a fuller, more independent adult consciousness. Though Sheila has found the "switch," the work has just begun. During the next week, she avoids physical contact with Neil. At one moment she wants to reach out and touch him, and the very next moment she feels herself recoil. She's ashamed of her reaction; she knows he's not really mean, but in her childhood consciousness, she wants him to break through her ambivalence, because she can't. She also wonders whether she's going to end up with all the blame for their sexual problems, which previously she had charged him with. Has she been ambivalent all along, and have her depressions and mood swings been excuses to avoid intercourse?

Next we turn to Neil's reaction to Sheila. In great detail he spells out every avoidance of intimacy that has taken place that week. He has withdrawn from Sheila whenever he decides that her avoidance means she doesn't want to be close to him or that she doesn't love him any more. Worse, maybe she has never loved him.

This separation experience releases hidden demonic anger in Neil, so there is real anger for Sheila to point at. He has the same problem she does: he holds an archaic childhood belief that he has an inalienable right to be loved as he wishes—which means she should not be ambivalent; she should just love him purely. She shouldn't have her own childhood demons to master. As he begins to suspect he really feels that way, he becomes angry inside and is afraid to say it aloud.

When she says that he should speak up and comfort her or get mad at her or do something other than act like such a goddamn martyr, he acknowledges that he's at fault. Her love or lack of love is so important to him that the least sign that she doesn't want him sends him back into a corner licking his wounds. He says, "I'm the kind of guy who, when the door is closed, even if by a thin cloth, won't enter. I will just sit down and cry."

He's afraid to try to break through her ambivalence with ardor. He's afraid that he'll be hurt even more if he tries and is still unable to win her intimacy. He's afraid that her silence indicates he's not doing a good enough job. Better to read the early warning signs and back off.

She has become a living trap baited with sexual allure and the promise of love. If he's careful, patient and sensitive to her precise mood, maybe he can get some of the bait without being injured. But if he makes a mistake, he'll pay dearly for it. Her ambivalence and avoidance are part of a sophisticated dance that expresses her true malice toward him. In his childhood consciousness view, she plays with him as a powerful, angry mother-woman might with a needy child. It's the belief that organizes his behavior.

By listening to her, he's able to hear quite distinctly that she's not an evil-intentioned woman; rather, she's struggling to understand him and is battling her own false images of him as the hostile male. In the same way, his childhood view is that a woman is someone to be wary of, a human threshing machine, not the real adult woman talking to him.

They both see clearly that the only way out of their dilemma is to continue talking at exactly that point when the hostile image of the other becomes dominant. Silence only feeds the demonic images.

In pursuit of adult consciousness, Neil and Sheila wrestle directly with the archaic images of their childhood consciousness. Sometimes the two realities each seem simultaneously so real that Sheila and Neil call their basic sanity into question.

In a paradoxical way, we have to come in contact with the insane in us before we can go on to an enlarged sanity. Before Sheila could contain her demonic image of Neil, she had to become absolutely terrified of and infuriated with him. Before Neil could contain his demonic image of Sheila, he had to alternate between intense fury at her and abject hopelessness that she would ever love him.

Sheila contained the demonic image of the dangerous, angry, pleasure-depriving man at that moment when she felt both terrified of him and sympathetic to him with the same degree of intensity. Her demonic image was not contained when she only felt terrified of him. At that point, the demonic image dominated and suppressed any feeling of sympathetic understanding. It was also not contained when she felt so sympathetic to him that her terror and anger were totally suppressed.

We can contain the demonic only when both childhood and adult reality coexist with equal credibility and demand action. At that point of real confusion, we embrace a state of mind that has terrified us; we are poised between two contradictory realities and feel very close to the edge of insanity. In fact, it is what people who become psychotic report as the earliest stage of that process. What was familiar becomes "unreal" and what was of minor importance becomes more "real."

Until Neil discovered the love notes and became so wildly angry, Sheila's images of him were balanced. She could say that she thought he was a hostile man *and* that she understood him, but neither were very powerfully felt compared with her own feeling of being hurt.

Many of us are trying to break through that same fragile sort of intellectualized balance in the mid-life decade. In the marital dialogues of our early thirties, we may look at our demonic images and try to decide whether our spouse is or isn't demonic, but we don't usually have the fortitude or ability in that period of our life to carry our investigation to the crucial state where it all becomes so real. In our early forties, our searching demand for truth and coherency drives us to this point, as it did Sheila and Neil.

While Sheila and Neil are each extraordinarily sensitive to the other's demonic qualities, they have no desire to sweep it under the rug any more. They don't simply intellectualize about what they have learned just enough to paste together their relationship. They don't compromise themselves into an artificial solution. Instead, they stay with their experience, expose it, track it down, check it out and transform it. They are determined to know where childhood consciousness ends and adult consciousness lies, once and for all, no matter what the cost.

At the time of this writing, the outcome of Neil and Sheila's marriage is not known, but they know they must find out whether their image of each other is a distortion or part of the true character of each of them. If she ends up believing she's married to an untrustworthy, hostile man who secretly hates her, she'll have to leave him. If he ends up believing she's truly an insatiable woman who never loved him and who is incapable of truly loving a man, then he'll have to leave her.

But if Sheila discovers that the hateful man is in her mind, she'll be able to enjoy, love and be at ease with the real man. Perhaps even more important, she'll be well on her way to breaking up the stereotype that men are strong but hostile and that women are weak victims. She can then acknowledge her own strengths and hostilities and the similarities that exist between men and women. She'll have options in life. She will feel that this truly is her life, to do with what she may.

If Neil ends up believing that the insatiable, unloving, controlling woman is in his mind, he'll no longer need to be so fearful about displeasing her. He need not feel that his anger is controlled by her mood swings. Paradoxically, he can then afford to be angry when it is appropriate and not be ashamed of it. He can become spontaneous again, with a full range of emotions and a new vitality. When he's no longer afraid of the depriving, controlling mother of his childhood consciousness, he need not live within the constricting mold of the serious, martyred, devoted "good boy" who always does his duty.

Once we have learned to contain our archaic demonic feelings of greed, hate, jealousy and competition, they no longer *automatically* force our lives into untoward action. If we work on them long enough, we can not only defuse their power over us but learn to harness them. We can actually live off the powerful passions that as children we didn't have the mental equipment to experience without terror. We can tap our own primitive energy to power our life.

It is this fundamental task of deep self-renewal that is the force that drives all the mid-life experiences. Under the pressure of time, we finally become the adult self that we have struggled toward for so many years. Mid-life, then, is not a sedentary or bucolic period. In fact, mid-life is every bit as turbulent as adolescence, except now we can use all this striving to blend a healthier, happier life. For unlike adolescents, in mid-life we know and can accept who we are.

Section VI
The End of an Era:
Beyond Mid-Life

"THE LIFE OF INNER-DIRECTEDNESS FINALLY
PREVAILS: I OWN MYSELF."

The grip that early childhood consciousness has had on most of
our adult life is noticeably lessened after our mid-forties; intima-
tions of our own mortality begin to crowd out our fear of what
others think or will do. It is hard enough to discern our *own*
mind.

As small and helpless creatures, we started our mental life in a
frame of reference indexed by power and size. We live most of
our adult lives with the same frame of reference—judging ourselves and others by rank, status, money. We live competitive
lives in a competitive society, and we are often victims of the
jealousy, envy and humiliation that naturally follow in a world
organized by the childhood criteria of power and size. Finally it
begins to dawn on us: it is the only world we know, but it is not
the only world there is.

Even those who are successful and who don't want to face
their own aging begin to think they'd *better* develop another perspective in life as it becomes obvious at work that younger men
and women are hot on their heels, ready and able to make that
extra effort that seems less and less worth it to people over 50.
Women who have stayed at home realize that while they may
have developed a distinctive sense of style and an unflappable,
gracious social poise, it is substituting for the fresh-faced apple-
cheeked glow and spontaneity they once had. They may have
gotten giving a smashingly successful dinner party down to a

science and be remarkably efficient at juggling demanding volunteer work with being truly attentive and helpful to their husbands, but the uncritical enthusiasm of youth just isn't there any more.

From ages 16 to 45 we are working to gradually dismantle the four major false assumptions built up in response to our childhood demons. By about 50 we complete the work of dismantling the last false assumption, "There is no evil or death in the world. The sinister has been destroyed." This is helped along because events are forcing us to accept that there never will be any magical powers with which we can bend the world to our will. With that, we make the final passage from "I am theirs" to "I own myself." With that momentous awareness, we are finally able to step out of the familiar world of struggle for status into a yet-to-be-developed frame of reference. For the next few months or for years, we're in a fog of awe. Nothing is the same any more. We are nowhere despite being surrounded by the familiar. If we will allow it room, our new perception will force us to transcend the pettiness inspired by our former feelings of possessiveness and battles over control and competition—though the change is not completed easily. It does not happen immediately. *But the life of inner-directedness finally prevails.*

Some see this new noncompetitive frame of mind as a religious experience. Others put their new philosophy into effect by giving attention to the overlooked details of their everyday lives; they find new riches right at home. Others become teachers, benefactors or world citizens.

This major transition in life does not occur sharply at age 45. Cycles of work, family and marriage extend in varying degrees into the fifties. For some men the work plateau may not be reached in the early forties but later on, so the disillusionment with the "magical" payoff of work is delayed to the late forties or early fifties. For some, having a family of children who are still young or parents who remain healthy and active continues throughout the forties, supporting the illusion of safety in life despite contrary messages. For some women, the excitement of a new career or the luxury of having only a career and not also a home and children to worry about can lend a temporary new sense of power just as the old power of youthful attractiveness fades.

But sometime in our forties decade—and for most people, it is in the mid-forties—we step from the intense heat of the mid-life period to a cooled-down, post-mid-life attitude. We live with a sense of having completed something, a sense that we are whoever we are going to be—and we accept that, not with resignation to the negative feeling that we could have been more and have failed, but with a more positive acceptance: "That's the way it is, world. Here I am! This is me!" And this mysterious, indelible "me" becomes our acknowledged core, around which we center the rest of our lives.

It is perhaps reassuring to those of us with more mundane talents that even the two brilliant and perceptive giants of depth psychology, Freud and Jung, both had powerful mid-life experiences that first disoriented them and then shaped and gave meaning to the remainder of their lives. Though each of us experiences psychological transition in our own way, I think we can translate their experiences into quite a good idea of what the framework of life is like after ages 45 to 50 and also what we must go through before we emerge as our wiser, more philosophical selves.

FREUD

Freud's chief biographers, Ernest Jones and Max Schur, describe the period from ages 40 to 44 in Freud's life as a critical period in his personality development; it was when the last major change in his personality occurred. During this period, he undertook the monumental labor of the first self-analysis by the interpretation of his own dreams. At the same time that he was engaged in this project, he was writing the dream book, which he considered his greatest achievement and his gift to the world. Freud felt his "immortality" rested on his work of dream interpretation and on the book, as can be seen by his repeated statements to that effect in his letters. During these years, as side issues, he discovered the Oedipus complex and infantile sexuality and uncovered his own infantile amnesia.

While writing the book, he went through a kaleidoscope of moods. He wallowed in depression: "Curious state of mind which one's consciousness cannot apprehend . . . twilight thoughts, a veil over one's mind . . . scarcely a ray of light here and there. Every line is a torment." He also soared in an "indescribable sense of intellectual beauty." At this time he was also deeply dependent on a special friend, Fliess, whom he idealized.

He was as concerned as any of us with the visible signs of his own aging, as Schur reveals in *Freud: Living and Dying:*

But I should also have been very glad to miss growing gray. . . . I was already quite gray, and the gray of my hair was another reminder that I must not delay any longer . . . the thought that I should have to leave it to my children to reach the goal of my difficult journey forced its way through to representation at the end of the dream.

Schur comments on that dream and Freud's interpretation:

This dream and its interpretation depict the torment experienced in his self-analysis, which, as Freud expressed it, left his "legs tired" and hair gray. The dream reveals a sense of urgency, of racing against time to conquer the vast unknown. It also shows that Freud felt he was working for posterity but expected only slander and derision in return.

Just before he was 44, when his self-analysis was at its end and the dream book, his attempt at immortality, was completed, in a letter to Fliess, Freud expressed his feeling that although he had by now sacrificed most of his illusions, the struggle still hurt:

In many a dark hour it has been a consolation to me to be able to leave this book behind me. True, the reception it has had so far has certainly not given me any pleasure. Understanding is meager, praise like acts of charity. To most people it is obviously distasteful. I have not yet seen a trace of anyone suspecting what is significant in it. I explain this by telling myself that I am fifteen to twenty years ahead of my time. Then, of course, sets in the doubt (literally torment) that is regularly associated with forming a judgment *in propriis* (about oneself).

. . . Inwardly I am deeply impoverished. *I have had to demolish all my castles in the air,* and have just plucked up *some courage to start rebuilding them.* During the catastrophic collapse you would have been invaluable to me; in the present stage, I should hardly be able to make myself intelligible to you. I conquered my depression with the aid of a special diet of intellectual matters and now, under the influence of the distraction, it is slowly healing. . . . *No one can help me in the least with* what oppresses me; it is my cross, I must bear it; and heaven knows in the process of adaptation my back has become noticeably bent.

Even for Freud it was months later before the building of a new framework began, and it was accompanied by both bitterness and relief. Even Freud had to resign himself to life as it is—had to accept as impossible his childhood desire to be *magically* bigger than life will let any of us be:

Many thanks for your kind words. They are so flattering that I might almost believe some of them—if I were with you. However, I look at it a little differently . . . the inner voices to which I am accustomed to listen suggest a much more modest estimate of my work than that which you proclaim. . . . No critic . . . can see more acutely than I the disproportion between the problems and my solutions, and it will be fitting punishment for me that none of the unexplored provinces of the mind in which I have been the first mortal to set foot will ever bear my name or submit to my laws. . . . Well, I really am already 44 years old, a rather shabby old Jew, as you will see for yourself in the summer or autumn. My family insisted on celebrating my birthday. My greatest consolation is that I have not stolen a march on them with regard to the whole future. They can experience and conquer, so far as they will have the power to do so. I leave them only a foothold; I have not led them to a mountain peak from which they can climb no higher.

From this time on, Freud, as described by Jones, ". . . emerged the serene and benign Freud, henceforth free to pursue his work in imperturbable composure." Schur says: "The end of a period which was probably the most dramatic in Freud's life. It was during that time that all his great discoveries were made, at least in essence, or their foundations laid."

JUNG

At age 37, C. G. Jung parted with his mentor, Dr. Freud, and it was a period of immense turmoil for him, as he reveals in his book *Memories, Dreams, Reflections*, which was recorded and edited by Aniela Jaffe: "After the parting . . . a period of inner uncertainty began for me. It would be no exaggeration to call it a state of disorientation. I felt totally suspended in mid-air, for I had not yet found my footing. . . . I resolved for the present not to bring any theoretical premises to bear upon my patients, but to wait and see what they would tell of their own accord."

This is the first step of the last stage of the process; now we can finally become truly free of childhood consciousness: by suspending the system of thought that has provided our orientation to life and basis for decision making up to now.

When Jung tried to restabilize himself by focusing on his accomplishments to date, particularly his book on the hero myth, this only led him to ask himself what personal myth he was living in. At the same time, he had the series of dramatic dreams about "twelve dead" that was the origin of his theory of archetypes; the dreams led to his new understanding that dream content was part of the living being, not just vestiges of old experiences. "The dreams, however, could not help me over my feeling of disorientation. On the contrary, I lived as if under constant inner pressure. At times this became so strong that I suspected there was some psychic disturbance in myself."

A memory of himself as an 11-year-old boy playing with building blocks surfaced with a great deal of emotion:

THE END OF AN ERA: BEYOND MID-LIFE

"Aha," I said to myself, "there is still life in these things. The small boy is still around, and possesses a creative life which I lack. But how can I make my way to it?" . . . *This moment was a turning point in my fate, but I gave in only after endless resistances and with a sense of resignation.* For it was a painfully humiliating experience to realize that there was nothing to be done except play childish games.

Nevertheless, I began accumulating suitable stones, gathering them partly from the lake shore and partly from the water. And I started building: cottages, a castle, a whole village. . . .

I was walking along the lake as usual one day, picking stones out of the gravel on the shore. Suddenly I caught sight of a red stone, a four-sided pyramid about an inch and a half high. It was a fragment of stone which had been polished into this shape by the action of the water—a pure product of chance. I knew at once: this was the altar! I placed it in the middle under the dome, and as I did so, *I recalled the underground phallus of my childhood dream. This connection gave me a feeling of satisfaction.*

Naturally, I thought about the significance of what I was doing, and asked myself, "Now, really, what are you about? You are building a small town, and doing it as if it were a rite!" I had no answer to my question, only *the inner certainty that I was on the way to discovering my own myth.* For the building game was only a beginning. It released a stream of fantasies which I later carefully wrote down.

This sort of thing has been consistent with me, and at any time in my later life when I came up against a blank wall, I painted a picture or hewed stone. Each such experience proved to be a *rite d'entrée* for the ideas and works that followed hard upon it.

Jung broke his ordinary frame of reference in order to create a new one "but only after a great deal of resistance." He describes, with vivid exactness, his inner turmoil:

I stood helpless before an alien world; everything in it seemed difficult and incomprehensible. I was living in a constant state of tension; often I felt as if gigantic blocks of stone were tumbling down upon me. One thunderstorm followed another. My enduring these storms was a question of brute strength. Others have been shattered by them—Nietzsche, and Hölderlin, and many others. But there was a demonic strength in me, and from the beginning there was no doubt in my mind that I must find the meaning of what I was experiencing in these fantasies.

I was frequently so wrought up that I had to do certain yoga exercises in order to hold my emotions in check. But since it was my purpose to know what was going on within myself, I would do these exercises only until I had calmed myself enough to resume my work with the unconscious. As soon as I had the *feeling that I was myself again, I abandoned this restraint upon the emotions* and allowed the images and inner voices to speak afresh.

Had I left those images hidden in the emotions, I might have been torn to pieces by them. . . . As a result of my experiment I learned how helpful it can be, from the therapeutic point of view, to find the particular images which lie behind emotions.

Jung knew "that below the threshold of consciousness everything was seething with life." He knew he had to let himself plummet down into it in order to gain power over it—otherwise, he feared, he would become mentally ill:

Particularly at this time, when I was working on the fantasies, I needed a point of support in "this world . . ." It was most essential for me to have a normal life in the real world as a counterpoise to that strange inner world. My family and my profession remained the base to which I could always return, assuring me that I was an actually existing, ordinary person.

With the support of his familiar reality, Jung underwent a profound change in his public professional life. If such a change occurred today in a physician, it might be considered a predictable phenomenon of the mid-life transition or perhaps even a crisis:

I came to the decision to withdraw from the university, where I had lectured for eight years as *Privatdozent* (since 1905). My experience and experiments with the unconscious had brought my intellectual activity to a standstill. After the completion of *The Psychology of the Unconscious I found myself utterly incapable of reading a scientific book. This went on for three years. I felt I could no longer keep up with the world of the intellect, nor would I have been able to talk about what really preoccupied me.* The material brought to light from the unconscious had, almost literally, struck me dumb.

I therefore felt that I was confronted with the choice of either continuing my academic career, whose road lay smooth before me, or *following the laws of my inner personality,* of a higher reason, and forging ahead with this curious task of mine. . . .

Consciously, deliberately, then *I abandoned my academic career.* For I felt that something great was happening to me, and I put my trust in the thing which I felt to be more important *sub specie aeternitatis.* I knew that it would fill my life, and for the sake of that goal I was ready to take any kind of risk.

I even had moments when I stormed against destiny. But emotions of this kind are transitory, and do not count.

Finally at 44, seven years later, after his final dream of understanding, Jung wrote:

This dream brought with it a sense of finality. I saw that here the goal had been revealed. *One could not go beyond the center. The center is the goal,* and everything is directed toward that center. Through this dream I understood that the self is the *principle and archetype of orientation and meaning.* Therein lies its healing function.

When I parted from Freud, I knew that I was plunging into the unknown. Beyond Freud, after all, I knew nothing; but I had taken the step into darkness. When that happens, and then such a dream comes, one feels it as an act of grace.

As a young man my goal had been to accomplish something in my science. But then, I hit upon this stream of lava, and the heat of its fires reshaped my life. That was the primal stuff which compelled me to work upon it, and my works are a more or less successful endeavor to incorporate this incandescent matter into the contemporary picture of the world.

The years when I was pursuing my inner images were the

most important in my life—in them everything essential was decided. It all began then; the latter details are only supplements and clarifications of the material that burst forth from the unconscious, and at first swamped me. It was the *prima materia* for a lifetime's work.

During mid-life, both Freud and Jung found the *prima materia* that they sculpted on for the rest of their creative lives; from these mid-life discoveries, they derived immense personal strength. In the same way, we must all find the *prima materia* within our innermost self; from it we derive our understanding of the meaning of our life.

That doesn't mean that we'll be immune to the hazards of life after we hit 45 or 50 or that we'll ever again be able to ignore the specter of death or how limited our time is. Sickness, divorce, physical deterioration, reduced circumstances, forced retirement, the ingratitude of those we love, tragedies and disappointments—all the events that begin to pile up after 50—whittle away at all of us. Those of us who have made contact with our inner core face these inevitable hazards of later life with greater strength; we are able to bounce back because we don't get lost in how bitter the reversal is. We can't be reduced to nothing by any ordinary quota of misery; neither our present nor our past can become a source for prolonged despair or make us believe our life is meaningless. Our sense of meaning resides within us; it does not inhere in any extension of us that can be amputated by the wheel of fortune. They are giants among us that live through the muck of life with an unimpeachable dignity.

But there are also mean and crotchety old folks. They've not made contact with their inner core, and they cling to the childhood consciousness view that power and status are an index of human worth. As reversals occur to such people with increasing frequency as they age, they perceive themselves as losing the battle of life. They begin to attack life itself as meaningless as they slide downhill. Their envies and jealousies become larger, like warts on the nose, as their humanity shrinks.

Some of us awaken from this nightmare slide downhill and through a flash of insight and a tremendous commitment of will initiate changes leading back to our true inner self—to Jung's center, "the self [that] is the principle and archetype of orientation and meaning." Sometimes this occurs only after a severe loss, followed by a deep mourning reaction. The loss then becomes the source of an unintended and unexpected miracle: the men and women who came alive at the end of their life.

At any age, we can make the discoveries described in the mid-life chapter and find a new burst of vitality. At any age, we can challenge and conquer the last false assumption and touch the incandescent stream within us that causes a light of meaning to shine on our life from inside out.

Section VII
Individual Growth and Its Effect on Social Issues: Marriage, Careers and Women's Liberation

The theme of this book has been growth. Probably because of my experience as a psychoanalyst, I've come to understand "growth" in one special way: as the release from arbitrary internal constraints. I don't pay much attention to what happens after the release—that seems to take care of itself. It's the work of liberation, not prescription, that has been the focus of my attention.

Our individual growth is part of a historical social process. The arbitrary internal *constraints* of adulthood were once the internal *standards* of childhood, which we learned at home or at school (although we may have subsequently distorted them with our childish imagination). None of us can live without internal standards, for internal standards are what we and the culture define ourselves by; they are our windows onto the world, the point of view we use to interpret reality and choose actions. And society interprets who we are through our behavior.

Our earliest internal standards all had a "Thou shalt not" quality. Thou shalt not cross the street, hit your sister or satisfy your sexual curiosity. These are rigid rules, defined by others. But later in life we must be released from the rigid interpretation of these axioms in order to grow. We must learn to cross the street under safe but changing conditions, we must be able to hit our sister if conditions warrant it, and we must explore our sexual curiosity. In short, we must become self-defined, flexible and free; we must live closer to our impulses and further from the rigid rules of childhood in order to feel alive.

By freeing ourselves, we automatically re-form the values of the previous generation—which have been instilled in us as our internal standards—and thereby form our own generation's values—which in turn become the internal standards of our children.

We also respond to the changing collective values so produced. For instance, over the last ten years, our culture has become more sexually permissive. We've lost support for internal standards that are sensually restrictive—the code that most of us learned long ago was the "right" way. If those of us brought up with the old code now decide to experiment sensually, we will find that at first we can't fully enjoy the new experience, even if we've intellectually decided it's ethically all right to enjoy it. Thus our previously unquestioned internal standard about sensuality is exposed as an arbitrary internal constraint—an internal prohibition. After we've tested our new value a few times and discovered that the sky hasn't fallen in on us, we thereby strengthen the new value we've intellectually accepted.

By reconciling our childhood standards with our contradictory direct adult experience, which usually increases with age, and by responding to the shifting values of our culture, internal prohibitions are driven to the surface for us to work on and new values are created and passed on. As we saw in the case of Arthur, who felt a conflict between making money and being an "intellectual" (Section IV), the work we do on our own internal prohibitions also affects our mates and children. As we free ourselves, we free our families from the warp we have produced on their consciousness.

Growth is like a river; you can dam it up, slow it up, divert it, but you can't ever stop it. Which brings us to the next issue: how do the major institutions of adult life—marriage and work— help or hinder the essential growth toward adulthood?

Marriage

In what ways does marriage help or hinder the individual growth process? Aren't emotions so powerful that they dictate the form of a marriage? Yes and no. They are powerful but not all-powerful. Emotions are shaped and channeled by our ideas about marriage—our ideas and concepts guide our expectations and demands. Our ideology of marriage must conform to the direct experience of growth if individual growth is to be optimal within a marriage; otherwise, growth must be either sacrificed to a marriage or chosen instead of marriage.

Our prevailing concepts of adulthood and marriage are still static. This book is one of many efforts to reconcile our concepts with the phenomenon as it is experienced. As long as marriage is seen as a static arrangement between two unchanging people, any substantial change in either of those people must initially be perceived as a violation of the contract. It sets off guilt in one partner and developmental envy (see pages 284–89) in the other, because it's not "supposed" to happen. Supposedly, we're to be defined by our partner's need for security and to move only when the other is ready or with his/her agreement. Such a contract makes us other-defined; it distances us from self-directing impulses and adds an imprisoned quality to our life. The rigidly fixed rules of childhood that we're trying to get away from internally can be easily reproduced in marriage by accepting the ideology that it is a static arrangement.

Ideally, in a really happy, really adult marriage, change in one partner is met gladly by the other partner, who is not afraid of the growth, but welcomes it—intellectually, at least—as an interesting improvement in the relationship and also sees it as the beginning of his or her next induced-growth step. Then when developmental envy occurs, it is not cause for righteous indignation because an inadequacy has been exposed; it is the source of information.

The static concept of marriage fosters the conspiracies of marriage that warehouse and slow down growth; the growth concept of marriage encourages empathic separateness and a continuous, flowing rhythm of change. In a growth marriage, we are married and divorced many times in the sense that we are continually divorced from old arrangements and married to new ones. We negotiate from the present only—"But you were that way before" is irrelevant. No guilt about our new self surfacing. No responsibility to remain as we were. Only a responsibility to handle change with integrity and sensitivity to our partner.

What happens to the stability of a marriage with constant change? Isn't a static concept necessary to contain runaway growth? None of us wants to be abandoned and left behind by a partner who has outgrown us. This is the fear society has been responding to all along; this is why, until recently, the one who changes has been labeled irresponsible, sick or inadequate, while the one who wants things to remain the same has been considered the solid, sane one.

Now values are changing: the pioneer is often approved of, and even the sympathetic sometimes label the conservative partner "uncool" or old-fashioned. While it remains painful, divorce is now understood as occurring usually because two people have outgrown each other rather than as an indictment that two people have failed as adults. Society now grants permission to change—and with it, to change partners.

Perhaps the epidemic of divorce in the Western world is because our culture itself is in transition in its attitudes toward marriage: the static and growth concepts of marriage coexist right now in our society. If one partner embraces the ideology of growth while the other tries to stop the change because of the belief that marriage should be static, then divorce is inevitable. But as the society creates more partners who believe in the growth concept of marriage, we may see not only a new stabilization of marriage, but also a new form of the institution. Living through the rhythms of one's own growth against the pushes and pulls of the changes of a beloved partner over a lifetime creates a wonderfully dynamic relationship. Society may come to view marriage not so much as a fixed economic unit, but as potentially the best route to the highest level of personal unfolding.

On the other hand, we may be witnessing the beginning of a new form of married life in which we change partners whenever a new part of ourselves requires confirmation. All children will be members of extended families; everyone will have half brothers, half sisters, half mothers, half fathers and dozens of grandparents.

The cement of static marriages was loosened forever when we became a sexually permissive society. Once children have grown up believing in their right to be sensual and sexually free, they're never going to buy the same principle of fidelity that we all bought. In fact, once any of us discovers that our mate does not have to be our only sexual resource, the power of the sex drive will no longer serve as the cement it used to be during the rough times.

Perhaps as a society we're conducting a grand experiment by forcing this next generation of adults to do battle with sexual jealousy directly. If each partner sees his or her own sexual freedom as an inalienable right, battles over jealousy/possessiveness issues are inevitable. If they succeed in resolving these issues constructively, the present painful aspects of living within a growth ideology will be greatly diminished. If monogamy and fidelity prevail, it could be at a higher level of maturity: "I choose this because it's the best way for me, not because I'm told it's the only way."

Careers

What's the prevailing attitude in industry toward individual growth? Many industries have invested millions of dollars and thousands of hours attempting to introduce programs that encourage growth in their employees. But the prevailing value system of American industry flatly states that money, power and status are the only meaningful goals in life. These values derive directly from the fundamental motivational theme of the years from ages 20 to 45: to get big in order to erase the traumatic childhood consciousness of helplessness. We're offered magical immunity from death and biology if only we can climb a rank higher. If our energies are deflected from acquiring profit and achieving success by excursions into a time-occupying questioning of inner life, industry/society wants us to believe we will be punished by a bad report card; we will risk losing the rewards of rank. So the subject of an inner life is completely banished. We don't talk to work friends at all about deeply personal issues, especially if we're men. At most a few gripes about finances, the wife or the kids may be tolerated or a few weeks' indulgence may be granted if we're undergoing a particularly difficult divorce. In a career setting, the future becomes so dazzling that the present can hardly be seen, much less explored.

Some men who have totally bought into this value system reach a plateau during the mid-life decade and wonder what they've done with their lives. While they're floundering around looking for a new value system, they often put their careers and future with the company in jeopardy. With industry's prevailing value system, the manager witnessing this change, despite the employee's efforts to hide it, must say to himself, "What's wrong with this guy? He's lost his edge. Is he burning out? Are we going to have to get rid of him? Has he become deadwood?"

With the ideology of growth, an enlightened manager might say, "This is the best thing that could happen to this man and this company. He's been too good, a boy scout, and therefore defined his work too narrowly. He's taken very few chances, has been too competitive with his promising subordinates, and has added too much tension to the system, even though he's been an efficient and productive worker. When he transforms his view of the meaning of his life, it will give him a renewed interest in his work, because he will view it from a new perspective. His growth will translate into the growth of the company, because only a man of his age and experience can provide the necessary new insights."

From the growth-ideology point of view, the problem becomes an opportunity if both employee and employer can sit down and work out a solution without stigma. The solutions may range from costly sabbaticals to no-cost redistribution of tasks and responsibilities.

If a growth ideology pervaded industry, the whole mid-life work problem might be prevented. If during the twenty years of work before the crises of the mid-life decade every useful expansionist urge of employees was captured by an enlightened personnel policy, there might well be an explosion of new vitality in both industry and individual lives.

It could be started quite simply. Suppose every time an employee said, "I'm bored, ready to move on to new challenges or new responsibilities," the supervisor, instead of politely listening and thinking to himself, "There's no slot open for him," took that employee's statement as a mandate for action that must be fulfilled. Suppose the guiding policy was that those urges in individual employees were the true power source of the company. If an employee's statement of readiness was taken as authoritatively as a memo from the big boss, then that creative energy could be captured instead of suppressed, and both the company and the individual could grow organically. Why shouldn't the meaning of work for an individual begin to come from the ever-increasing fit of his talents with his job rather than from his rank in some meaningless hierarchy?

The product-oriented value system of American business has evident merit, but what are the human costs? Can we afford the heart attacks, ulcers, early deaths, and ruined families? Doesn't the static career concept have to move to a growth ideology for the same reason that our static marriage concepts must move: because the costs of ignoring the unstoppable growth processes are too great?

Our Response to Change

To talk about transforming the attitudes of our institutions toward growth and change is to talk about a very long-range goal. But how do we handle the demand for growth in our private lives in the meantime? On a personal level, how do we handle the dilemma of the need for security versus the desire for freedom?

All adults need the right mixture of security and freedom.

Without a sense of what is necessary for our security, the search for freedom becomes mania and anxiety. But without a sense of freedom, clinging to security becomes deadness.

What does it mean, to have security? Most people would say it means being sure of the love, loyalty or protection of someone else. More precisely, it means having a workable mental and emotional structure—that is, a set of patterns of action and thinking that gives us the sense of being grounded in and sheltered by a familiar and comprehensible reality. We need to live in some kind of reality structure. When we grow, we wander in an uncharted area. But if we wander long enough, we begin creating a new structure. That's the way we're built; there's no fighting it.

What this need for structure tells us is that there is a rhythm to growth that must be heeded. When we move too far too fast, our anxiety tells us to slow down and build a new structure before going further. If we've stayed in one place too long, our sense of stagnation tells us to get moving. Growth is not one long, uninterrupted climb up a hill; there must be time out for "just living." Self-conscious "growers" always hurrying to the next goal miss as much of life as those dug in for the duration.

One growth rhythm is dictated by pauses for rebuilding or reshaping our reality structure. This has to be distinguished from the stopping and starting we do as we respond to outdated childhood fears. Anxiety is generated by both sources: we get anxious when we really have moved too fast and should slow down and also when we are about to transgress an outdated internal standard that should be discarded. One anxiety is a signal that we must slow down to consolidate the growth we've gained; the other is a signal to push ahead past the anxiety or else risk not growing any more. In the first section, we described the seven-step inner-dialogue mastery process, which is the route of emancipation—through it, we are able to separate the past from the present.

We also talked earlier about our enslavement to the fear of the childhood demonic. Let me reiterate, in a somewhat different way from the discussion in the first section, the demonic fantasy of being a prisoner. This is a deep-seated fantasy that represents our earliest experience and retains much of its otherworldly primitive power throughout our lives.

THE DEMONIC PRISONER FANTASY

We are born slaves to sadistic parents. They produced us for their benefit and consumption. We are their property, which they can dispose of as they wish at any time they wish. As long as we don't try to escape, life can be bearable; we'll be granted a limited range of freedom. If we try to escape, we'll be hunted, caught, tortured, mutilated and annihilated, maybe even eaten. They've just been waiting for us to make the fatal mistake and assert our desire for freedom. All along they've known we were just pretending to be contented as slaves.

If we assume that this fantasy is the primitive organization of the demonic childhood world which we're trying to master by adult thinking, we have a shorthand way of understanding our daily fluctuations from optimism to severe states of despair. We are optimistic when we're free of this fantasy, despairing when we believe in it.

The unconscious fantasy that we will have to be slaves forever makes up the erratic rhythm of growth; it accounts for wild fears, when rational considerations don't warrant such anxiety, and explains for me some of the mystery that reigns between joyful living and intractable despair.

This is the dialectic of the struggle toward adult independence, then: a contest between the ever-present adult need to be free and the primitive terror of helpless child-slaves forever subject to arbitrary punishment and destruction.

When we've changed too fast and too radically and have lost the security that comes from having a workable structure for reality, we'll be truly relieved when we stop and rest. But we will also have a sense of victory, accomplishment. When we retreat from a growth step because we're not "supposed" to be that free, our diminished anxiety will be mixed with the taste of defeat. We'll have opted for an outgrown illusion of safety.

And the illusion of safety for the price of a corresponding restriction of self is always available in the network of false ideas that make up our childhood consciousness. The ideas of childhood consciousness exist as permanent constructs below the surface of our minds. Though they've been presented chronologically here, at the time when they first surface to be challenged, they always exert an effect—stronger before we challenge them and weaker after a little testing. The struggle against these outmoded ideas of childhood is the critical message of this book.

Each major false assumption has its own specific cost. When we believe we'll always be our parents' child, we must continually look for an authority to live under who knows the one right way. When we believe that doing things our parents' way will bring results automatically or that when we falter or tire, someone else will step in, we will always be dependent persons. We will persevere in a creative direction only when we have someone else's approval. Our lives will be filled with resentment at those who don't "let" us grow and who neglect to straighten out our lives. And so on. Each false assumption exacts its limitation on a free-ranging, fully alive mind.

On the other hand, we need a structure of patterns and values to live within. But we must help build that structure, not just be slaves to the values our parents passed on. The temptation to think, "I'm not meant to be free," to hide behind a restrictive, safe self-definition is tremendous, and we all do it sometimes. But if we're to realize our dreams and our potential, we must transcend that archaic biological fear of change.

And when transcending that fear, we must be prepared to accept the sadness that comes with a real transformation of self. This sadness is not the depression we commonly experience when we are temporarily set back, either by growth-stunting internal constraints or by external circumstances. Rather, it is the sadness that arises *because* we are shedding our shackles and deactivating the demonic prisoner fantasy. After all, the prisoner fantasy is a deeply rooted, albeit distorted, link to the loving, safety-providing parents who had our total faith in earliest childhood: the ones who kept us from inflicting innumerable disasters on ourselves when we were small, because they loved us. We know we are caught in this ambivalence about the "forgotten" demonic prisoner fantasy every time we create a neurotic drama in our lives, either when we claim to be invulnerable—the special child/superman/superwoman/rescuer—or when we act totally vulnerable, the helpless victim who must be rescued. Every time we cast ourselves in either of these roles, we are perpetuating our connection to the childish fantasy and forfeit a piece of our internal freedom. When we choose instead to live off the stuff of current, adult reality, we gain more freedom for ourselves—and suffer more sadness, at the loss of an era inevitably sacrificed to that monster, Time.

We must learn to distinguish between the anxiety deriving from too rapid change and that deriving from the demonic prisoner fantasy, and we must learn to distinguish between the sadness which accompanies growth and the depression which occurs because growth is stalled. This is perhaps more important in our lifetime than in that of previous generations because there have been such rapid and pervasive changes in values on the fundamental issues of life—work, love, family, sex. We are all now being required to turn inward and question the values that were previously accepted as givens in this country. In the last ten years, the value changes have been qualitatively different from any that have occurred in the past. They have struck at the heart of the family and marriage: today, one-third of all first marriages in this country end in divorce. This is a fundamental blow to the security of millions of daily lives. It requires new patterns for living and painful soul-searching on a massive scale.

Women's Liberation

Clearly the issue that cuts across all the other social issues relating to growth is the changing role of women. It has occurred rapidly, is pervasive, and undermines the security patterns of all of us—men, women and children. Being a woman nowadays is where the action is.

A role change is really a self-definition change, so that women's liberation requires a woman to license herself to use her own power. In the course of the relicensing, she'll have to transgress an outdated arbitrary internal rule and do battle with the demonic prisoner fantasy—which, once defeated, releases enormous personal power. So we have an insight into the energy source of the women's movement: it is a life-or-death liberation from primitive captivity, not just creating a new social role to fit a new historical period.

But that insight, so firmly anchored in the actual experience of women making the change, is the hardest for a woman to hold on to. "What primitive internalized rule? Where is it? I can't see a rule, but I can see a world run by men and for men, a world that has confined women to powerless roles."

That is undoubtedly true. It is also true that men must change their own self-definitions as well as their concept of women. However, this is not the whole truth. There are still two fronts for women to challenge—the external political structure and the limiting internal self-definition. And the most ferocious opponent is within. On some level every woman knows this; women talk about losing nerve and holding themselves back, as men rarely do, yet periodically they lose this insight.

One reason women lose this insight is that they fail to distinguish between the needs of a political movement to which they are committed and their own needs as individuals to grow. The particular needs of an individual woman get lost in the demands of the political movement because the movement furnishes such powerful emotional support for individual growth; consequently, the two interests often seem to be indistinguishable.

Individual men and men's social-system bias against women are appropriate targets for the political movement; stirring rhetoric and black-and-white analysis of issues are necessary fuel to keep the momentum of change going. But an individual woman needs to think in those terms only in the consciousness-raising stage of her personal emancipation; after that, she needs a balanced deployment of her aggressive energies. Some energy must be used to educate her men, some to learn new skills, and much must be targeted on working out her own internal prohibitions. Nothing less will do if real growth is to occur.

So much unnecessary misery occurs when all a woman's aggression is directed at the men in her life, for everybody suffers and nobody benefits. Women now in their mid-life decade are especially vulnerable, for they are the ones who are most dramatically caught in the crunch, most of them having lived fifteen to twenty years of their adult life with the very limited wife-and-mother self-definition. Now they have the opportunity—in fact, the painful necessity—to change that self-definition radically.

Added to the difficulty we all face in holding on to the slippery insight that our own internal prohibitions hold us back more than *any* external obstacle, women in mid-life have the added load of dealing with an existential anger. There is no answer to their question, "Who's going to give me back those fifteen to twenty years?" And powerful anger always makes clear thinking terribly hard, for the anger seeks a target, any target. And for the woman seeking redress for twenty lost years, that target is usually her husband, as if he single-handedly created the social system that both he and she bought into when they married. He may well have benefited more from the system than she has; he may in fact still believe it is true that indeed women can't add, subtract or handle money, that they are too "soft" to take the rough jostling of the business world, that they are not capable of sustained serious thought that would help them produce important scientific discoveries, effect statesmanlike political settlements, or make tough corporate decisions. In short, the husband may be a raving male chauvinist. However, even if this is so, every woman's *first* project must be her own mind, her attitudes about herself, her own emotional constraints. It is a false syllogism to insist, "He benefited, I'm deprived and angry, so he deserves to suffer.'' This is as far as many women get in their thinking on this matter, and it is responsible for much of the chaos produced in so many people's lives today by the issue of women's liberation. When political necessity is confused with what is needed in one's own personal life, this false thinking is strengthened, and a steel trap is sprung on both victims.

In short, given the radical social changes that have occurred in this century, we can be sure that there are more issues to confuse us than we are likely to be able to resolve in our lifetime. Therefore, it is all the more important that we truly commit ourselves to the idea of nurturing our own growth. It is a lifetime process. We must learn to recognize and root out the forces that stop us from growing or lead us into dead ends. We must always remember to look first for the enemy within. And we must find a way to teach this to our children.

Epilogue

Since I introduced this book with the transition incident in my life that first suggested to me that growth necessarily involved the painful shedding of hidden childhood assumptions, it seems fitting that at the end of the book I bring the story up to date.

While physicists and chemists can write about their subject matter without personally undergoing the processes they are describing, most clinicians and writers are writing about themselves when they write about others. I am no exception. I have not been immune from any of the processes described here, nor has anyone else I've known well. Since, thank God, the culture has not yet totally homogenized us, of course we each create our own forms, grow and experience change with differing intensities.

At 43, I find myself in the midst of all the struggles outlined in the mid-life section. I've modified my career: I no longer present myself only as a practicing psychiatrist who secretly writes unpublished papers to himself. Now I officially write as well as treat patients. In the past I was never sure whether I wrote because I was a "real" writer only temporarily in the closet or because writing required a discipline that forced me to crystallize the ideas and observations floating until then vague and half formed in the back corners of my mind. I found out during the course of writing this book that I'm not a "real" writer. And though initially this was a painful disillusionment, I'm now quite satisfied to present ideas clearly, even if inelegantly, as long as every so often there is a touch of beauty.

My wife has undergone her own profound transformation, triggering thunderous reverberations throughout our marriage. Often I was left painfully behind, stewing in the juices of developmental envy, fighting to return her to our earlier conspiracies

335

of mutual dependence which I was not ready to relinquish. Sometimes I saw the light and did pursue the growth step her growth was forcing in me. Out of our experience came a jointly authored paper, "Individual Growth and Marital Consequences."

We now seem to have emerged from under the black cloud of those years, both of us quite different from the people we were before. The sense of vitality we have now, together and apart, speaks for itself and tells us we did something profoundly right in muddling through our quagmire.

Our children are off to college, all four of us are living reasonably comfortably at the edge of the unknown. We have experienced our fair share of death, tragedies and disappointments—and maybe more than our fair share of good luck.

Index

Achievement-aspiration gap, 231
Adolescence
  conflicts of, 71–76
  and psychosis, 45
Adult consciousness
  vs. childhood consciousness,
    17–18, 25, 31, 37–38, 72, 97,
    102–104, 125, 289, 300–307
  and divorce, 213–214
Adulthood
  criteria for, 88–90
  nature of, 16
Aggression, and anger, 241
Ambivalence, in consciousness,
  304–305
Anger, demonic, 18, 255
  and internal prohibitions, 19–
    21
  and protective devices, 25
Anxiety, and change, 328–331
Authenticity, in men, 245

Behavior, and rewards, 77–81,
  86–87
Bergman, Ingmar, 94, 95
Berman, Dr. Ellen, 122–123
Blue-collar families, and

evolution of consciousness,
  149–151
"Both Sides Now" (Mitchell),
  165
Bryson, Jeff, 130

Career development, of women
  executives, 263–266
*Career Development for Women
  Executives* (Hennig), 263–
  266
Careers, 205–206
  vs. childbearing, 97–99, 133–
    134
  and individual growth, 325–
    327
  and marriage, 121–130
  for middle-class women, 97–98
  for working-class women, 96
  see also Work
Change
  and anxiety, 328–331
  and consciousness, 41
  and separation situations, 25
Childbearing, 206
  vs. career, 97–99, 133–134
  and roles, 100

Childhood consciousness
  vs. adult consciousness, 17–
    18, 25, 31, 37–38, 72, 97,
    102–104, 125, 289, 300–307
  and divorce, 214
  reality of, 54–55
Childhood demons
  mastery of, 31–38
  origins of, 22–25
Children
  and illusion of safety, 222–225
  and marriage, 127–134
  needs of, 103
  self-centeredness of, 102
  and work, 176–177
Child Studies Through Fantasy
  (Rosalind Gould), 26–28
Clichés, and truth, 170–172
Commitment, in women, 260
Competition, and two-career
    marriage without children,
    121–122
Consciousness
  adult vs. childhood, 17–18, 25,
    31, 37–38, 72, 97, 102–104,
    125, 289, 300–307
  changes in, 41
  and divorce, 213–214
  evolution of, and
    socioeconomic class, 148–
    151
Conspiracies
  breaking, 279–280
  confronting, 280–291
  and coupling, 119
  and divorce, 291–292
  and internal prohibitions, 137,
    141–142
  living with, 292–293
  malignant, 111–113
  nature of, 109–111
  of one-mindedness, 147–148

and parents, 144–147
and responsibility, 139–140
shifting, 199–204
and traditional marriage, 131–
  134
Contracts, making and breaking,
  159–164
Coupling, 120–136
  and conspiracies, 119
  and feelings of inadequacy,
    109–113
  and life style, 108–109, 135
  and self-image, 114–116
  and sexuality, 117–118
Coward, Noel, 276

Death
  male response to, 229–241
  and mortality, 229
  of parent, 226–229
Demands, vs. opportunities, 75
Demonic images, 305–306
  and marriage, 193–199
  see also Anger, demonic;
    Childhood demons
Demonic prisoner fantasy, 329–
  331
Dependence, parental, 54
Depression, 238
  transitional, 157–159
Destructiveness, *see* Anger,
  demonic
Differences, negotiable, 203
Divorce, 324
  aftermath of, 213–215
  and conspiracies, 291–292
  and the enemy, 210–213
  and power, 207–210

Envy, developmental, 284–291
Equality, and friendship, 63
Extended family, 215

Extramarital sex, 270–271
  see also Infidelity

Failure, vs. success, 107
Fairness, concept of, 30
Family
  extended, 215
  loss of intact, 220–222
  parents as, 62–63
Fantasy
  demonic prisoner, 329–331
  omnipotent, 26–28
Fear, types of, 169
Femaleness, stereotyped, 131–134
Femininity, 246
  and independence, 87
Fliess (friend of Freud), 312
Freedom
  from parents, 71–76
  and security, 327–328
  see also Independence
Freud: Living and Dying (Schur), 312
Freud, Sigmund, 311–314, 317, 318
Friendship, and equality, 63

Gould, Rosalind, 28
Greed, controlling, 295–300
Groups, supportive nature of, 62–63
Growth, individual, 321–322
  and careers, 325–327
  and change, 328–331
  and marriage, 323–325
  and women's liberation, 331–334

Heller, Joseph, 49
Hennig, Margaret, 263–266
Hölderlin, Friedrich, 316

Identity formation, and emancipation from parents, 67–70
Illness, of parent, 226–228
Illusory safety, and false assumptions, 39–42
Images, demonic, 305–306
  and marriage, 193–199
Immortality, *see* Safety, illusion of
Inadequacy (feelings of), and coupling, 109–113
Independence
  and parents, 49–53, 57–60
  of women, 87, 95
  see also Freedom
Individuality, *see* Independence
Infidelity, 274
  questioning the rules of, 275–277
  see also Extramarital sex
In-laws, and marriage, 92
Inner-directedness, in middle years, 309–319
Intimacy, vs. space, 206
"I Travel Alone" (Coward), 276–277

Jaffe, Aniela, 314
Janus (ancient Roman deity), 161
Jones, Ernest, 311, 314
Jung, C. G., 311, 314–318, 319

Knievel, Evel, 244

Lewis, C. S., 169–170
Lief, Dr. Harold, 122–123
Life style, and coupling, 108–109, 135
Limitations, rule of necessary, 30–31

Living together, 120–121
Look Back in Anger (Osborne), 43
"Love and Hate: How Working Couples Work It Out" (Murphy), 128–129

Maleness, stereotyped, 131–134
Marriage
  change patterns in, 277–279
  as conspiracy, 111–113, 201–204
  and demonic images, 193–199
  early, 66–67
  as illusion, 81
  and individual growth, 323–325
  and in-laws, 92
  sex renegotiated in, 267–271
  traditional, 130–134
  two-career, with children, 127–130
  two-career, without children, 121–127
  see also Monogamy
Masculinity, relief from, 236
Memories, Dreams, Reflections (Jung), 314
Men
  and breaking work immunity pact, 239–241
  and changing meaning of work, 241–245
  roles of, 94–96, 104–107
  and work, 173–176
  and work as immunity from death, 229–236
  and work as protective device, 236–239
Middle-class families, and evolution of consciousness, 150–151

Middle-class men
  role of, 95
  and work, 174–176, 231
Middle-class women
  role of, 96–98
  and work, 176, 177–178
Middle years, and inner-directedness, 309–319
Mitchell, Joni, 165
Monogamy, and oedipal conflict, 271–275
Mother
  ideal, 102
  love, 294–295
Motherhood, 99–104
  criteria for, 89–90
Mourning, after death, 227–228
Murphy, Mary, 128–129

Nietzsche, Friedrich, 316

Obligation, need for freedom from, 180
Oedipal conflict, and monogamy, 271–275
Omnipotence
  fantasies of, 26–28
  of parents, 28–29
One-mindedness, as conspiracy, 147–148
Opportunities, vs. demands, 75
Osborne, John, 43
"Other Worlds, Of" (Lewis), 169

Pain
  and death, 228
  and self-deception, 166–168
Parenthood, effects of, 133–134
Parents
  challenging, 45–46
  changed attitude toward, 207

and conspiracies, 144–147
dependence of, 54
as family, 62–63
and identity formation, 67–70
illness or death of, 226–229
and illusion of safety, 222–225
independence from, 49–53,
    57–60, 71–76
omnipotence of, 28–29
and responsibility, 71–76
roles of, 45, 91–92
and sex, 64–66
and values, 184–192
Passions, controlling, 295–300
Pasteur, Louis, 17
Payoffs (automatic), and
    behavior, 77–81, 86–87
Plath, Sylvia, 22
Power, 203–204
and divorce, 207–210
and illusion of safety, 222–225
and women, 246–263
Prohibition, and traditional
    marriage, 131–134
Prohibitions, internal
and conspiracies, 137, 141–142
and demonic anger, 19–21
and work vs. children, 176–
    178, 182
Protective devices
and demonic anger, 25
omnipotent fantasies as, 26–28
Protector myth
and women, 246–263
and women executives, 264–
    266
Psychosis, and adolescence, 45

Reality
of childhood consciousness,
    54–55

current vs. demonic, 24, 32–
    33, 36–37
testing, 33–34
Resentment, role of, 179–180
Responsibility
and conspiracy, 139–140
and parents, 71–76
Revenge, and work, 21
Rewards, and behavior, 77–81,
    86–87
Risking
and emotional growth, 42
and reality, 36
and safety, 61
Role models, male and female,
    78
Roles
of men, 94–96, 104–107
of parents, 91–92
sex, 93–94
and talents, 81–82, 84–85
of women, 96–104
Rubin, Lillian B., 149, 181
Russell, Alys, 154
Russell, Bertrand, 154–156, 159,
    160, 163, 171

Sacks, Dr. Sylvia, 122–123
Safety, illusion of, 217–218, 220–
    225
and false assumptions, 39–42
Safety, and risking, 61
Scenes from a Marriage (film),
    94–95
Schur, Max, 311, 312, 314
Security, and freedom, 327–328
Self-confidence
and accomplishment, 73–74
in marriage, 123–124
Self-deception, and pain, 166–
    168

Self-definition, change in, 332–333

Self-image
  and coupling, 114–116
  and success, 237
  and work, 173

Self, *see* Identity formation

Sensitivity, natural vs. forced, 180

Separation situations, and childhood demons, 24–25

Settling down, and single people, 206

Seven-step dialogue, and mastery of childhood demons, 31–34

Sex
  and coupling, 117–118
  and parents, 64–66
  renegotiated in marriage, 267–271
  roles, 93–94

Sheehy, Gail, 14

Single life, pros and cons, 120

Socioeconomic class, and evolution of consciousness, 148–151

Space, vs. intimacy, 206

Spock, Dr. Benjamin, 13–14

Status, as myth, 81

"Stroking," 238

Success
  vs. failure, 107
  and immunity from death, 230–236
  and self-image, 237
  and work, 132

Talents, and roles, 81–82, 84–85

Transformation, act of, 25

Transition, and depression, 157–159

Truth, and clichés, 170–172

"Two-Professional Marriage, The: A New Conflict Syndrome" (Berman-Lief-Sacks), 122–124

Uniqueness, dangers of, 54–55

University, and independence from parental assumptions, 60

Values, and parents, 184–192

Whitehead, Alfred North, 154

Whitehead, Mrs. Alfred North, 154

Wolfe, Thomas, 171

Women
  independence of, 95
  and power, 246–263
  roles of, 96–104
  and work, 176–182, 257–259
  see also Femininity; Motherhood

Women executives, career development of, 263–266

Women's liberation, and individual growth, 331–334

Work
  breaking male immunity pact, 239–241
  changing meaning for men, 241–245
  and male immunity from death, 230–236
  as male protective device, 236–239
  and revenge, 21
  and success, 132
  varied meanings of, 172–183
  and women, 257–259
  see also Careers

Working-class men
    role of, 95–96
    and work, 173
    see also Blue-collar
        families

Working-class women
    role of, 96
    and work, 173, 176, 177
Worlds of Pain (Rubin), 149–
        151, 181

ABOUT THE AUTHOR

Dr. Roger Gould is a psychoanalyst and associate clinical professor of psychiatry at U.C.L.A. His private practice focuses on individual growth dilemmas and includes consultations with corporations about the emotional growth of their employees. He and his wife, Renée, a policy analyst, are codirectors of a research project studying women's lives and public policy.